Class Matters

Inequality and Exploitation
in Twenty-first Century Britain

Charles Umney

T0366432

First published 2018 by Pluto Press
345 Archway Road, London N6 5AA

www.plutobooks.com

British Library Cataloguing in Publication Data
A catalogue record for this book is available from the British Library

ISBN 978 0 7453 3709 8   Hardback
ISBN 978 0 7453 3708 1   Paperback
ISBN 978 1 7868 0245 3   PDF eBook
ISBN 978 1 7868 0247 7   Kindle eBook
ISBN 978 1 7868 0246 0   EPUB eBook

This book is printed on paper suitable for recycling and made from fully
managed and sustained forest sources. Logging, pulping and manufacturing
processes are expected to conform to the environmental standards of the
country of origin.

Typeset by Stanford DTP Services, Northampton, England

Simultaneously printed in the United Kingdom and United States of America

Contents

List of Figures

List of Tables

Acknowledgements

Thanks to the following people for advice on early drafts, or else other encouragement: Susie Ioannou, Madeleine Fullerton, Roy Umney, Sofia and Lily Umney, Ian Greer, Emma Peplow, Alex Johnsen, John Blackburn, Vera Trappmann and John Ward.

Introduction

Capitalism has been around for something like 500 years, and has held sway over for the vast majority of the earth for about 30. The reason this is worth pointing out is because, for many of its supporters, capitalism is far from perfect but it is the model that most fits with the reality of what human beings are actually like. A common argument goes as follows: humans are competitive, and some humans are much better than others (cleverer, harder-working and so on), and so a system which relies on competition and inequality, while it might seem a bit harsh, is basically appropriate. To try and do otherwise (i.e. build a system based on cooperation and equality) might be tempting but is ultimately utopian and thus doomed to fail.

But these kinds of argument, while posing as pragmatic, are also utopian in their own way. If capitalism really fits that well with human nature, then governments would not have to intervene so frequently and extensively to stop it falling apart. Anyway, as soon as we understand the comparatively short historical roots of capitalism, we are forced to recognise it for what it is: a system with a particular set of rules, among many others with different rules that have existed in the past, and which might exist in the future. Given that life on earth still has about five billion years left to run before the planet is engulfed in the sun's death cycle, it seems presumptuous to imagine that the system we have currently is the one that is best suited to the human condition.

The point of saying this is not to speculate about what the world might be like over the rainbow. It is simply to observe that, while we are in the middle of an era, it is very difficult to see beyond it. Various things about the world that appear second nature to those living within a specific system can start to appear very strange when looked at from a wider perspective. For example, in feudal Britain most people did not consider whether the belief in the king's right to rule being bestowed directly by God would appear ridiculous from the vantage point of the twenty-first century. Likewise, it is possible that, in centuries to come, people may also see something ridiculous in a system whereby supermarkets load their shelves with completely unnecessary quantities of food that gets thrown in the bin at the end of the day, while some people struggle to afford proper nutrition. So this book is, in part, an attempt to make life under twenty-first-century British capitalism look strange.

One of its strangest elements is the question of class. Most people do not particularly want a society divided along class lines. But rather than do anything about this, people tend to invent ideas (e.g. 'meritocracy', 'social mobility') that make it seem a bit less offensive. Hence, it is often argued that the ideal society should be one of 'equal opportunity', where every individual succeeds or fails on their own merits. This way, we would still have a class-divided society, but at least we would know that the people at the bottom truly deserved to be there.

Until recently, people that talked too much about class were considered to be dinosaurs from the age when poor children toiled day and night, losing their fingers amid the power looms of northern England in order to avoid the workhouse. The mainstream centre-left in Britain, supposedly sympathetic to working-class concerns, swallowed this argument whole, and it was elevated to one of the central dogmas of British politics from the 1990s until about 2015. But now this line looks very dated. Instead, the fashionable thing to say about class is not that it doesn't matter, but that the way in which it matters is changing. Nobody really disputes that, for instance, the 'Brexit' referendum of 2016 revealed substantial differences in the worldviews and aspirations of people from different socio-economic backgrounds, though how to interpret this is more controversial.

Initially, the re-emergence of class was driven by conservative voices. There is a powerful story that can be told about British politics (and indeed politics in any number of countries), about the divide between cosmopolitan elitists who love globalisation, and the ordinary people who are menaced by it. People on the right have been very good at playing on this idea, and they have, at times, used it to make discussion of class almost inseparable from neuroses surrounding nationalism and immigration. After assuming power, Theresa May tried to embody this worldview, though not very persuasively. But however bad things became for her, they were much worse for the centre-left,* who found themselves rendered irrelevant by their failure to find their own way of addressing

---

* By which I mean your Blairs, Browns, Milibands, etc.

the topic of class that didn't involve either empty platitudes or borrowed nationalism.

The reason British politics has suddenly become interesting is because we have the opportunity to see whether a more radical version of the left can do any better. Jeremy Corbyn's leadership of the Labour Party throughout 2017 was highly successful: to understand that this is the case, you need to compare its results not with previous election victories such as 1997, which might as well be 200 years ago given how much has changed since then, but with what is happening to equivalent parties in other countries in 2017. In France, Germany, the Netherlands, Greece, even in the US, established parties of the mainstream left look increasingly weak and directionless. In the UK, by contrast, following the 2017 general election there was actual enthusiasm and optimism.

Many people argue, however, that the current progress of the Labour Party was mainly based on its resonance with idealistic (and comparatively highly educated) young people offended by Brexit, rather than any kind of reconnection with the 'working class'. The fact that they gained ground in places like Kensington and Canterbury while losing it in places like Sunderland provided some symbolic support for this idea. Indeed, for some, after briefly starting to matter again after Theresa May's 2016 conference speech (where she really did talk about class a lot), class is now once again being replaced, this time by age, as the most important divide in British politics.

Ultimately, the problem is that the way class is invoked in British politics is usually inconsistent, shallow and self-serving. It obviously matters, but we need to find better ways of understanding it. That is the point of this book. In it, I look to revitalise a very different way of thinking about class which is barely recognised today, and which is rooted in a Marxist analysis of the relationship between *labour* and *capital*. Looked at this way, class can help us to understand why, for instance, young people (even those from affluent and educated backgrounds) might be increasingly dissatisfied with the status quo in this country, to an extent which cannot be even remotely understood by crude divisions of people into socio-economic categories defined by letter classifications (e.g. A, B, C1, C2, D, E). Understanding what labour and capital are, and why the relationship between them matters, enables not just a vague and moralistic rhetoric about elites versus everyone else, but also sheds light on the wider workings of the British economy, government and society.

THE REST OF THE BOOK

I will continue as follows. In Chapter 1, I provide an overview of the ways in which the concept of class has been used and abused in Britain in recent years, taking in both political jargon and academic research. In Chapter 2, I discuss the Marxist view of class, showing how it differs from the ideas discussed in Chapter 1 and identifying what I see as its most important elements. In Chapter 3, I provide a general overview of the way the British economy has changed in recent decades, with a particular focus on the way in which the 'balance of power' between labour and capital has shifted in favour of the latter. I argue that the Marxist ideas explained in Chapter 2 are important for understanding these general trends.

After this, the second half of the book engages with a series of specific topics such as work, technology and government, arguing that, in each case, Marxist theories about class are important and helpful in allowing us to understand them better. In particular, it helps us to explain how and why these things take the (often strange) form that they do in our society, as well as the ways in which they may be evolving. Firstly, I look at work: the place around which millions of people's lives revolve. I use insights gained from my analysis of class to consider why the experience of being a worker is, for so many, one of exploitation, alienation, frustration or boredom. Next, I examine government, making the argument that, in numerous fundamental respects, British political institutions are inevitably structured by the need to help capital at the expense of labour. This discussion of government carries over into Chapter 6, where I present a more in-depth discussion of the political context as it relates specifically to 'equalities' issues, with particular attention paid to gender and immigration. In Chapters 7 and 8, I consider how class relationships impact the evolution of new technology and the role of the media respectively. Finally, at the end of Chapter 8 I return to the British political scene and consider what the book's analysis tells us about its possible futures.

1

The 'Economy that Works for Everyone'

PLATITUDES

I will govern for the whole United Kingdom and we will look to build an economy that works for everyone, not just the privileged few.

Theresa May, after becoming prime minister of the United Kingdom, July 2016

We want to see a break with the failed economic orthodoxy that has gripped policymakers for a generation, and set out a very clear vision for a Labour government that will create an economy that works for all not just the few.

Jeremy Corbyn, leader of the Labour Party, May 2016

Class is a communist concept ... it groups people together and sets them against each other.

Margaret Thatcher, 1992[1]

Very few people claim they want an economy that only works for some. Given this, we might wonder why senior politicians keep talking about how they want an economy that works for everyone. If everyone agrees on this, why keep bringing it up as if it were controversial?

The idea of the economy that 'works for everyone' is a platitude. It is something that is sufficiently vague that nobody could really disagree, and which nobody ever gets around to defining. British politics runs on these kinds of statements. Certain things are so roundly accepted as good that their actual meaning is rarely questioned: important platitudes of the last decade have included 'balancing the budget' and 'social mobility'. More recently, these have been usurped by 'taking back control' and, as things have become more and more chaotic, 'certainty' and 'stability' (these last ones looking more grimly ironic by the day). These are all empty phrases on to which listeners can impute anything they like. Conversely, there are other phrases with equally little definition that are used to signify Bad Things: 'red tape', 'Westminster elites', 'magic money tree' and so on.

The platitude of the economy that works for everyone is a particularly important one, because of the sense of fuzzy warmth it provides. It conveys the idea that British society could and should be one big harmonious unit, where the prosperity of one means the prosperity of all, so long as a few issues can be ironed out. As with a healthy human body after the removal of an inflamed appendix, once a specific problem has been dealt with, the remaining entity is basically one in which all the different bits act in harmony. This is a good, uplifting message.

But such an economy has evidently not arrived and seems unlikely to do so in the imminent future. So the business of politics becomes the business of identifying new problems that can explain the delay, and this is where the message becomes less inspirational. There is no shortage of groups or entities that act as the social equivalent of the inflamed appendix, and politicians have competed to find the most relevant ones. On this basis, in the years following the financial crisis of 2008, the political right clearly did much better: migrants, the European Union, the unemployed and benefits claimants* evidently captured voters' imagination more than left-wing concerns like inequality, 'the bankers' and 'irresponsible capitalists'.[2] There has been a shifting astrology of blame which has, at times, become surreal and dreamlike, even extending at one point to people who don't have alarm clocks† or who leave their blinds closed.[3] Sure signs of unacceptable sloth.

The idea of class poses a problem for these kinds of platitudes, because it suggests that there are more deep-rooted and intractable divisions in society that cannot be resolved without significant upheaval – hence Margaret Thatcher's rejection of the very concept, in the quote above, as one imported from communist ideology. It alludes to tensions that are imprinted on the heart of society and *define the way it works*, when actually it is much easier to parcel out smaller, more manageable evils, whether they are real or not. So it seemed, until quite recently, that class had become very unwelcome in mainstream political discussion.

---

* Benefits claimants are a vastly larger group than the unemployed, but these two groups are often referred to as if they are synonymous.

† In early 2011, Nick Clegg tried hard to popularise the phrase 'Alarm Clock Britain' as a (wholly unsuccessful) means of signifying the kinds of no-nonsense hard workers he wanted to identify with the Liberal Democrats.

The Labour Party had a big hand in this. In its New Labour period, it had a quaintly uplifting message: yes, class *used* to matter and it used to be terrible, back in the pre-war era when people worked in hellish factory conditions. But now we've had Labour governments, along with the National Health Service (NHS), the welfare state, workers' rights, and so on, and as a result class is not a problem anymore. It still exists, but if we can make sure we have 'equality of opportunity' (as if this is possible when people start life under such different conditions) then class divisions don't have to be divisive.

Since then the Labour Party's abandonment of class has come back to haunt it. The political right in Britain became far keener to talk about class than before. Politicians such as Theresa May and Nigel Farage sought to build a close association between the idea of the 'working class' and a particular set of opinions, most notably related to immigration. They cultivated a widespread conventional wisdom that 'ordinary people' were sick of immigration and the EU, while 'liberal elites' loved immigration and hated native British people. This message, while dependent on some fairly self-serving stereotypes, proved quite resonant, and did the Labour Party very severe damage, particularly in the general election defeat of 2015 and in the Brexit referendum, which led to huge internal tensions and agonising. In 2017, as May began to look increasingly weak and Labour appeared to be gaining ground under Corbyn, the issue of class once again became hazy in British politics. For instance, we were told that age is now a far more important division than class, and had largely usurped the latter as a means of explaining people's voting choices.[4]

This erratic and unfocused discussion of class, sometimes dismissive, usually vague, always self-serving, comes about mainly because the concept is nowadays generally understood as a kind of cultural identification. It is associated with certain accents or certain kinds of job, or the kinds of music or TV programmes people like; who their friends are, the values they emphasise and the kinds of newspapers they read. Consequently, some of the people who talk about class most often are self-conscious liberal broadsheet journalists, fretting over whether or not they are allowed to pass judgement on people who read *The Sun*. There is a vast body of academic research on how to categorise people into different classes according to these social and cultural differences. I will summarise some of this later.

While recognising the insights that some of this literature can provide, I want to get away from this kind of thing. In the Marxist reading, class is about something different. It is not, at root, about culture, but about the *position people occupy within the structure of an economy*, including the economic function they fulfil and the demands and imperatives they face as a result. Some people own businesses and invest money in them in order to make a profit. Other people depend on their ability to sell their time and skills in exchange for a wage. Some have managerial roles whereby they need to control and regulate the second group in the interests of the first, while others might be involved in moving money about, or maintaining social order. Often, the interests of people in these different positions conflict.

The basic argument here is that these economic roles matter more than cultural or social identifiers: they are the building blocks of the capitalist economy, and the differences and conflicting interests between them not only affect people's experiences and the pressures they face in their own lives, but also have much bigger implications for wider society and government. So class is not just about classification: if we look at the most important changes in British political economy since the 1970s (which I will consider in Chapter 3), we can see that these changes did not just *affect* class relationships, but they were also *affected by* them. Before getting on to this, however, I will look in more depth at how discussion around class has developed in Britain over the last decade.

CLASS SINCE THE FINANCIAL CRISIS

Britain, like many other countries, had a brief glimpse of what we might call 'class consciousness' following the financial crisis of 2008. The financial sector was identified as the main cause of the downturn, and for a while the phrase 'the bankers' became closely associated with various adjectives: greed, trickery, short-sightedness. There was a consensus that large financial institutions had taken on too much risk in order to make more money for themselves, and that everyone else was facing the consequences.

On the surface this seems like a fertile context for class conflict. There was, certainly, a lot of protest, and groups on the radical left momentarily seemed marginally more relevant than they had done for years. Most notable here was the Occupy movement, which began in the US and spread to various other countries. Occupy groups gained publicity by staging highly visible protests in centres of financial activity, including outside St Paul's Cathedral. They set up tents and stayed there for several months, holding debates, making banners and so on.

These movements were highly successful in some respects. Mainly, they got people talking about the things they thought were important. The use of words and phrases such as 'inequality' or 'corporate greed' in the media spiked following their protests, and declined again as Occupy's profile diminished.[5]

But to what extent was Occupy about class? It aimed itself at bankers and the politicians with whom they were presumed to be in cahoots. They argued that these people had stitched the system up and had become extremely rich at everyone else's expense. They had a slogan to this effect: 'the 1 per cent versus the 99 per cent'. The problem with this slogan is that it is vague. For one thing, it relies on the conspiratorial idea that society is governed by a tiny elite out for themselves, as opposed to a chaotic society in which elites are as confused as everyone else. With the benefit of hindsight, which of these seems to work better as a description of the Cameron–Clegg years? Or the minority Conservative Brexit government? Capitalist economies are more confusing and unpredictable than this.

The slogan also buys into the 'economy that works for everyone' platitude. There is this tiny group who need to be brought down a peg or several, but beyond that everyone else exists on the side of righteousness. Lumped into the 99 per cent are everyone from students, the homeless, professional and blue-collar employees, the unemployed, the retired, small businesses and, implicitly, large businesses that work in 'good' areas like manufacturing rather than duplicitous financiers with their hocus pocus.

This 'intuitive populism'[6] was its main selling point, directed at a '1 per cent' which is highly opaque but found colourful personification in the actions of particular individuals, such as the former Royal Bank of Scotland boss Fred Goodwin. Very obvious, unambiguous bad guys, who made it easy to parcel off a small niche of society as the villains who were ruining it for everyone else. If this is class politics, it is a very narrow and personalised version.

Occupy deserves credit for pressuring British politicians, even Conservative ones, to talk a lot more than they used to about inequality and corporate greed. But these terms are fuzzy. Fighting against inequality, for instance, has long been a rallying cry of the left, but the word 'inequality' is surprisingly easily subsumed into dry and technocratic language. What is inequality, really? Often, it is encapsulated in an esoterically calculated figure (i.e. the Gini coefficient) that sometimes gets higher (which is bad) or lower (which is good), and which can be manhandled in support of any argument. For example, Britain's Gini coefficient may well decline if economic instability takes a chunk out of elite incomes, as occurred in 2010–11,[7] but this does not mean that anything particularly profound or emancipatory has happened.

The danger of this technocratic fuzziness is that the left's rhetoric fizzles out, and this is indeed what happened in the years immediately after the crisis. David Cameron, the prime minister at the time of Occupy's activity, was able to reel off his own statistics that said inequality was falling, enabling every potentially damaging exchange on the topic to disperse into a fog of numbers. Politicians on the centre-left were repeatedly naive about how widely the anti-inequality message would resonate. Concern with inequality is not a new thing in Britain: the number of British people who think that the gap between rich and poor is too wide has been very high for years and looks like remaining so. But what declined throughout the 1990s and 2000s was people's inclination to actually do anything about it. By 2010, the number of people supporting policies that redistribute wealth had sunk to about one in three, compared to over half in 1991.[8] The effect of several years of austerity and high-profile attacks on welfare recipients (such as the harshly punitive 'bedroom tax') did not have a substantial effect on this general lack of interest.[9] Corbyn's strategy relied on the idea that people were starting to care again, but this cannot be assumed.

So while the old (pre-2015) centre-left put too much faith in people's outrage at inequality, the right were highly adept at finding a narrative which was in many respects less accurate (the idea that the financial crisis was a result of Gordon Brown 'spending all the money' on benefits claimants) but, paradoxically, felt more real. They realised that very few people identified as 'the 99 per cent'. Instead, they pursued a strategy of flattery. David Cameron and George Osborne developed a category that people actually *wanted* to feel like they were part of. This was the idea of 'hardworking people', and it was given its appeal by the sense, reinforced by government, that there were a lot of lazy people about. Everyone knows a lazy person with whom they like to contrast themselves.

The hardworking person became the model citizen of the austerity era: they accepted that we were 'all in it together', and that you had to pull your weight by making sacrifices without complaining. This idea was fleshed out in sometimes poetic ways. The hardworking person was enraged by the sight of their neighbours' curtains being drawn (George Osborne talking on the radio: 'It is unfair that people listening to this programme going out to work see the neighbour next door with the blinds down because they are on benefits'). They were cruelly bullied by trade unions, who admittedly are also made up of hard workers, but of the kind that complain (Sajid Javid: 'these [anti-union] reforms will stop the "endless" threat of strike action hanging over hardworking people'). And their main interests were gambling and alcohol.*

In policy terms, Cameron and Osborne's legacy now looks very humble indeed. They fell a long way short of their self-imposed deficit-reduction targets. Indeed, their whole rhetoric and agenda was built around eliminating the UK budget deficit by 2020, but this objective was ditched as counterproductive and unachievable by their successors, Theresa May and Phillip Hammond. They advertised themselves as the only choice for 'stable' leadership, but then Cameron had to resign after accidentally leaving the European Union. Nonetheless, they cemented a highly successful political demonology for the early twenty-first century. The economy that works for everyone is possible, if by 'everyone' we mean 'hardworking people'. They flattered enough people into identifying with this category to win elections, and were very pointed in showing who did not fit. Consider how the role of the unemployed moved from victim to perpetrator in Conservative election posters, from Thatcher's first election (an image of people queuing outside an unemployment office with the headline 'Labour's not working') to Cameron's 2015 re-election (a picture of David Cameron with sleeves rolled up so as to look energetic, with the headline 'let's cut benefits for those that refuse work').†

This was a far more (electorally) effective variant on the 'economy that works for everyone' line than the Occupy vision (and even more so than the weak dilution thereof upon which Ed Miliband ran the 2015 election). In the latter case, the barrier to a good economy was a

---

* In 2014 Grant Shapps (then Tory chairman) tweeted a celebratory image in response to the latest Osborne budget reading thus: 'BINGO! Cutting the bingo tax and beer duty to help hardworking people do more of the things they enjoy.'

† The value of comparing these two posters was inspired by Imogen Tyler's keynote speech at the *Work, Employment and Society* conference at the University of Leeds, September 2016.

highly opaque and hard-to-define group that many people ultimately suspected were untouchable anyway. The hardworking people phrase, by contrast, enabled the Conservatives to present themselves as the improbable conquerors of Labour's territory. Until very recently, Labour itself accepted their narrative (and many people in the party clearly still do). As the then shadow Work and Pensions Secretary Rachel Reeves underlined, Labour had become desperate to show that 'we are not the party of people on benefits. We don't want to be seen, and we're not, the party to represent those who are out of work … Labour are a party of working people, formed for and by working people.'[10] Here, the glib division between the 'working class' and those who are out of work is taken as read. As I will argue later, according to the Marxist view this is one of the most stupid things anyone can possibly say about class.

During Theresa May's first few months in office, the Conservative version of class warfare assumed a fuller expression. A Conservative MP hoped, in a French newspaper, that May might be the first politician of the new 'post-liberal' settlement,[11] being unafraid to recognise that many people's lives have been much damaged by social and economic liberalism. On assuming her position, May gave a speech in which she repeatedly used the phrase 'working class' and put strong emphasis on themes of social and economic justice. For example, she talked about

> fighting against the burning injustice that, if you're born poor, you will die on average nine years earlier than others …
>
> If you're from an ordinary working class family, life is much harder than many people in Westminster realise. You have a job but you don't always have job security. You have your own home, but you worry about paying a mortgage. You can just about manage but you worry about the cost of living and getting your kids into a good school …
>
> I know you're working around the clock, I know you're doing your best, and I know that sometimes life can be a struggle. The government I lead will be driven not by the interests of the privileged few, but by yours.

Why did this approach fail for her? Probably not because it is a weak line: it isn't (as evidenced by the pressure which mounted on Corbyn throughout 2017 to say more right-wing-sounding things about immigration, and the number of people in the Corbyn movement who share a similar critique of liberalism). More likely, she just expressed it in an implausible way – you can't say these things and then lecture nurses on live TV about how naive they are to ask for a pay rise.

The most interesting thing for our purposes is what right-wing people mean when they talk about the 'working class'. At her first party conference, May was using this language, sometimes in a self-contradictory way. She wanted to create 'a programme for government to act to create an economy that works for everyone – an economy that's on the side of ordinary working class people'. The first half of the quote is the platitude we have encountered many times already. The second half, though, seems to define a specific group within society and explicitly put government in its corner – so, by definition, *not* an economy that works for *everyone* – what about the liberal elites? It is, in its fuzzy and self-serving way, a message of class conflict.

This kind of language built on the way Cameron and Osborne were implicitly using the idea of class. By 'working class' in the above quote, May essentially means the same thing as Cameron's 'hardworking people': a kind of fuzzy-but-warm haze that almost everyone thinks they are a part of. But she was drawing out a particular element of this far more strongly than before. In passages like the following, the meaning becomes much sharper:

> [I want] to put the power of government squarely at the service of ordinary working-class people. Because too often that isn't how it works today. Just listen to the way a lot of politicians and commentators talk about the public. They find your patriotism distasteful, your concerns about immigration parochial, your views about crime illiberal, your attachment to your job security inconvenient. They find the fact that more than seventeen million voters decided to leave the European Union simply bewildering.

Here, various things are meshed together. There is a concern about job security lifted from the trade union movement and the political left. It is true that this has been threatened by 'liberal elites'; May was aware of just how much this is the case, having been an integral part of these efforts in the Cameron government. Then there is the old-school Tory stuff: the EU, patriotism, law and order, and so on. These themes are presented as if they are all part of the same big basket of Working-Class Issues. So the working class is defined as people who worry about job security, who love the Queen, who want the death penalty and who want to leave the EU. And, of course, who dislike immigration. May was the most anti-immigrant British prime minister for a very long time, with a tendency to make sure that anti-immigration sentiment remained high-up on the list of working-class issues as she defined them. So her key line was probably this one: 'if you believe you're a citizen of the world, you're a citizen of nowhere. You don't understand what the very word "citizenship" means.'

This is a very important quote. Here, the elite opponents of the working class are *cosmopolitans*. In other words, people that revel in a world of open borders and diversity; put succinctly by the musician Wynton Marsalis as meaning that 'you fit in wherever you go'.[12] It is obvious that many people have lost some very important things because of globalisation: international competition and economic restructuring (most importantly the decline of heavy industry in Britain) have rendered working lives in many regions insecure, and caused the fragmentation of communities that once had more cohesive identities and senses of purpose. Employers and investors are highly mobile, and their decisions to move elsewhere has serious consequences for those that depend on them for work. So, unsurprisingly, many people do not want to fit in wherever they go, and may distrust things that do. It is easy to see why, in this context, it has been an open goal for the Conservatives to conflate support for migration and free movement in the EU with anti-working-class elitism. It is also worth noting that the most cosmopolitan thing in the world is capital, but we will return to this later.

This caused serious problems for Labour, and will keep resurfacing irrespective of periods of electoral optimism. It is supposed to be 'the party of the working class', but the associations that go with this term have, as we have just seen, been changing in a way that is much more conducive to Conservative talking points. In some quarters, it seems that the phrase 'working class' has become largely synonymous with criticism of immigration. It has become unusual to find a politician or journalist who uses this term without then segueing into this topic. For instance, *The Sun*, which always used to complain about class politics, now features leader columns with titles like 'Rage of the Working Class'. But what is the working class raging about? Only one thing, apparently:

Our population has just rocketed by 513,273 in one year, 335,600 from migration. It is not racist to protest at the calamitous effect this is having on working people who bear the brunt of it.

Prosperous middle class home owners in London love all the Polish plumbers and cleaners. For working people the influx has meant low pay, stagnant for a decade as housing costs have soared. It means schools and surgeries are full up.

It means being branded 'thick' by supposedly educated Remain supporters too dim themselves to see that the rational desire for our Government to control immigration has nothing – zero – to do with prejudice or narrow-mindedness.[13]

Obviously, we are not just talking about a British phenomenon here. The tying together of this kind of 'identity politics' and the working class has fatally undermined centre-left parties in many countries. This is perhaps most obvious in the United States, where Donald Trump worked hard to befriend the leaders of predominantly white trade unions (notably in the building trades, whom he will needed for his border wall) while preparing for conflict with those more likely to represent immigrant workers and ethnic minorities (e.g. in the public sector).[14]

But despite all this, the UK Labour Party actually performed surprisingly well in the 2017 elections compared to sister parties in other European countries such as France, Greece, Spain, Iceland or the Netherlands. This resilience coincided with a strong shift to the left under Jeremy Corbyn's leadership, a fact which caused much surprise and worry among commentators wedded to liberal political orthodoxy.

How did this happen? At first, it seemed like Corbyn would not manage to reverse Labour's downward spiral. In the initial stages of his leadership, he appeared more afraid of talking about class than the Conservatives. In his 2016 conference leader's speech, a week before May's, Corbyn did not use the phrase 'working class' at all. He used the woollier term 'working families'. The success of what we might call the 'Conservative class warrior' as described above was one reason why Labour preferred to keep things vague, relying on broader condemnations of inequality and reiterations of the 'economy that works for everyone' platitude. It was unnerved by the rawer kind of class conflict expounded by the Tories which centred on nationalism. Labour appeared snookered, prompting various doom-laden prophecies from even the most sympathetic observers.[15] Brexit brought these anxieties to almost intolerable levels for Labour and was the central cause of a failed leadership coup in 2016.

The situation became much brighter with the general election of 2017, which left Labour in an unexpectedly strong position having attracted more votes than most commentators, and most of their own MPs, had thought possible. Suddenly, doom-mongers became optimism-mongers.[16] But it is wrong to imagine that Labour's agonising around class has been resolved: almost certainly, it will come back. Their most high-profile constituency triumphs in 2017 came in places like Kensington where they attracted new support from anti-Brexit rich people, or in places with a heavy student vote like Canterbury. Meanwhile, there were swings *away* from the party in places like Sunderland which had voted very strongly for Brexit. The fact that the biggest sources of new Labour support were among the young and the highly educated[17] suggests, at least on the face of things, that Labour remains highly vulnerable to the 'right-wing class warrior' argument.

On the other hand, the face of things can be deceiving. The argument of this book will be that a lot of the discussion and analysis mentioned so far is based on very shallow readings of class, which sees it as a means of sorting people into categories, rather than something which in many respects *defines the way in which society works*. Let us take a stereotypical Corbyn-supporting educated young person working in a graduate job. (By 'young person', we shouldn't imagine a teenager: Labour support was higher in each age band up to those in their forties). Their voting choice *may* tell us that Labour had simply realigned to hoover up a more privileged demographic, thus moving away from their 'working-class base'. But it may also tell us something else: perhaps the problems that used to be associated with this 'working-class base' are now starting to spread across society more widely. Insecurity, the boredom and frustration of working life, the sense that government is powerless to act to address urgent and distressing social problems because it needs to avoid offending 'the markets': these are all 'class issues' and they affect a very wide spectrum of people indeed.

The point is that we need, urgently, to consider how we understand the idea of class. Class is clearly important in Britain today. As we have seen, it has become a fashionable topic for some surprising people, and the source of terrible worry for others. But the way in which the term is used and understood has been manipulated in a political and self-serving manner. In some ways it appears to be almost worthlessly vague, such as when it is associated with 'hardworking people'. At other times, it becomes darkly and misleadingly specific, as in the conflation of 'working class' with anti-immigrant sentiment. In trying to get beyond this, I will start by looking at some other, more academic, discussions around class in twenty-first century Britain.

CLASS AND CLASSIFICATION IN ACADEMIA

Phillip Mirowski has argued that since the 1970s there has been a concerted effort by politicians to designate more and more people as 'middle class'.[18] This, he suggests, is a good way of minimising social conflict, since if everyone feels middle class they presumably have more invested in the status quo. The previous section, however, showed a slightly different picture emerging in relation to current British politics, whereby politicians allude much more frequently, and in a more celebratory way, to the 'working class', all the while associating it strongly with nationalism and patriotism. But what about when we move away from front-line politics?

There are various academic writers who have sought to rehabilitate class as a key focus when analysing society. Probably the most high-profile recent work is *Social Class in the 21st Century* by Mike Savage (written with several colleagues at the London School of Economics). This book was informed by a large piece of research called the 'Great British Class Survey', conducted in conjunction with the BBC. People were asked to fill in an online questionnaire about their earnings, job and living situation, as well as various questions about their social networks – the kinds of people they know and socialise with. The survey then assigned respondents to one of seven categories, which they identified as the new class structure in Britain. These are the elite, the 'established middle class', the 'technical middle class', the 'new affluent worker', the 'traditional working class', 'emerging service workers' and the 'precariat'.

In developing this sort of categorisation, Savage is seeking to do various things. First, he wants to offer a more nuanced hierarchy, moving beyond the vague terminology of 'working' and 'middle' classes. In this sense, the book is about classification: he argues that we need to be able to delineate people's class positions accurately, and then understand the characteristics of each category. This, he suggests, also serves an important political purpose. It helps us to empathise more successfully with those at the bottom of society, and to be more critical of the unfair advantages accruing to those at the top. For this reason, the first paragraph of Savage's book puts emphasis not on class itself but inequality. Ultimately, it is claimed, understanding class helps us fight inequality.

Another of Savage's objectives relates to the idea of 'social mobility', which is rarely far behind when the issue of inequality is raised. Social mobility is when someone born into a poor family has plenty of opportunities to make it up the social scale, and presumably when people from affluent backgrounds see their life prospects decline (though the latter point is rarely as celebrated by those who have turned social mobility into a catchphrase). Savage says that these class distinctions are an important barrier to social mobility. If you're born in the elite, you have friends and contacts who are also in the elite, and you know how to conduct yourself in a way that other members of the elite like, so you tend to stay in the elite.

Third, to make this social mobility argument, Savage highlights different kinds of 'capital' – meaning attributes that someone possesses or develops which they can use to enhance their class position. These are: economic capital (referring to someone's wealth and income), cultural capital (their tastes and preferences) and social capital (their friends and social networks). People who have a lot of these kinds of capital tend to use them to get more and climb higher, thus breaking social mobility and reinforcing class divisions.

In this sense, Savage is highly influenced by the French sociologist Pierre Bourdieu, who pioneered the use of 'capital' in this way. Bourdieu argued that vast portions of our lives and societies are shaped by different classes' access to these kinds of capital. People from more affluent class backgrounds have certain kinds of interests, certain contact networks, certain senses of humour and certain ways of expressing themselves, and this is not even to mention the additional advantages that being born with money can buy (better education, more secure living conditions and so on). He used the idea of 'symbolic violence': the things that more affluent people like are held up as the most important things needed to get ahead in society, whereas the things working-class people like and the way they behave are presented as what not to do. The fact that a certain set of mannerisms and cultural reference points get you much easier access to influential social networks, for instance, is a kind of 'symbolic violence'.

Bourdieu is celebrated for giving a rich depiction of the lives of people in different class situations, and, in particular, showing how these distinctions reproduce themselves from generation to generation.[19] Ultimately,

Bourdieu provides a very good way of explaining why social inequalities do not change, and why there is little social mobility. Bourdieu's work, as shown by its influence on writers such as Savage, is probably the dominant way of addressing class in academic sociology; it's an exercise in classification, characterising the nature of differences and showing why they don't go away. As I have already noted, after the 2017 election there was a popular argument that age had replaced class as the most important factor influencing voting choice.[20] This is interesting. If our concern is mainly about defining a set of classes and showing why the differences between them matter, this development poses a problem: why bother, when it seems that age is more important in explaining people's worldviews anyway? I will come back to this in the final section of the book, where I consider the situation in Britain following the 2017 general election.

Notice that the bottom of Savage's scale is something called 'the precariat',* which is drawn from the work of Guy Standing, another academic with fairly high media visibility and a flair for coining neologisms.[21] Standing has become a very influential writer on class, because he posits the existence of an entirely new class, and a 'dangerous one' into the bargain.† The precariat, for Standing, is a diverse group, with the defining feature being *insecurity*. For instance:

1. Their 'industrial citizenship' is insecure. By this, Standing means that they have little security in the world of work. They will lack legal or institutional protection against job loss, work opportunities may be short term and prone to dry up, they will have little access to opportunities to gain skills that could enable them to access better jobs; and they will generally have nobody to speak up for them at work (such as trade unions).
2. They will also have income insecurity, and will likely not know whether they will be able to provide for themselves and their dependents in the medium term. This is partly a natural result of point one, but also reflects various other things: the weakening of welfare 'safety nets', for instance. People in the precariat are also less likely to have family or community networks they can draw on for support. In this sense, the precariat is connected with the idea of

---

* This is a portmanteau, mixing together the words 'proletariat' and 'precarious'.

† The subtitle of his book *The Precariat* is 'the new dangerous class'.

'disaffiliation', which French sociologists have been writing about for some years:[22] 'disaffiliated' people, like the precariat, are cut off from access to both secure work and other sources of support and income provided by wider society.

3. They also, apparently, do not *feel* like part of the 'traditional working class'. They do not identify with trade unions, the traditional representatives of this group, and they do not necessarily value the same things the post-war trade union movement valued (such as wage growth and job security). Instead, they might demand other kinds of social protection; things like a 'universal basic income', for instance (we return to this idea later).

Point three – that the precariat has completely different needs and aspirations from the 'traditional working class' – is probably Standing's most controversial point, and he is often criticised for not providing enough evidence. Expressed this way, the question becomes not simply 'how do we define different classes?' but also 'what do different classes want?' In this sense Standing is no doubt unsurprised by the tying together of class and attitudes towards immigration described in the previous section. For him, one of the dangers of 'precarity' is how easily it can be associated with nationalist political projects: insecurity becomes the rejection of globalisation which becomes the rejection of foreigners. Hence, if nothing more positive can be offered to them, in the worst-case scenario he sees the precariat as the core demographic of future fascist movements.

So the state of the art in academic discussion of class tends to emphasise the need for finer distinctions, taking into account the relative decline of 'traditional working-class' jobs and the growth in white-collar or service work. It also emphasises *barriers* between classes, examining how class distinctions (e.g. in access to different kinds of social, economic and cultural capital) reinforce and reproduce themselves, acting as a brake on social mobility. There is also a growing concern with insecurity among those at the bottom, as exemplified by Standing's work on the precariat.

One thinker who does not feature heavily in the work of high-profile British academic analysts of class such as Savage or Standing is Marx. To some extent Marx is seen as too blunt. After all, he focused primarily on the relationship between only two groups – worker and capitalist – whereas nowadays we want to see more nuance. The kind of economy he was analysing (principally Britain in the nineteenth century) was one where mechanised industry was just emerging, and in which the new actors on the scene were the emerging 'proletariat' of factory workers and the 'bourgeois' mill owner. But the UK economy is highly complex, featuring huge amounts of professional, knowledge-based and service-based work, which obviously presents a challenge for this kind of binary distinction.

Another reason why Marx appears at odds with the spirit of the age is that he has very little interest in 'social mobility', at least in the warm and fuzzy way we understand it today. Who could deny that people should be able to rise in the social hierarchy if they have good ideas and work hard? As we shall see, Marx does talk a lot about social mobility in a sense, but in a way that inspires less enthusiasm: he looks in some depth at the *downwards* social mobility of people who may have once been self-sufficient small producers, but who were reduced to the status of disposable factory hands by the development of capitalist industry.

It is true, then, that if our main purpose is to find increasingly fine ways of categorising different groups of people, and explaining the barriers between them, Marx's writing offers little help today. But thinking about class should not be purely about classification, however nuanced, as an end in itself. As I said earlier, for Marx class is more about the position and function that people occupy within the structure of an economy, and the way in which these different roles interact and conflict. For instance, someone who depends on selling their time and skills in exchange for a wage may have conflicting interests with someone who depends on making a profit by manufacturing and selling goods at a competitive price. This is the case even if they both have the same views on the relative value of the opera versus *The X Factor*, have the same accents and went to the same school.

The key point is this: when talking about class, our objective should not be simply to provide a comprehensive categorisation of groups of people and the differences between them, but *to consider how the interactions between people with different economic roles affects the working of society as a whole*, from the experiences people have at work, to the development and application of technology, to the economic and social policies pursued by governments. Unlike Bourdieu or Savage, whose emphasis is on how class divisions persist, Marx's interest is on how the conflict between different classes leads society to *change*, and hence to the undermining and disruption of the status quo rather than its preservation.

2
Alien Powers:
Class in Marxist Thought

One important difference between Marx and the other writers discussed in Chapter 1 is that, for him, class is less about cultural and social attributes and more about the way the economy is structured, particularly in the workplace. Marx's focus was primarily on *commodity production*. In other words, those workplaces where goods are produced, to be sent out later into the marketplace for sale. Of course, there are many other kinds of workplaces, where tangible commodities are not produced (for instance in the service industry, finance or the public sector). I will come to these later, but for now I will focus on how Marx thought class distinctions worked in commodity production.

Marx utilises something generally called a 'labour theory of value'. In broad terms, this is the belief that the value of a particular commodity is determined by the amount of labour that has gone into it. Things which require more labour, tend to be more valuable.* In the productive workplace, commodities are produced using a combination of two main inputs: human labour and machinery. Machinery can reduce the value of commodities, by reducing the amount of human labour required to make them. Commodities are then sold and the money reinvested to make more commodities.

---

* There are a lot of caveats that need to be explained here, which are discussed in Marx's work and which have also been discussed at great length ever since. When talking about how much labour goes into a commodity, Marx refers to 'socially necessary labour time'. What this means it that, if I spend two days making a chair that is identical to one that was made in a factory in ten minutes, my chair is no more valuable than the factory one. What determines value is therefore not the actual efforts of particular individuals, but the amount of labour it *should* take to make something given the technology available. If new chair-making technology is invented that reduces the amount of labour required to make a chair, then we would expect the value of chairs to decline. However, also note that 'value' here is not the same as price, since sellers make all sorts of decisions about pricing in order to gain competitive advantages against their rivals, selling commodities below or above their value. The point, though, is that Marx would expect the real prices of things, over time, to follow the same trends as their value, which in turn follows 'socially necessary labour time'.

The owner of the factory hopes that s/he makes a profit in this process. But where does this profit come from? This is where class divisions come in. According to Marx, workers produce more value in a day's work at the factory than they receive in wages. The difference between the value the worker produces and the value of their wage goes back to the factory owner (i.e. the capitalist), and Marx calls it *surplus value*. If the capitalist can then successfully sell these commodities at their value, then this surplus value is converted into hard profit.

How is the capitalist able to gain this surplus value? If workers aren't being paid the full value of what they've produced, why don't they just make and sell things themselves without the capitalist taking a cut? This is because of a very important point: one of the defining characteristics of capitalism is, for Marx, the fact that the 'means of production' (the technology, organisational resources and other equipment needed to produce commodities) are owned by the capitalist. The worker can't do these things on his/her own, because they don't have access to the equipment and investment power they need. Admittedly, at some stage they may have done. In pre-capitalist Britain, many would have worked in their own homes using their own equipment (e.g. small-scale weavers). But under capitalism the most modern and efficient machinery becomes concentrated in the hands of capitalists, and workers therefore have no choice but to sell their time and skills to them in exchange for a wage.

Broadly, Marx concerns himself with two main classes: *labour* and *capital*. Labour refers to those people who do not own the means of production, and who depend on being able to sell their time and skills to those that do. Capital refers to those that do own the means of production, and who depend on hiring labour and extracting surplus value, in order to make a profit. If we consider class analysis as primarily a means of *categorising* people, then this is obviously quite blunt. Even setting aside the fact that there are many people who don't easily fit into either of these categories, there is so much variation *within* them: it refuses to distinguish between the vast discrepancies in skill, status or pay levels between individuals within the class of 'labour', for instance. The worker involved in designing the iPad, versus the worker involved in its manufacture.

But this is to miss the point. We are not talking here about ways of sorting individuals into particular categorisations, but as a means of explaining the processes and pressures that define capitalist societies. Take 'capital', for instance. As Anwar Shaikh points out, capital should not be taken to denote a group of individuals with shared cultural and social characteristics, but an economic *process* which is enacted by particular individuals or groups.[1] Money is invested in order to make something, which is then sold, hopefully for more money than was originally invested. Then this augmented sum is reinvested and the cycle begins again. Marx represents this with a very simple formula: M-C-M'. Money is invested (M), used to make commodities for sale (C), and a larger sum is created (M'). When anyone enters into this process, he or she is acting as capital.

If the M-C-M' cycle is broken, and the people with the money stop investing it (and either fritter it away on personal consumption or just hoard it under their mattresses), they stop being capitalists. So, when I refer to *capital* from now on, I mean all those people or agencies, be they the sole owners of a company, shareholders, major investment organisations or whatever else, who are involved in investing money in order to extract 'surplus value'. Likewise, when I refer to *labour* I mean all those people that depend on their ability to sell their time and skills to capital as a means of carrying out this process, usually in exchange for a wage. By fulfilling this function, they create surplus value which the capitalist can then try to realise as profit and reinvest.

I need to stress something very important here, which takes my analysis of class a very long way away from those discussed in Chapter 1. 'Labour' as a class under capitalism is not necessarily something you *are*: it would be insultingly reductive to pick a particular individual with all of their complexity, and say 'this person is labour'. It is something you *do*; a role you fulfil within the wider economy. Someone could be within the 'elite' according to the kinds of cultural activities they like, food they eat and people they meet, but if they end up spending eight hours a day selling their time and skills to someone else in exchange for a wage, then for that period they are acting as labour and experience the pressures and demands that go with this role.

Therefore, the point is not to claim that these categories are exhaustive, nor that they explain the life conditions of everyone who fits into either of these broad groups. Obviously they do not. But they do offer a way of understanding the kinds of pressures and conflicts that characterise all capitalist societies. The twenty-first century British economy is highly diverse, with a huge service industry and a much more high-tech manufacturing sector compared to the cotton mills of Marx's day (to name just two of the most obvious differences). But this book will argue that these pressures and conflicts continue to play out in similar ways, even if the surroundings look very different. Capitalists *need* to keep extracting, realising and reinvesting surplus value, and if they don't the economy will stop growing. The importance of this cycle characterises our world as much, if not more, than it characterised Marx's.

So this analysis is, in some respects, quite 'depersonalised'. Unlike other writers, I am less interested in the personal attributes that make someone 'working' or 'middle' class, (or whatever other categorisation we might develop). Consequently, I am also less interested in language such as 'corporate greed' or 'irresponsible capitalism'. Certainly, there is greed and irresponsibility in the corporate world, as elsewhere. But more interesting is what happens when capitalism is simply working as it is supposed to. In this respect, Marx's distinction between labour and capital leads to various important points, which we will now examine.

CONFLICT IN THE WORKPLACE

For Marx, capital can only function if it is continually able to extract surplus value. In other words, if it is able to get more value out of workers than it gives them in the form of a wage. Whether capital is invested by a kindly old philanthropist, or by a predatory multinational investment fund, it has to extract this surplus value, otherwise no profit can be made and the business will fail. If large numbers of capitalists are unable to do this, then the economy will stagnate or contract. The quantity of surplus value that a worker can furnish in a given working day is variable. If workers can gain higher wages or shorter working hours without a corresponding increase in productivity (e.g. through new working methods or technological improvement), then surplus value diminishes.

This means that, by definition, capital has an interest in trying to limit wages and extend working time. Labour, conversely, has an interest in the opposite: most workers would ideally like to reduce working time and raise wages. This is the kind of observation that seems very obvious, but in Marx's view there is something odd, even irrational about this situation. It suggests that, under capitalism, the process of making things to satisfy human needs – one of the most important activities in any society – is built on a massive conflict of interest. Capital needs to get as much from labour in exchange for as little as it can get away with, and this basic fact creates the additional need for all sorts of other things: management, control, supervision and so on.

For capital, the drive to extract more surplus value becomes both art and science. It is something that capitalists try to measure and calculate as precisely as possible, and they are continually inventing new techniques and methods that can help them in this effort. For example, in pre-capitalist societies, Marx suggests, things like rest and communal times were regulated by social and cultural expectations – mealtimes, for example, were a social experience and a lynchpin of community interaction – but during the capitalist working day they become things to be strictly measured, monitored and haggled over.[2] Office workers are expected to eat at their desks, call centre workers' trips to the toilet are meticulously counted and professionals are judged on whether or not they are replying to emails at two in the morning. The capitalist, Marx argued, would inevitably seek to find ways around limits to working hours (for instance through government legislation), through various 'small thefts' of the worker's time.[3]

In Marx's view, wages and the length of the working day reflect a balance of power between the distinct class interests of labour and capital: who is more organised, and which side is more able to get their way? The capitalist wants as much surplus value as s/he can get, but there are limits, particularly their inability to push workers beyond what can be tolerated socially and even physically: 'Capital ... takes no account of the health and the length of life of the worker, unless society forces it to do so.'[4]

The point here is that the division between labour and capital in capitalist economies means there is a continuous conflict of interest around the amount of surplus value that gets extracted. Today, as I will show, there is no shortage of examples of 'bad employers' who commit cynical 'small thefts' against workers. But the mistake is to attribute these instances to the greedy personalities of those involved. Capitalists need to extract as much surplus value as they can. If they don't, then others will outcompete them. So this 'greedy' behaviour has a 'rational' basis: every other capitalist does it, and they need to remain competitive. The way this conflict plays out in modern British workplaces will be the subject of an in-depth examination in Chapter 4.

Before moving on, we also need to recognise that, according to Marx, the inevitability of class conflict under capitalism would also produce the likelihood of *class consciousness* and resistance. In other words, the people comprising the classes of capital or labour are likely to, over time, start to identify shared interests with other people in the same group, and act accordingly. Marx is therefore interested in the development of forms of collective organisation on the part of workers, most obviously trade unions.

In the *Communist Manifesto* he argues that whether individual confrontations between workers and employers were won or not is less important than the 'main thing', which is that workers became more confident about, and committed to, organising collectively to advance their interests against capital. Capital, however, can also be class-conscious (arguably it finds it easier to be so than labour), and when it is it can have a very powerful voice. Consequently, Marx is not surprised to find institutions like unions being treated as 'heinous crimes' to be legislated against severely,[5] following collective lobbying of government by capitalists. He comments on the hypocrisy of liberal theorists who defend free trade but not the freedom of workers to organise. This is a remark which, as I will show, has very obvious relevance today.

The idea of class consciousness among labour is probably the single area where it is easiest for the theorists of classification to blow vast holes in Marx's argument. It does seem fairly evident that the shared 'class' identities we find emerging in reality are much less likely to reflect the broad division between labour and capital as Marx defines them, compared to the more nuanced gradations identified by writers like Savage. Marx's definition of labour, for instance, would include a relatively glamorous job such as working in digital software design, alongside lower-skilled and lower-status work such as on an assembly line. Obviously, there are likely to be major social divisions between these groups that are probably better understood in terms of ideas like social and cultural capital, and this poses a big problem for the Marxist version of class consciousness.

Nonetheless, I have already said that Marx's ideas around class should be looked at as a means of explaining the pressures that shape the development of society as a whole. In this respect, there are two reasons why his ideas around class consciousness and interest have an obvious relevance. First, because it puts us on the lookout for more subtle signs of 'resistance' against capital among workers even in apparently quite sedate environments without any stereotypical hallmarks of class consciousness (such as militant trade unions). I come back to this point in Chapter 4. Second, because the Marxist view enables us to see how class conflict is reflected in various different areas of British life, such as in the way government policy evolves, or the way culture and media operate. I will discuss this extensively later. First, I will identify some of the key aspects of Marx's analysis of class which will resurface throughout the rest of the book.

DEPENDENCY AND DISCIPLINE

Since workers depend on selling their time to capitalists in exchange for a wage, it follows that their well-being (under capitalism) is also highly dependent on the smooth running of the M-C-M' cycle. If this process is interrupted (for example, if enough surplus value cannot be extracted, if goods cannot be sold profitably or if new profitable invest-ments cannot be found) then the result may be a crisis which leads to unemployment or wage cuts. Capitalism therefore means that workers are at the mercy of a process which is largely out of their control. If that process falters, labour suffers, as has been the case since the crisis of 2008, which precipitated a long and deep decline in British workers' relative pay as capitalists sought to return to profitability (see Chapter 3).

For now, the point is that, in Marx's argument, capitalism tends to create a larger and larger group of people who are dependent on selling their time to the capitalist, and who, as a result, are ultimately in a vulnerable position with limited control over their own destiny. For Marx, it is important to stress, this includes those people who have waged jobs, but also those people who either have no job at all or who drift erratically in and out of the labour market. Marx does not distin-guish too sharply between these groups because they share an important characteristic: they are all separated from the 'means of production' and in this sense they are all dependent on capital. When capital moves to make redundancies, or to take on staff, people are buffeted between these categories by decisions over which they have no say.

The vulnerability of labour in this context is often discussed using highly fatalistic and quasi-scientific language, such as the jargon of 'supply and demand'. It is fairly common to hear people justify life-ruining things like redundancy using these kinds of highly abstract and self-consciously neutral terms. For instance: we might agree it's a shame that many train guards are being laid-off, but accept it as inevitable due to advances in ticket machine technology. Supply has come to outweigh demand, and so there must be an inevitable adjustment to these market conditions. In this kind of argument, supply and demand are spoken about as natural 'laws' to which humans must adapt, in the same way as we must learn to cope with the law of gravity, or our inability to breathe under water.

But this is not how Marx sees it. The balance between supply and demand is, in some key respects, regulated directly by capital. By seeking to grow, capital expands the demand for labour, but by investing in labour-saving technology or by laying people off for whatever other reason, it can also decrease this demand. Capitalists can choose whether to invest in technology that directly replaces workers without improving 'customer service' (such as ticket machines), or invest in technology that improves service without necessarily making people redundant (such as expanding or improving train capacity). So it is nonsense to talk about the supply and demand for labour as if they were neutral laws of economic gravity. '*Les dés sont pipés.** Capital acts on both sides at once.'[6]

I need to add another point. For Marx, it is a misconception about capitalism that it is against what would now be polemically termed 'big government'. In Marx's view, government plays a very important, and often quite coercive, role in managing and manipulating the supply of dependent labour. In the first volume of *Capital*, he considers the mass movement of people from the countryside to emerging cities in the early years of the industrial revolution. They were drawn by the 'carrot' of job opportunities in capitalist industries, compared to a life of grim rural struggle. But they were also pushed by the stick. Government, Marx argues, was highly active in depriving people of the means to support themselves in the countryside. For instance, by violently enforcing the enclosure and privatisation of common land that they were using for subsistence. And then, he says, once people lost access to the land, they were apt to be treated as 'voluntary criminals' and subjected to more legislation, such as restrictions on begging, which stretch all the way back to the Tudor period but which intensified in capitalism's early years.[7,†]

So in Marx's view the idea of 'meritocracy' – i.e. that capital was capital and labour was labour because of the superior ingenuity and hard work of those in the former group – is the worst kind of 'insipid childishness', and a kind of all-ages fairy tale.[8] Instead, he argues that a bullying government was an essential component in the birth of the modern

---

*   'The dice are loaded.'

†   There is an interesting aside here: Marx also discusses public policy around international migration. But whereas in our time this idea is associated with neuroses around immigration, Marx writes about restrictions on emigration, for fear that people leaving the country would jeopardise the labour supply.

capitalist labour market, forcibly pushing people into a vulnerable position in order to increase labour market supply in capitalist industry's formative years.

Marx uses the term 'industrial reserve army' to describe those people who were not employed but who drifted in, out and around the labour market, ready to be called upon by capital. These people often existed in the most desperate poverty. If we follow Marx's argument, it is ridiculous to draw a clear dividing line between the 'working class' (who are in work) and the unemployed (who are not), as is conventional wisdom today (recall the Rachel Reeves quote in Chapter 1). The reason this is wrong is because their fates are tied closely together. By its very existence, the 'reserve army' exerts a disciplinary pressure on those *within* work since the more unemployed people there are, the more the worker fears for his or her own position. It is therefore a source of labour market supply which, to some extent, can be manipulated to weaken the bargaining power of labour. Consequently, the reserve army is not a burden on capitalist economies: it is a resource, which 'belongs to capital just as absolutely as if the latter had bred it at its own cost'.⁹

Finally, I want to note another implication of Marx's argument. He does not believe that unemployment and poverty can ever be eradicated on a lasting basis in capitalist societies, because capital depends on these things both as a ready resource and for disciplining the in-work population. If there was no unemployment and poverty, labour would be less scared to demand higher wages and reduced working time, and so would become insufferably overconfident from capital's perspective. It is for this reason that he criticises influential liberal theorists such as Adam Smith, whose social conscience was demonstrated by his arguments in favour of the education of workers. Marx believed that other thinkers, like the French politician and writer Germain Garnier, though apparently much crueller in their outlook, were more in tune with the nature of capitalism. Whereas Smith wanted to see improved education for the poor, albeit 'in prudent and homeopathic doses',¹⁰ Garnier countered that such education could actually be a big problem for capital. This is because capitalists depended on the disposability and malleability of the worker, and their total dependence on the requirements of capital, which unnecessary education might jeopardise.

On the face of things, these kinds of comments seem a long way from the 'knowledge economy' which supposedly drives modern Britain, though as I shall argue later, this kind of rhetoric does need puncturing.

They do, in fact, fit much more closely with current employment policy, which emphasises quickly pushing people into low-skilled jobs rather than providing them with training and skills.[11] In any case, these themes of dependency and discipline will recur throughout the book.

SUBORDINATION OF THE INDIVIDUAL

Marx is frequently characterised in quite a blunt way as a 'collectivist' thinker, i.e. someone who is primarily concerned with group categories and with little interest in the specific characteristics and concerns of individuals. This is not necessarily fair, since much of his argument relates to what he sees as the subordination of genuine individuality in the capitalist workplace. Capitalism is 'individualistic' in the sense that if you lose your job you are on your own. But in many other respects it is all about enforced collectivisation.

Under capitalism, as we have seen, workers produce things in order that they can be sold on the market. While the things they produce may have 'use value' (i.e. a practical or recreational purpose), the reason they are produced is so that the capitalist can realise their 'exchange value' (i.e. how much one can expect them to sell for) in order to make a profit. This is another occasion where something which appears as a statement of the obvious is actually, according to Marx, revealed as a somewhat strange and specific state of affairs when considered from a wider perspective. Producing things purely so they can be sold for profit leads to all sorts of peculiar nonsense: large amounts of unnecessary commodities that go unsold because demand was not as high as first thought; the expenditure of untold billions and unquantifiable amounts of human effort on the creation of an advertising industry, whose sole purpose is to convince people that they need things that they self-evidently don't; periodic crashes and crises when invested money cannot return a profit. One might ask: why don't we just decide what we want and then produce it as a 'use value', and be done with it?

The fact that, under capitalism, things are produced primarily for sale in a competitive market, means that, in Marx's words, 'the process of production has mastery over man'.[12] In other words, human needs are subordinated to the service of something much more abstract – the continuation of the M-C-M' cycle. For Marx, however, note that 'human needs' here do not just concern *what* is produced but also *how* things are produced. In this respect, he argues that there is something fundamentally anti-human about the way production is organised under capitalism. He believes that the main thing that distinguishes humans from animals is our ability to enter into a self-directed creative process. A spider's web or the honeycomb of bees are impressive creative achievements. But such creatures do these things by instinct only. Humans have purpose. They can decide and design their own work in order to fulfil their own individual objectives.[13]

If we accept Marx's view, then it suggests there is something wrong with the very structure of capitalist workplaces, because they are characterised by the exact opposite situation. Workers produce the things they are told to produce in the manner they are told to produce them, for the sole purpose of returning a profit to someone else. In this process, the full spectrum of human creativity is stunted:

> [Capitalist manufacture] not only subjects the previously independent worker to the discipline and command of capital ... [but also] converts the worker into a crippled monstrosity by furthering his particular skill as in a forcing-house, through the suppression of a whole world of productive drives and inclinations, just as in the states of La Plata they butcher a whole beast for the sake of his hide or his tallow ... the individual himself is divided up, and transformed into the automatic motor of a detail operation.[14]

As machinery progresses, Marx argues that we have a process of rapid 'socialisation', i.e. the bringing together of individual workers (who may previously have been working on their own account as small-scale producers) into a large collective group with a narrowly defined division of roles, as in a factory. In this sense, capitalism is a highly *collectivist* system rather than an 'individualist' one. This socialisation occurs under the control of the capitalist and new technology is used to pursue the ends they define. As such, the machine is no longer a tool the worker can use to express him or herself, but instead comes to sweep aside individual initiative and decision making:

> In no way does the machine appear as the individual worker's means of labour. Its distinguishing characteristic is not in the least ... to transmit the worker's activity to the object ... Rather [the worker's efforts] ... merely transmit the machine's work, the machine's action, on to the raw material – supervises and guards it against interrup-

tions. Not as with the instrument, which the worker animates and makes into his organ with his skill and strength, and whose handling therefore depends on his virtuosity. Rather, it is the machine which possesses skill and strength in place of the worker, is itself the virtuoso ... The worker's activity ... is regulated on all sides by the movement of the machinery and not the opposite.[15]

In this sense, machinery, from the point of view of the worker, is an '*alien power*'. They have no control over it, but its demands come to define the physical and mental actions they must perform for large stretches of their life. Marx suggests that as machinery progresses it takes on more and more complex tasks, meaning that labour's jobs become more menial and workers themselves become more interchangeable. The machine, under capitalism, becomes the worker's enemy. In the early years of industrialisation this was rendered very vividly by the Luddites: clandestine bands of workers who destroyed new industrial equipment in Yorkshire, Derbyshire and neighbouring counties, and whose name has become associated with a distrust of technology. Individuals acting as labour are often deprived of the capacity to show initiative or creativity. Instead, they 'now produce only for society and in society ... individuals are subsumed under social production; social production exists outside them as their fate'.[16]

So Marx believes that, for labour, there is the continual danger that the capacity for individual expression will be stunted, as workers' initiative and creative agency becomes more and more subordinated to a production process designed by and for capital. This is not just about technology, but also the development of various forms of management supervision. For Marx, there must *always* be a requirement for some form of supervision over the worker, because of the inherent conflict of interest between labour and capital.[17]

Liberal theorists are fond of conflating the 'free market' with the freedom of individual humans, arguing the purest state of freedom exists when people are able to buy and sell as they want. In Marxist terms, this is ridiculous. It completely overlooks the workplace, which is, after all, the central facet of many people's lives. When we look at the workplace, we might suppose that the more anarchic (i.e. the more competitive and unrestricted) the marketplace, the more intense the discipline that needs to be exerted over the worker therein.[18] Domenico Losurdo has shown how liberal philosophers during the industrial revolution, while they vaunted 'freedom' in the marketplace, advocated ever fiercer and more intrusive control over employees.[19] Jeremy Bentham's concept of the panopticon – a building where a central observer could continually survey every other person in every other room – could have been applied to a prison, but could also have been applied to the workplace. And this is not to mention the alarm and violent responses provoked by the revelation that workers were trying to form trade unions to represent their interests.[20] I return to this idea of workplace control in Chapter 4.

ALIEN POWERS AND LOSS OF CONTROL

The final point to emphasise about Marx's writing on class is the most complicated and arguably the most important. Even though dividing society into labour and capital is fairly blunt as a way of categorising individuals' experiences and social status, it has a much greater value in a different respect. Different pressures and imperatives act on people depending on where they sit in the economic structure of society – whether they rely on their ability to sell their time and skills in exchange for a wage, or whether they depend on extracting profit, or whatever else. As I have shown, the main such imperative is the need to maintain the M-C-M' cycle, which is urgent for both capital and labour, but the process of doing so involves all sorts of conflicting interests and forms of control. How these pressures play out has significant implications for the way in which society develops and changes. Why is this?

Capitalism is highly dynamic, and needs to expand. We have seen that to be a 'capitalist', in Marx's definition, is to be defined primarily by the processes and imperatives you enact rather than your personal characteristics. You have to extract surplus value, realise it as profit, and then reinvest it in expanded form. If you don't do this, your business is outstripped by competitors and you fail. Therefore, according to Marx, the need for capital to get continually bigger is comparable to a religious duty: 'accumulate, accumulate! That is Moses and the Prophets!'[21]

This means that individual capitalists are driven by a force outside of themselves – competition. Competition forces the capitalist to extract more surplus value from his or her workers, or fall behind. The competitive marketplace is a funny thing in Marx's thinking: on the one hand, it is the product of a lot of different individuals pursuing their own interests in the ways they see fit. In this sense it appears to be quite anarchic and subject to individual strategising. But as individual capitalists are pushed to compete harder to gain over their competitors, the collective result is a pressure that acts on all these individuals and which is beyond any of their control. 'As much as the individual moments of this movement arise from the conscious will and particular purposes of individuals … their own collisions with one another produce an *alien social power* standing above them.'[22] Competition exerts a 'reciprocal compulsion'[23] on capitalists that strips them of their autonomy and binds them to a system which imposes its rules on them.

As we have already seen, this has important implications for capital in the workplace. Conflicts around wages and working time do not simply 'depend on the will, either good or bad, of the individual capitalist. Under free competition, the immanent laws of capitalist production confront the individual capitalist as a force external to him.'[24] Limiting wages and cutting break times becomes an imperative rather than a preference.

We should note that at this point we do run into quite fundamental philosophical differences that set Marx apart from other thinkers. Liberal theorists such as Hayek also refer to the way in which the individual under capitalism is buffeted by pressures that are out of his or her control; the difference is that, for him, this is all part of the fun. He warns, for instance, against 'planning designed to protect individuals or groups against diminutions of their income, which although in no way deserved yet in a competitive society occur daily, against losses imposing severe hardships having no moral justification yet inseparable from the competitive system'.[25] It is sad that people suffer morally unjustifiable hardship, but the only alternative is not to have a competitive system, and nobody wants that.

Furthermore, the idea of alien powers has much wider ramifications for society and, especially, for government. The last thing governments want are economic crises. If capitalists are not successfully extracting and reinvesting profits in their country, then they will not have economic growth. So governments in capitalist societies are dependent on the well-being of capital as a class; if capitalists are not investing, then the government has serious economic and social problems.

For this reason, government is also subject to 'alien powers'. When they impose potentially unpopular measures, such as austerity policies, they tend to rationalise this in a certain way. They appeal to abstract imperatives which are forcing their hand. British capitalism must be *competitive*. We have to reduce the tax burden and labour regulations in order to increase *business confidence*. Borrowing must be decreased so as to win the approval of *the markets*. These italicised phrases are highly abstract concepts which are 'alien powers' in the Marxist sense. They are amalgamations of the competitive interactions between thousands of individuals, which become a collective entity that has coercive force over capitalists and governments. I come back to this idea in Chapter 5.

There is another sense in which the idea of 'alien powers' applies here. Labour and capital perceive the world around them very differently. Various writers, particularly inspired by the French philosopher Henri Lefebvre, have distinguished between the two ideas of 'place' and 'space'.[26] 'Place' refers to something concrete. A place is where people live and work, where they develop roots and communities, and so on. 'Space' is something calculating and impersonal: to think about the world in terms of 'abstract space' is to think unsentimentally about how you can configure a supply chain most profitably. When capital invests in the construction of a factory in a given area, the lives of workers and their families are configured around this. Communities, networks and services spring up, and over time that place might even develop a distinctive local culture built around the nature of work in the area. But capital is not sentimental, and if it becomes more profitable to relocate that factory elsewhere, it will generally do it. In this sense, the way capital perceives geography itself is alien and remote from the perspective of labour. Things which become completely central to the latter can be discarded remarkably easily by the former.

The consequences of this kind of remoteness are all around us. For example, in Britain James Meek reported on Cadbury's relocation of production from its Somerdale plant near Bristol to Skarbimierz in Poland.[27] Two groups of people in different countries found themselves being played off against each other by capital:

Sometimes, globalised consumer capitalism links communities [in Britain and Poland] ... links them, in that strange way of globalisation, without doing anything to bring them together ... I asked [a Polish worker] how she felt about what had happened to the British factory. 'I never really thought about it', she said. 'We lost so many jobs here in Brzeg ... We didn't feel sorry that others lost theirs ... it's somewhere else in the world. We don't physically know these people.'[28]

Capital's remote calculations in abstract space had severe implications for the Somerdale workers' sense of place. Something had been lost that others would struggle to understand. In many cases this had unsurprising political consequences.

> [The workers interviewed] all voted in June [2016] for Brexit. A few years ago [one of them] joined Ukip … as we talked about chocolate-making's lack of industrial glamour, a certain amount of bitterness towards the public in general spilled out … 'People didn't get the history. It didn't mean anything to them. They didn't care whether they were going to get their Crunchie from Poland.'[29]

People's lives thus come to be governed by forces whose workings are distant and nebulous, but whose actions have painful consequences.

The point here is that the division between labour and capital within societies, even if broad and not necessarily comprehensive (see the next section), reveals important insights into the way society works. This is not just about the way different people interact with each other at work – it has much wider implications for the way in which societies and governments evolve and change over time. In the chapters that follow I will pick apart these implications in greater detail.

BEYOND PRODUCTION

I have said that Marx's analysis of class focused on commodity production, i.e. making goods for sale in the market. What about other things, such as the service sector, finance or the public sector? If physical commodities are not being made for sale in these contexts does that mean Marx's argument about labour and capital does not apply? What about small entrepreneurs and the self-employed?

Many service industry workers – for instance in areas such as warehousing, logistics, retail or call centre work – clearly act as labour, in Marx's terms, for various reasons. As Mandel argues, they share the central characteristic that they are separated from the means of production and required to sell their labour power.[30] Usually, the people that employ them are capitalists, in that they intend to profit from their investment. In addition, these kinds of workers are often essential parts of the M-C-M' cycle. Surplus value cannot be realised without logistics workers or retail workers. Where more complex commodities are concerned, we can also say that people in areas like customer support are an important part of this cycle.

Because they are part of realising the M-C-M' sequence, these kinds of workers are likely to experience the same kinds of pressures that commodity producers do. Their break times are barriers to the expansion and acceleration of this cycle, and their wages come out of the surplus value created in production (since the costs of transporting and selling commodities is a deduction from the profit made on them). For this reason, Marx devotes large sections of the second volume of *Capital* to explaining how capital is constantly seeking to increase the speed of circulation so profits come back faster.[31]

So the 'realm of circulation' – where goods are traded once they have been produced – is very important, and what happens there is very closely linked to what happens in production. For one thing, I have already argued that the force of competitive pressure in the marketplace acts as a kind of alien power over capitalists. A competitive marketplace sharpens their instincts, intensifying drives to extract more surplus value and intensifying the need for discipline over labour. But it is also important to note that there is large potential for disruption in the circulation process, and this can have serious consequences. Blockages or interruptions in circulation, perhaps because of limits to the size of the market or other logistical barriers, can mean a lack of profitable investment opportunities. This, in turn, leads to capitalists opting not to invest and instead sit on their money.[32] By accumulating large 'hoards' of money that can't be invested immediately but which cannot simply lie idle, the seeds of the banking and financial systems emerge (see Chapter 3).

It is therefore clear that various positions which do not easily fit into the labour–capital relationship nonetheless revolve around it in some way. People in managerial roles, for instance: the reason for their existence is the conflict of interest between labour and capital, which creates a ubiquitous need for supervision in the workplace. As capital becomes more sophisticated the role of management assumes more complicated forms, as shown in Chapter 4. Various professions emerge which are, in key respects, defined by the need to maintain the smooth running of capitalist processes – accountancy and legal professions, for instance, to say nothing of advertising and marketing work. The financial sector is a more complicated issue to which I return later. The public sector is a special case, which will be discussed in some depth in Chapter 5. In the meantime, we now turn to Chapter 3, which presents an overview of the way in which the British economy has developed in recent decades, and considers the ways in which the Marxist ideas already surveyed might apply.

3
Changing Class Dynamics in Britain

INTRODUCTION

In Chapters 2 and 3, I examined the way in which Marx uses the concept of class, comparing it to other perspectives from politics and academia. The purpose of this chapter, by contrast, is to paint a broad-brush picture of how the British economy has evolved over recent decades, with a particular focus on the way in which the relationship between labour and capital has changed.

It is practically impossible to discuss economy and society in Britain over the last 40 years without talking about inequality. The story is striking – as we shall see, an extended decline in inequality that followed World War II was dramatically reversed during the 1980s, and has followed a more ambiguous path since then. Because of this reversal, most people on the left in Britain see inequality as the central evil of British society, and complaining about inequality dominates left political rhetoric today. However, in Chapter 1 I argued that this was a problem. Inequality is a woolly and abstract term, and has been employed in ways that do not resonate widely. Admittedly, identifying inequality as the main social enemy has been effective in some ways, since any politician from right or left generally now needs to at least pretend to care about it. However, it has produced a fairly limited political discussion, with a fixation on technocratic measures like tinkering around with tax rates. I agree with the author who says:

> Reducing social inequalities to income alone – the size of people's wallets – is a very myopic approach. One reason why, for all the talk about inequality in the wake of the 2008 financial crisis, there has been limited public outrage and no sustained political effort to attack it is, I suspect, the exclusive focus on income and wealth in mainstream debate.[1]

As Branko Milanović has shown, increasing inequality in Britain is not simply a product of national circumstances, but part of a much wider pattern of the changing global distribution of wealth.[2] The big global winners since the 1980s have been the 'emerging middle classes' of countries such as China and India, as well as those who were already in the top 1 per cent of the world's wealthiest (for the most part, people who were already rich in North America and other developed countries). The biggest losers are 'working-class and lower-middle-class Americans, Europeans and Japanese', who remain on the 80th percentile of global wealth but have descended to that point from much higher.[3]

One of the stories these figures tell is that labour's position in countries like Britain is declining. But this decline needs to be understood on more levels than the abstract technical question of income distribution. In this chapter I will look in greater depth at important changes in the relationship between labour and capital in Britain, including the increasing difficulties for British workers in representing their own interests and having a say in their workplaces, as well as key policy interventions that were more or less explicitly designed to strengthen capital's hand. There have also been important changes in the structure of the British economy (such as the growing importance of finance and *financialisation*), which have made capital more unreachable – harder to negotiate with and to restrain. In short, British labour has become more vulnerable and more subject to fierce discipline from capital and government – a process which has been more visceral than can be encapsulated in a Gini coefficient.

INEQUALITY AND THE BALANCE OF CLASS POWER IN BRITAIN

'Class Compromise'

Most analyses of British political economy since World War II show a sustained low level of inequality (comparatively speaking) from 1945 through to the 1970s. They then show it rising very sharply during the 1980s, before assuming a murkier pattern over the last 25 years. Figure 1 shows two lines.[4] One is the Gini coefficient, which is the most commonly used statistical method for calculating income inequality in a country. The other line is the 90:10 ratio, which quantifies the relationship between the consumption of those on the 90th percentile of British society versus those on the 10th percentile. Both measures fit this rough outline. Figure 2[5] takes a longer-term view and shows another possible measure of inequality: the percentage of all national income going to the richest 1 per cent. Here, there is a striking U shape, with the 1980s once again the turning point.

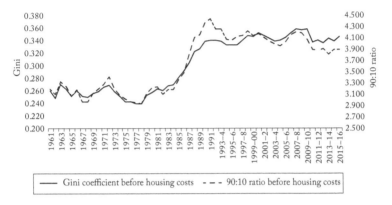

Figure 1   Measures of UK inequality: Gini coefficient and 90:10 ratio
Source: https://www.ifs.org.uk/tools_and_resources/incomes_in_uk

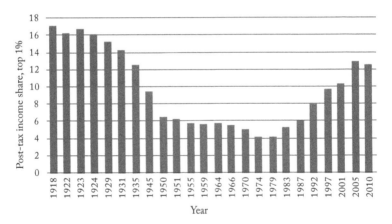

Figure 2   Measures of UK inequality: proportion of national wealth going to top 1 percent
Source: http://www.dannydorling.org/books/injustice/figures/fig-14.pdf

In Marxist terms, the retreat and resurgence of inequality reflects shifts in the balance of class power between labour and capital. The post-war period is often described as one of 'class compromise' or 'social compact',[6] in which labour benefitted from a political commitment to full employment and welfare state expansion, both of which mitigated the fear of unemployment for workers, in turn enabling rapid wage rises and the sustained growth of consumer demand. Moreover, this 'compromise' rested on the fact that labour was comparatively well-organised, with high levels of trade union density and a large proportion of workers' terms and conditions being set by collective agreements negotiated between employers and unions.

It is important to stress that this period of decreasing inequality is an outlier when put into historical perspective. The Marxist historian Eric Hobsbawm referred to it as a 'Golden Age' in which labour managed to make material concessions from capital that would have been unthinkable in the years before, and the years after. Trade unions were the main manifestations of workers' power. In Britain, in the decades leading up to World War II, collective bargaining had gradually progressed from a proscribed activity to something that was institutionalised nationally; during the war, the need for urgent increases in productivity and good labour relations catalysed the creation of government institutions in which employers and trade unionists would negotiate wages across entire industries, minimising the scope for disruption and conflict.

In this respect the groundwork was laid for a more 'coordinated' approach to the labour market which insulated workers against market forces. During the post-war period, collective bargaining was a powerful means of 'taking wages out of competition'; in other words, by setting up national standards, they weakened the pressure on capital to use wage cuts as a means of competing with each other, forcing them to compete on other things such as efficiency, product quality, marketing and so on.[7] The 'alien power' of competition which pushes capital to extract more surplus value in exchange for less pay was temporarily restrained by these measures. It is therefore not surprising that union membership has tended to be associated with narrowing inequality,[8] and, conversely, that the declining scope of collective bargaining and union influence implies the opposite. Note how the sudden and rapid drop in the number of workers whose terms and conditions are decided by collective bargaining (see Figure 3)[9] coincides with the pick-up in inequality identified previously as well as the stagnation in the wage share.[10]

Before getting carried away with the idea that unions were driving the rise in worker prosperity over this period, we should remember that market conditions were highly favourable to labour. World War II had reduced the labour supply (since lots of people had been killed or

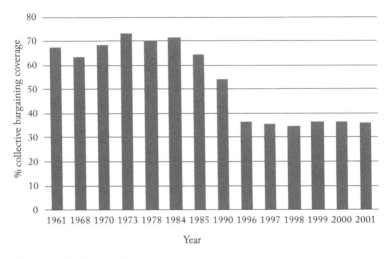

Figure 3   Declining collective bargaining coverage

injured), and the reconstruction effort had increased demand. Hence collective bargaining and the coordination of wage policy at national level arguably also served to *protect* capital from potentially more rapid wage rises that may have been possible under the circumstances. The Marxist economist Ernest Mandel argued that government efforts to expand the planning of wages, rather than leaving them up to the market, were not so much for the benefit of labour but a (temporary) means of providing stability for capital, preventing labour costs getting out of hand due to labour market tightness.[11] Moderate union leaders who were willing to remain on good terms with government and employers were a necessary condition for this. So was the increasing concentration of capital into fewer, larger, 'monopoly' firms which cultivated extensive bureaucracies, and which were shielded from market pressures. These provided readily identifiable counterparts for industry-level collective bargaining between labour and capital.

No Compromise

The key point is how fragile the post-war era was. It rested on the assumption of a sustainable compromise between two 'partners' (i.e. labour and capital) who would continue to find mutually acceptable compromises over wages and working conditions. The problem is that, as we have seen, these classes inevitably engage with each other on a vastly unequal footing, and with conflicting interests at the core of the relationship. Therefore any institutional compromise between them, while it may stabilise things for a time, is likely to be doomed in the long run of history.

As Howell has shown in some detail, the strength of trade unions during this period was significantly overestimated, including by unions themselves.[12] The institutional resources available to British unions remained weak in comparison to a country like Germany (with stronger legal protection of collective bargaining at industry level and institutionalised 'co-management' at workplace level). By contrast, to advance their demands against management, British unions relied more on being able to mobilise people on the shop floor, particularly through strikes – a situation which came to a head in the late 1970s and the fabled 'winter of discontent'. Their belief in this approach even led them to reject attempts, for instance under Jim Callaghan's Labour government, to institutionalise more strongly collective bargaining over wages and other aspects of work on a national scale.[13] They saw this as unnecessary. But they underestimated how forcefully Margaret Thatcher's government would attack their capacity to conduct strikes, and overestimated how strongly they would be able to resist those attacks.

So the post-war 'compromise' was dismantled surprisingly easily. First, labour was incapacitated very effectively by the blunt force of government legislation; the Thatcher government introduced policies that stringently regulated the conduct of strikes and other forms of union activity. Employers felt more up for a fight, and more willing to take radical steps to minimise the influence of organised labour, typically justified in terms of increasing international competition. The vanguard here was Rupert Murdoch's dispute with print unions at Wapping in 1986. Here, Murdoch's company, News International, which at the time owned four British newspapers, sought to relocate its production from Fleet Street to Wapping. Workers at the new site would need to agree to new restrictions including no-strike clauses and more 'flexible' working arrangements. In the strike action that followed the breakdown of talks over the move, 6,000 workers taking part in the action were dismissed, and the new site was put into operation with the help of members of a different, more employer-friendly union. The strike continued for over a year and ended in defeat, with production on the new terms beginning in earnest at Wapping.

The dispute is significant because it shows an employer who had become impatient with the collective bargaining of the post-war decades, and who wanted to escape these restraints. News International was therefore at the forefront of a trend: capital was becoming emboldened to stage big showdowns with labour. It is also significant because of the extent to which government enthusiastically and explicitly intervened on the side of capital, particularly through extensive policing and the use of new legal restrictions on trade unionists. Thatcher's government had outlawed secondary strikes, where workers not directly involved in a dispute go on strike in support of another group. It also imposed limits on the number of people allowed to stand on picket lines (a major tool in trying to enforce a strike), and made offences against these rules punishable in the criminal courts.[14] Combined with the role of the police, reprising their highly politicised function initiated during the miners' strike a year earlier, there was an intensified sense that the law and the government were not entirely neutral mediators between labour and capital.

Aside from a more aggressive outlook, the forms assumed by capital were also becoming harder to pin down. Large, 'vertically integrated' firms (where multiple functions from sales to research to production were performed in one organisation) began to shift towards 'vertical disintegration'; in other words, subcontracting and outsourcing. This meant that the 'bargaining partners' with which unions had to try and engage became smaller, more diffuse and under fiercer competitive pressure.[15]

Companies, influenced by new managerial ideas around 'organisational culture', also expanded their use of human resource management techniques and sought to use this as a replacement for dealing with trade unions.[16] Team-building exercises and the employee suggestion box enabled managers to present a veneer of caring without the inconvenience of independent collective representation. Government also did its bit to make collective bargaining harder. Institutions that had been established to regulate conditions in given industries on a national scale were dismantled – the National Dock Labour Board being a case in point.[17] Industries that had served as bastions of union strength were cut back or privatised.

One thing many on the left share with conservatives is their romanticisation of small businesses against the corporate juggernaut. This sentiment is intuitively presented as part of the 'inequality' narrative of corporate elites versus the little people; the latter term presumed to include both workers and 'small businesspeople' who should no doubt be considered in 'the 99 per cent'. But we can now begin to see that this is misplaced. Evidence shows that societies dominated by larger firms tend to be more equal than ones with high numbers of small businesses.[18] What I have said so far gives us some idea of why this may be: larger corporations are more tangible 'bargaining partners' enabling a more organised labour market, and they are also less likely to be under intense competitive pressure. As such, the belief that inequality is inherently bad and that small businesses are inherently good is self-contradictory.

These developments had unsurprising results. The share of national wealth going to labour began to decline, in comparison to the share going to capital. Özlem Onaran has estimated that, once we exclude elite managerial salaries, the percentage of gross domestic product taking the form of workers' wages reduced by about 11 per cent between 1975 and 2008.[19] During this time we also see a steady rise in the proportion of the British labour force in low-waged jobs, from around 12 per cent in the mid-1970s to just over 20 per cent in the late 1990s[20] (the increase tailing off after this until the crisis period). Moreover, Costas Lapavit-sashas has shown how the productivity of British workers over the same period increased far more rapidly than wages, suggesting that employees are producing more for their employers while getting less in return.[21] Correspondingly, the Marxist economist Michael Roberts estimates a significant (albeit temporary) upswing in the rate of profit (i.e. the amount of surplus value returning to the capitalist in relation to the amount of capital invested) over the Thatcher years.[22] These are the predictable outcomes of a shift in the balance of class power.

All of this is not to draw a simple cause-and-effect relationship between 'disorganisation' (i.e. declining union strength and collective bargaining coverage) and inequality. Correlation does not mean causation. To some extent, both may be consequences of wider changes: 'globalisation' and the opening up of labour forces in other parts of the world, technological change, and even the increasing role of finance in the UK economy (to which I will turn shortly). However, it is clear that union decline has exacerbated the problems facing labour and made the latter more vulnerable; more likely to come through these transitions in worse shape than it might otherwise have done. The point, then, is that organised labour has been effectively *disciplined*: British workers have less capacity to challenge capital collectively, and have become more vulnerable to its fluctuations and demands. Furthermore, as I argued in Chapter 2, capital cannot function without this discipline.

Again, when discussing workforce discipline, we should recognise that we are talking about an international trend rather than a national one. Comparable comments could be made of many countries. These trends have been even more severe in the United States, and slightly cushioned but nonetheless present in major continental European economies such as Germany and France. They are also evident in emerging economies like China (although this case is more controversial).[23] This means that Thatcherite legislation in Britain can only really be the 'how', rather than the 'why', of this disciplinary programme. Indeed, Thatcher herself was very honest that she was acting under the coercion of alien powers, as exemplified in her mantra of 'there is no alternative'.

From a capitalist perspective – the most important perspective in capitalist society, after all – this was largely true. As we saw in Chapter 1, capitalism cannot function unless surplus value can be extracted, realised and profitably reinvested. So while it is probably true to say that British Conservative politicians do not like rising equality and an organised labour market, the more important point is that *capitalism as a system* does not like these things.

The economic crises affecting Britain in the 1970s, which Thatcher's government was mandated to address, were in part a consequence of what Marxists have termed the 'profit squeeze'.[24] Wages were rising, diminishing the surplus value accruing to capitalists. Union strength was also weakening the supervisory functions of firm-level management. The tax regimes and institutional commitments (such as collective bargaining) imposed on business during the post-war period were also becoming an intolerable burden. Rising equality was, ironically, therefore also a source of imbalance, as labour extracted more in wages at the expense of surplus value. In that sense, reasserting the dominance of capital was, ironically, a necessary *rebalancing* from capital's perspective. Governments cannot ignore this logic, though a more precise discussion of how they relate to it will need to wait until Chapter 5.

New Labour, 'Partnership' and Labour Discipline

The 1980s experienced a great leap forward for class power and inequality in Britain. What has happened since then? Since the 1990s, the trajectory of inequality in Britain has been more ambiguous. It appears to have been hindered by the minimum wage introduced under New Labour, which supported incomes at the lower end of the labour market.[25] Also under New Labour, increases in welfare payments may have reduced overall levels of poverty and inequality.[26] In the latter case, however, changes benefitted children and pensioners far more than workers without children, whose relative position may even have got worse under Blair and Brown. Support, in other words, was aimed at future and former members of the workforce, rather than strengthening the position of labour itself.

New Labour used taxation and welfare policy to adjust incomes in a way that mitigated inequality statistics, while largely continuing and even exacerbating the class discipline of the Thatcher years. While trade unionists were afforded some (limited and loophole-ridden) new rights, the main bulk of anti-union legislation remained in place. Indeed, even the union-friendly legislation of the time generally came with an explicit agenda of fostering 'partnerships' between workers and employees, in which it was understood that labour deserved a voice, but not to the extent that it might actually challenge the prerogatives of capital.[27] Partnerships – as manifested through things like the union-learning agenda[28] – were supposed to follow the theory that a more 'constructive' (i.e. management-friendly) form of trade unionism could make life easier for employers while also strengthening trade unions' presence in the workplace.* Evidence suggests that partnership strategies, while they might put unions on better terms with managers, tend not to create a strong counterbalance to management, with partnership workplaces typically suffering more problems of management bullying, lack of meaningful dialogue or problems with working time, than ones where unions took a more oppositional approach.[29] British capital is arguably too short-termist and authoritarian to allow meaningful partnerships to emerge – an idea to which I will return shortly.[30] This calls into question the central New Labour idea that there can be widespread 'mutual gains' between labour and capital in the workplace (rather than one advancing

---

* The union-learning agenda was a scheme, supported by the Union Learning Fund, to involve trade union representatives in administering workplace education and training schemes. This had obvious potential scope for common interest between labour and capital, which led it to be criticised by some observers as a kind of co-opting of unions into a non-threatening and excessively employer-friendly attitude. Others, however, contested this, arguing that by channelling more resources to representatives in the workplace, these kinds of initiatives could strengthen independent trade unionism, even setting aside the actual content of training initiatives (see endnote 82).

at the other's expense), but the rhetoric of partnership was very important in making the party respectable to centrist opinion.

With regard to welfare policy under New Labour, there is something else that needs noting. While many benefits increased quantitatively, there was also an important qualitative change in the way the benefits system was administered. Like his American analogue Bill Clinton, Blair greatly expanded the use of 'conditionality' in the benefits system, where recipients were expected to meet certain objectives and targets or risk being sanctioned. In other words, supposedly more generous welfare services also become more punitive, seeking to push recipients into the lower end of the labour market and make it harder for them to turn down the jobs offered, however bad they might be.[31] In these measures, we can see an infrastructure developing that allowed government to take a more direct role in monitoring and manipulating the industrial reserve army.

Post-Crisis

The economic crisis that destroyed New Labour as a political force had ambiguous effects on inequality as a statistical measure. It has been argued that the crisis and subsequent austerity measures reduced inequality, since top incomes took a significant hit while certain benefits for those on the lowest incomes (again, particularly pensioners and children) were protected.[32] This provided the Cameron government with the ammunition to claim, somewhat optimistically, that their tenure had been an egalitarian one. This smoke and mirrors serves to highlight the problems of thinking about inequality in the abstract. When we look at the power relations between labour and capital, once again the picture is a little different.

The biggest victims of the post-2008 period have been wage earners, particularly those at the lower end of the labour market. More optimistic analyses of living standards and inequality under austerity have tended to overlook the divergence between pensioners and wage earners, with the former's condition remaining stable but the latter's becoming notably worse.[33] In the crisis's aftermath, as unemployment rose, investment stalled and companies sought to cut costs, the biggest declines in income being among those in low-paid jobs.[34] Consequently, the current crisis is quite distinctive in the sense that, unlike in previous crises where profits were severely hit, the share of wages in relation to profits has not appreciably increased.[35] It is also distinctive, not necessarily in the *depth* of wage declines (though this has been extensive), but in the *length* of the squeeze on wages (see Table 1).[36] Hence, while worklessness has declined since its post-crisis heights, poverty has remained stable and in-work poverty has increased.[37] There has been a sort of 'squashing', where middle-income families are less distinguishable from poor ones – the fact that this is happening while median household incomes are rising reflects how the incomes of elderly people have made solid gains owing to the protection of pensions and benefits.[38]

Table 1 TUC data on crises and earnings decline

Crisis	1865–7	1874–8	1921–3	1976–7	2007–14
Duration of earnings crisis (years)	2	4	2	2	7
Depth of real earnings decline (%)	–10	–1.7	–8.2	–6.6	–8.2

The majority Conservative government that took office in 2015 also greatly expanded the disciplinary apparatus surrounding labour. For one thing, there is the Trade Union Act. This was an incoherent and melo-dramatic piece of legislation, albeit one which is likely to have significant effects.[39] Its main provision was to impose new restrictions on whether or not trade unions are allowed to call a strike. It has some contradic-tions: the central conceit is the need to curb strike action at a time when strike action is at a historic low, and it demands high voting turnout in trade union strike ballots while simultaneously limiting participation (for instance, by preventing unions from holding strike votes online). These contradictions are interesting and tell us something about the relationship between government, capital and labour: I will return to the subject in Chapter 5. For now, suffice to say that the Act is a particularly route-one form of labour discipline inspired by Thatcherite retro-chic.

More sophisticated than this were welfare changes spearheaded by Iain Duncan Smith, albeit building on New Labour initiatives. The con-ditionality and punitive sanctions were expanded and intensified, being applied to the disabled and long-term ill, and increasingly to those in low-paid jobs who were reliant on benefits to support wages.[40] In the case of disabled people, it seems likely that the process of forcing people to attend 'fit for work' assessments, and the efforts to pressure people back into the labour market at any cost, contributed to a great many early deaths.[41] Once again, *discipline* of the labour force is the central issue: not of trade unionists this time but over people in and around the 'reserve army'. According to Jay Wiggan, these changes have increased competition for the lowest-paid jobs, and pushed people into accepting the terms of those jobs without reservation.[42] In other words, people's expectations of what they can get from capital are being forced downwards.

Table 2   Countries' experiences of economic and wage growth, 2007–15

	Real wage growth, 2007–15	Real wage decline 2007–15
Positive annual GDP growth, 2007–15	Norway Slovak Republic Sweden Germany France Luxembourg Austria Czech Republic United States Ireland Belgium South Korea Japan Israel	United Kingdom
Negative annual GDP growth, 2007–15	Denmark Latvia Slovenia Spain Finland	Italy Portugal Greece

While these trends are not unique to the United Kingdom (as we have seen), I should stress that this country is highly specific in some respects. As Table 2 shows, it is the only OECD (Organisation for Economic Co-operation and Development) country that experienced wage decline *at the same time* as the economy was growing.[43] This reflects the extent to which the 'British model' has been based on forcing people into low-wage employment, and how successful we have been at creating a tightly disciplined labour force which imposes minimal demands on capital. To understand this more fully, however, it is important to look more closely at the way in which the position and character of labour and capital have changed over the same period.

FINANCIALISATION, CAPITAL AND CLASS DISCIPLINE

In understanding the changing relationship between capital and labour, we need to recognise wider contextual factors in the British economy. We know that since the 1970s there have been shifts in the way government has regulated labour–capital relations. Regulations over trade unionists and benefits recipients (i.e. labour) became much tighter, while regulation over the decisions capital could make in investing, trading and in the labour market, became much looser. One particularly important area of deregulation was in finance, notably with the Thatcher government's 'big bang' of liberalisation which consolidated London's place as a hotspot for the international financial services industry, and correspondingly increased Britain's reliance on this sector. Understanding the way in which the *character* of capital in Britain is changing requires attention to these developments.

Britain, alongside the United States, is arguably the 'purest, most advanced form' of so-called 'financialisation'.[44] This term describes a trend whereby capital looks more and more towards purely financial channels as a source of investment and profit (i.e. as opposed to producing commodities for trade in the 'real' economy).[45] There is an extensive literature on the way in which capital has been diverted from productive investments towards financial ones, particularly in Britain. More interesting for this book is how this affects the relationship between labour and capital.

According to Lapavitsas, financialisation means three key empirical developments.[46] First, companies have become less reliant on bank loans in financing their operations, and more on their own financial activities, such as trading in securities, bonds, equity and foreign exchange. Second, the role of banks has changed as a result, towards lending to consumers and also towards greater involvement in commercial investment banking. And finally, households themselves have become more embroiled in the financial system through escalating private debt and the extension of retail financial services, such as mortgages, credit cards, student loans and so on. This trend is by no means unique to Britain, but it is particularly pronounced here.

How does the financialisation of the British economy affect the way capital relates to labour, and vice versa? For one thing, it has changed capital's priorities. Financialisation implies a fixation on so-called 'shareholder value'; i.e. the prioritisation of maintaining and bolstering share prices ahead of productive investment in equipment or personnel.[47] In this sense, things like business psychology and speculation come into play; the watchwords become 'confidence' and 'expectation', since share prices are greatly influenced by all kinds of hard-to-predict contingencies. Because of this focus on shareholder value, financialisation means we are more likely to see capital pursuing 'downsize and distribute' strategies rather than 'retain and reinvest' ones. In other words, efforts to reduce firm resources and labour costs in the short term will take precedence over longer-term investment in developing the workforce and technology/infrastructure, in order to improve the perceived health of the firm from the perspective of investors.[48]

Fichtner's study of hedge funds – the shock troops of financialisation – provides a good illustration of this kind of activity.[49] Even by capital's standards, hedge funds are highly opaque, suffering very few regulations around transparency and reporting. When they invest in non-financial companies, they often play a highly 'activist' role in trying to increase the company's share value, by forcing down its operating costs (e.g. money spent on productive investment and labour expenses). In such cases,

> Initially, the hedge fund typically communicates its demands to the management of the target company in private. If the management is not willing to fulfil its demands, the activist hedge fund will typically launch a public campaign to build up pressure. In most cases they are able to attract like-minded investors (mutual funds, banks or other hedge funds) that buy in on the target company stock in anticipation of a success of the hedge fund... In some cases activist hedge funds cooperate by forming a 'wolf pack' that has more financial clout to enforce its demands *vis-à-vis* the target company.[50]

This makes financialisation quite frightening both for management and labour at workplace level. Their position becomes much more dependent on the perceptions of financial investors who may move their money around quickly and unexpectedly, and according to sometimes unpredictable criteria. Such investors – like investment institutions and professional fund managers – are remote from the day-to-day life of the workplace, and consequently are 'generally much more mobile and rapidly threatening than the old forces of the product market'.[51] The cumulative effect of all of their individual transactions becomes like a swarm guided by the 'collective power of opinion',[52] which can lose or gain confidence in a firm's management for opaque reasons.*

This swarming of financial investors, all pursuing shareholder value, is more commonly known in business journalism as 'the markets' and it is the archetypal 'alien power' as I have used the term. To watch the business news is to realise that 'the markets' cannot be reliably predicted, and experts' explanations of their behaviour (whether the share price of a particular firm has gone up or down, for instance) are only ever offered as rationalisations after the event. They are thus hard to read and their mood is only discernible in their reactions. From the perspective of the workplace, 'the markets' force management to compete for investment, which often means shedding costs and demonstrating an immediate-term path to greater profitability. As such, workplace-level management comes to seem like an innocent victim of financialised pressures: it's the shareholders and investors that are really turning the screws. Hence it is perhaps not surprising that financialisation-era protest movements such as Occupy have little to say about class divisions in the workplace.[53]

While Marx's analysis of finance remains underdeveloped (he died before finishing the third volume of *Capital*), it is clear that he was interested in its unpredictable and opaque elements. Financial capital appears, to Marx, as 'the most irrational form of capital', where money seems to create more money out of thin air rather than through the manufacturing of commodities.[54] The circulation of financial investments is, as we have seen, often quite remote from workplace reality, and so from the point of view of managers and workers their movement seems highly arbitrary, even as they hold life-and-death power over many firms.[55] The more esoteric and 'psychological' influences that come into play with regard to finance is something Marx hinted at but which remains underdeveloped in his work.[56] I will try to develop it more in Chapter 5, showing the implications it has for government policy.

All of this means that financialisation has made British capital more short-termist, more concerned about 'market confidence' relative to

---

* For instance, when United Airlines beat up one of their own passengers due to the fact they had overbooked a flight (quite shocking, but still one of early 2017's more uplifting news stories), their share price unsurprisingly fell. But the extent of this fall was very unpredictable. It is only by observing the data after the event that these kinds of things are worked out and ad hoc explanations can be offered. This is not a science: it all depends on what mood investors are in at the time.

investing in workforce or productive infrastructure of the workplace in the longer term. As a result, there is evidently a connection between the extent of financialisation in the British economy and the country's weak industrial productivity growth,[57] with inevitable knock-on effects including stagnant wages. Financialisation has also made capital less willing to tolerate having to deal with labour. Daguerre directly blames the emergence of the financial class for the collapse of the post-war 'social compact' between labour and capital.[58] Indeed, the subordination of financial capital was probably a necessary condition for the creation of cohesive collective bargaining institutions and wages policy in the aftermath of World War II.[59] International statistical research also indicates that the extent of financialisation is inversely proportional to the reach and influence of regulatory labour market institutions.[60] And Lucio Baccaro and Chris Howell have shown how, right across Europe, states have been proactive in reshaping methods of labour market regulation so that they impose less of a burden on capital, instead maximising the discretion of employers to act in a rapid and unencumbered way in response to market pressures.[61] The short-term pressures implied by financialisation probably also contribute to the difficulty of establishing meaningful workplace 'partnerships' between unions and capital.[62]

LABOUR DISCIPLINE AND 'PRECARITY'

There has clearly been a shift in the power balance between labour and capital since the 1970s. In some respects the signs have been very obvious: declining trade union strength and collective bargaining, greater wage inequality, more low-wage work. In other respects the pattern is more ambiguous. The make-up of British labour has, during this time, itself become more complex: more ethnically and culturally diverse, with higher rates of female participation and higher rates of inward and outward migration.

One complex issue is the question of insecurity. If capital has become more 'impatient', and labour has been under greater disciplinary pressure, we might also infer that work has become more insecure. This is certainly the idea underpinning the 'precariat' concept (see Chapter 2), and the assumption about growing insecurity has become a truism, especially but not exclusively on the political left. But what this actually means is complicated, and some of the most important assumptions of this argument are not borne out by hard data.*

One obvious measure of work insecurity is so-called 'atypical' work (i.e. short-term contracts, agency work and other forms of more casualised employment relationships). There has been an international trend towards greater levels of atypical work from which Britain has not been excluded, though its progress across the labour market has been uneven.[63] These trends have given rise to much discussion of 'precarity', which, as we saw, refers partially to short-term work but also tends to encompass a range of other factors (such as unpredictability of income, low prospects for a stable career and an inability to exercise agency over the conditions and patterns of work). One problem with this broad definition is that, as Choonara points out, some of these factors (e.g. the need to do jobs as defined by management with little scope to exercise your own skills and agency) apply much more widely to *labour* itself under capitalism and hence can't really be used to characterise a distinct 'precariat' class.

The idea of a growing precariat fits nicely into the story of financialisation narrated in the preceding section; a more disembedded and rootless form of capitalism with fewer commitments to labour and more commitments to short-term shareholder value. The problem is that existing data for the United Kingdom tend to show only fairly modest increases in forms of atypical employment, and overall levels that are relatively low by international standards.[64] It is in supposedly more highly regulated countries such as France that temporary work has risen more rapidly.[65] In Britain, the rise has been more ambiguous and modest, increasing from 5 per cent to 8 per cent of the workforce between 1984 and 1997, before stagnating and indeed declining since then.[66] Choonara shows that the amount of time, on average, British people spend in their jobs has actually remained relatively stable over this period, suggesting there has not been a mass shift to hiring and firing at will, and individuals remaining in one job for several years remains the norm. While things like zero-hours contracts have expanded significantly, they remain a small proportion of the workforce as a whole.[67]

---

* In clarifying my own thoughts about the issue of insecurity and 'precarity', I found Joseph Choonara's work helpful, particularly two presentations; one at the Centre for Employment Relations, Innovation and Change doctoral conference, University of Leeds, May 2016; one at the International Labour Process Conference, University of Sheffield, April 2017.

One explanation for this may be that, to put it bluntly, the UK labour market has already been more 'precarious' than those of other European countries for a long time, but that this is manifested in different ways. For instance, it is one of the easiest European countries in which to fire someone. So much so, that according to some observers there is actually little obvious scope for further deregulation that would make much difference, leading to more extreme proposals to undermine job security (such as the Beecroft report which the Coalition government considered in 2012) being ditched.[68] On the face of things, we might surmise that British capital does not feel the need to demand the mass casualisation of labour. To some extent, economic crisis and austerity has had an impact: while it has not led to massive increases in temporary work overall, temporary work has been a disproportionately large component of job growth under austerity. Moreover, the level of 'involuntary temporary work' (i.e. where workers want permanent work but cannot obtain it, rather than being in temporary work because they find it convenient) has also increased in the last decade.[69]

Standing, as one of the primary popularisers of the precariat thesis in the United Kingdom, has sought to counter potential criticisms by arguing that Britain has seen 'casualisation by stealth' using other means. For instance, there have been repeated increases in probationary periods during which workers can be made redundant more easily.[70] In this respect, the Coalition government of 2010–15 was particularly innovative, with measures such as the imposition of fees to bring employment tribunals making it much less risky for employers to terminate people's contracts, and precipitating a rapid and dramatic fall in the number of cases brought for unfair dismissal.[71]

Self-Employment and the 'Gig Economy'

Another potential kind of precarity is the abuse of 'self-employment'. This is, indeed, an area in which Britain probably leads its European neighbours. Self-employment accounts for a very large proportion of the employment growth we have seen since the crisis, and the number of self-employed workers now approaches the size of the public sector workforce, which has been shrinking.[72] In liberal discussions, there remains a widespread assumption that self-employment is a form of freedom, albeit one purchased at the cost of heightened insecurity and unpredictability, and even that its expansion is creating a new upwardly mobile voting constituency for the Conservative Party to hoover up. Consider the following passage from *The Telegraph*:

> An army of public sector workers, heavily unionised, with generous pay, lots of time off, and lavish pensions. Councils stuffed with bureaucrats doing non-jobs, and quangos recruiting a growing army of diversity workers. An over-manned and feather-bedded public sector that is intent on voting itself ever more generous pay and conditions. That may well be many people's idea of the dominant force in the British labour market.*
>
> And yet, here is something surprising. That dominance is not really true.† In fact, the total number of self-employed workers is fast catching up with the numbers in the public sector. The 'gig economy' is triumphing over everything else. As that trend gathers force – and there is no reason why it should not – people who work for themselves are going to become an ever more powerful economic and political force.[73]

It is important to move beyond the kind of hyperventilating naivety embodied here. It is true that some self-employed workers welcome the trade-off between freedom and risk.[74] It is equally true that self-employed workers are more vulnerable: their earnings have fallen much more dramatically than the employed since the crisis.[75] For journalists and some politicians, these risks are all part of the mythology of the free worker who does not need their life to be planned out for them.‡ Enthusiastic liberals have little time for those who end up in self-employment but don't buy into this mythology. Uber drivers recently launched a successful legal challenge to their company, in which they argued that their self-employed status was unfair and that they should be treated as employees with the holiday and sickness rights that entails.

---

* 'Many people' here should be read as meaning '*Telegraph readers*'.

† This is one of the least surprising things to have ever been described as 'surprising' in a national newspaper.

‡ Work and Pensions Secretary Damian Greene: 'Just a few years ago the idea of a proper job meant a job that brings in a fixed monthly salary, with fixed hours, paid holidays, sick pay, a pension scheme and other contractual benefits. But the gig economy has changed all that. We've seen the rise of the everyday entrepreneur. People now own their time and control who receives their services and when. They can pick and mix their employers, their hours, their offices, their holiday patterns. This is one of the most significant developments in the labour market. The potential is huge and the change is exciting.'.

Some were not impressed at this challenge to 'freedom'. One, who accuses these workers of 'missing the point of self-employment', argues:

> [Uber's] … main argument both in court and in the email Uber UK have sent out this weekend claims that drivers work for Uber precisely because they value being their own boss and being self-employed. In doing so, they therefore have the freedom to choose when, where and how long they drive for. Uber says this can be substantiated by drivers' opinion polls. It worries me with this case that there is a constant attack on our democratic rights freedom of choice, of freedom to set up new types of company that have undoubtedly benefited millions – of freedom of choice for people who do prefer to be self-employed … The representatives of the Uber drivers in this case argue that these self-employed people should not have the right to be self-employed and this does not undermine their flexibility and freedom.[76]

Note the almost religious invocation of the words 'flexibility' and 'freedom': freed from the burden of sickness and holiday pay – what a relief!

The recent government-initiated Taylor Review into 'gig economy' practices provides a nice case study in capital's ability to continue getting its own way. The review advised the creation of a new status with weaker employment rights than a standard employee but more than the self-employed. This was framed as a step-forward for workers' rights, but only seems as such until we recall that the court decisions mentioned above suggest that gig economy workers *already* have rights, it's just that they usually go unenforced. In other words, creating a new status rather than focusing on enforcement is a step backwards, rather than forwards.[77] The authors write: 'we want to incentivise employers to provide certainty of hours and income as far as possible and to think carefully about how much flexibility they can reasonably expect from their workers'.[78] All well and good, except that we should, by now, be aware of how limiting this phrase 'as far as possible' actually is in a capitalist economy.

Sometimes, a self-employed person acts as *labour* in the same way as a waged employee, it's just the legal terminology that differs. 'Platform capitalists' like Uber are great achievements in the art of labour discipline, marshalling and directing thousands of 'workers' over whom they exercise a significant amount of control, with much less danger of having to make reciprocal commitments. Thus speaks the CEO of the crowdworking platform CrowdFlower:

> Before the Internet, it would be really difficult to find someone, sit them down for ten minutes and get them to work for you, and then fire them after those ten minutes. But with technology, you can actually find them, pay them the tiny amount of money, and then get rid of them when you don't need them anymore.[79]

Like the productive worker who is separated from the means of production, such workers are also separated – this time from the organisational mechanisms (i.e. the app and its database) that link customers with the service. It is this ownership of the 'means of circulation' that enables the company to makes its profits.

Elsewhere the abuse of 'self-employed' labour is more brutal, as in the construction industry,[80] or certain parts of the service sector. In some cases, workers are essentially pushed into self-employment despite being tied to one 'employer' just like any other worker. See, for instance, Geraint Harvey et al.'s study of fitness instructors who are nominally self-employed: this means they have no employee rights but nonetheless are only allowed to operate in a particular gym (and sometimes have to pay 'rent' for the privilege).[81] A self-employed person who is only allowed to deal with one company at a time: here it seems to be capital that is 'missing the point of self-employment'!

Feeling Precarious

Nonetheless, despite rises in self-employment and fluctuations in other kinds of 'atypical' work, it seems much of the 'precariat' argument overstates how instantly disposable the British labour force has become. Hence, in understanding employment in Britain, it is equally important to focus on what is happening *within* 'stable' jobs, rather than becoming fixated on increasing casualisation as the central narrative. By doing the latter, we miss ways in which workers in ostensibly secure work are experiencing tougher discipline. As Choonara points out, saying that someone has 'stability' in their job is not necessarily a good thing. It may also indicate a lack of opportunities to find something better, or the need to cling on to a bad job because of fear of the alternative (something particularly important post-2008).

This observation may help to explain why, as Duncan Gallie and his colleagues have shown, in spite of the mixed picture in terms of job casualisation, British workers evidently *feel* more insecure.[82] Insecurity, however, is not captured so much in statistics on temporary or agency employment, but in other more complex ways. More than fearing actually losing their jobs, British workers seem to fear future pay reductions, as well as more qualitative worries such as losing the ability to decide how their work should be done, or being pushed into less interesting roles with fewer opportunities to develop skills. Discipline in this context does not mean rendering labour completely disposable, so much as squeezing more out of it in the workplace in the form of intensifying pressures and diminishing rewards.

Robert MacDonald has argued that statistics relating to job tenure and the kind of contract someone has can mask other forms of insecurity that need to be picked up through qualitative analysis.[83] This is particularly important among young people. MacDonald finds growing numbers of young people who describe themselves as being trapped in low-paid jobs with little path to advancement, and a rising sense of there being no way out of this predicament. Indeed, when temporary employment did increase in the UK (as in the 1990s), this was heavily concentrated among young and old, rather than those in-between.[84] Tracy Shildrick finds that young people are often scarred by their experiences of casualised and low-paid work, losing confidence in their capacity to navigate in the job market.[85] Transitions from school into work are becoming more difficult and risk-laden, a situation which is exacerbated by the retrenchment of services such as careers advice under austerity.[86] And Lisa Russell highlights a growing disjuncture between young people's aspirations and the British economic system's capacity to meet them.[87] When discussing young workers, it should be added that, in general, young people tend to be less informed about, and less engaged with, trade unions.[88]

There is another reason why the sense of insecurity may be increasing in Britain. Even if overall rates of 'atypical' employment have not increased dramatically, insecure contracts have proliferated more evenly across the workforce as a whole. As Janet Smithson and Suzan Lewis put it: 'It is possible that the public perception of rising levels of insecurity may be more to do with whom it now affects (graduates and professional workers as well as manual workers) than with an overall rise in the phenomenon.'[89]

In other words, sections of the workforce which have been considered relatively privileged have begun to feel the vulnerability inherent in being a source of labour under capitalism more strongly. I come back to this in some detail in Chapter 4. For now, consider a phenomenon such as internships, which are helping to normalise low pay and insecurity in high-status careers such as the media or creative industries. The importance of internships is growing among graduate workers, increasingly becoming as important as a degree itself in some fields.[90] *Unpaid* internships, which are an important way of accessing more glamorous careers,[91] have a curious parallel with workfare policies, despite being typically targeted at young people from much more affluent backgrounds. Both normalise the idea of 'experience' as something you get *instead* of pay, rather than *while doing paid work*. Despite the differences in access to social, cultural and economic capital among the average creative industries intern versus the average workfare victim, in both cases internships contribute to labour discipline: they displace more secure and well-remunerated opportunities, and create new reserves of highly malleable labour with lowered expectations.[92]

It seems that work insecurity is becoming more egalitarian in Britain. The link between university education and pathways into a secure working life has weakened.[93] Casualised and unreliable contracts are creeping into areas such as academic research and lecturing.[94] Kim Hoque and Ian Kirkpatrick also find that agency work and temporary contracts have risen among managers and public service workers in the UK, leading to these kinds of workers feeling increasingly marginalised in their jobs.[95] I pick up these threads in Chapter 4, after a brief summary of the conclusions that can be drawn so far.

CONCLUSION

The picture that comes across in this chapter is obviously a complex one. For various reasons, including the growing financialisation of the British economy, capital has become harder to negotiate with. As such, the labour market has become more disorganised, with weaker tools for labour to represent its interests. Government has intervened more or less explicitly in support of capital, either by forcibly disrupting trade union strength, by liberalising key industries, or by creating an expanded apparatus for monitoring the reserve army as with 'workfare' policies. This has had the effect of expanding the prevalence of low-paid work and a more diffuse *sense* of insecurity at work. Insecurity has spread more widely across the labour force, coming to encompass (particularly young) people in seemingly more privileged contexts.

In making these observations, key themes outlined in Chapter 2 resurface: the bundling-up of more and more people into an antagonistic and dependent labour–capital-type relationship, as well as the role of government in disciplining both the working and non-working populations. Earlier, I stressed the *fragility* of the comparatively egalitarian post-war era. The lesson in this respect is a fairly simple one: given that capitalism is based on conflicting class interests, a system based on 'class compromise' is always going to be unstable, and the institutions of this compromise (collective bargaining, taxes designed to support an expanded welfare state and so on) eventually become unworkable 'rigidities' which constrain, rather than support, capital.[96]

There is also the theme of alien powers. From a Marxist perspective, these changes have not simply happened because British capital and politicians are horrible. We have seen that the structure of capitalist economies imposes imperatives on people within it, and first and foremost on capitalists themselves. They need to extract surplus value, and they need to expand. They need to be competitive and meet the terms of 'the market'. It is certainly true that Margaret Thatcher's political project was inspired by an ideological commitment, which many Conservative (and Labour) politicians sincerely believed in for philosophical reasons. But it was not just this. From the perspective of the continued survival of capitalism, it was very important to break out of the profit squeeze caused by (comparative) union strength and rising wages in the 1970s, plus the 'rigidities' implied by welfare systems and collective bargaining. The relationship between capital and labour had to be reworked.

4

Jobs

[From a supervisor's notebook:] And if I were determined to live solely on the flesh of my own staff ... the greatest challenge to present itself would be maintaining each of them in an edible state while also regulating my consumption of these bodies. Perhaps I should try to keep them alive; in that case I could simply restrict myself to ingesting only those elements capable of regeneration, such as blood. Even so, I do dream about their armpits and elbows.[1]

In this chapter, I will examine the various ways in which British capitalists try to consume labour – figuratively speaking, of course. I argued in Chapter 2 that the first site of conflict between labour and capital is the workplace. Capital has a built-in imperative to extract more surplus value from labour, but it needs to do this while maintaining pay and conditions at a rate which does not negatively affect profits. The ways in which it contrives to accomplish this are highly varied: sometimes they are brutally simple and sometimes elaborate and subtle. It requires knowledge and technique to suck out as much blood as possible, while leaving the 'armpits and elbows' intact so that work continues to get done.

Capitalists might try to squeeze out more surplus value through seemingly benign methods, such as changes to working techniques that increase efficiency. It could also mean downward pressure on wages, either in cuts, freezes or below-inflation increases (in other words, a 'real-terms decrease'). It might try to offload other commitments to labour, such as pensions or holiday provision. It might seek to speed things up: the faster the M-C-M' cycle moves, the more profit is made (at least in the short term). Then there are cases of what Marx called 'small thefts' against the employee: reductions to lunch breaks, getting people to stay later or to take their work home with them, and so on.

All of this suggests that, underpinning the relationship between labour and capital, is the need for *control*. Whatever the context, capital must find ways of controlling labour: it is no use having workers unless they spend their time doing what you want them to do. Managers have, for at least a century, sought to turn the art of control into a science. In the early twentieth century, Frederick Taylor pioneered 'scientific management'. He was concerned that factory workers of the day were exercising too much agency over their own time. They were dictating their own pace of work, finding ways to create downtime and manufacturing space for socialising with each other on the job.

The human being is a social animal – and, for that matter, one which is not programmed to spend eight hours a day performing repetitive tasks for no particular reason – so this kind of procrastination might seem quite natural, even a necessary safeguard in the face of crushing boredom. But for capital and management it is a problem which needs to be solved. The answer for Taylor was quantification: he used time-and-motion studies to develop tables of how many times the average worker could perform a given action in a given time, which could then be used to set extensive numerical targets for employees. This method depended on breaking down tasks as far as possible into simple, repetitive actions. The assembly line was the archetypal 'Taylorist' instrument, since a worker would just perform the same action over and over again at a rigidly predictable pace that was defined by management science and enforced by machinery. What can be simplified and measured can be controlled.

In this kind of situation, Marx's argument that capitalist work arrangements crush the individual seems to make a lot of sense. The worker's creative process, a defining characteristic of what makes him or her human, is supressed by the need to comply with a template laid down elsewhere. But let's be fair and modern: while this might fit the stereotypical Taylorist system, it all seems a far cry from today's 'knowledge workers' at high-tech enterprises, who apparently sit around on bean bags drinking artisanal tea before brainstorming over a game of mah-jongg. Nonetheless, I aim to show in this chapter that even the hippest workplace has rules.

WORKPLACE CONTROL

Culturally, it is frowned upon in the United Kingdom to talk in a critical way about management and employers. People who do this risk one of two outcomes depending on the age of the person they are talking to: being accused of reliving the 'Winter of Discontent' (something which remains bizarrely scandalising despite all the various much worse things which have happened since), or being likened to French workers, who kidnap their human resource managers, set fire to tyres and stage mass protests if they are asked to stay five minutes late at work (it is said).

There have, in fact, been some notable scandals surrounding 'bad employers' in Britain in recent years. Certain cases tend to act as lightning rods for criticism, and the individuals involved are presented as sacrificial offerings so that everyone else can carry on as normal. For instance, in 2016, the British media went through a few weeks of being obsessed with Phillip Green, the former owner of (among many other things) British Home Stores. He extracted vast sums of money from the company for his own enjoyment while its employees' pension fund accrued a crippling deficit.

It is true that Green's case is a particularly bad one, with added irony: at one point he was an adviser on cost-cutting to the 2010–15 Coalition government. People like this become the 'unacceptable face of capitalism',[2] whose very existence makes all the other faces of capitalism, by definition, acceptable. Cue various commentators rushing to reaffirm their faith in the system now that the bad apples have been found out.[3] Once these people have been publicly shamed, the economy can go back to working for everyone.

In Green's case the victims were his workers, but the scandal wasn't really about work; it was too glamorous. A well-connected member of the elite who avoids huge amounts of tax was frittering away people's security in retirement. It is much rarer that there is such a furore over the way people are actually treated by their employers in the workplace itself, although the damage done to human dignity is often just as severe. The most significant case in this respect is the recent controversy around Sports Direct. This broke when the *Guardian* newspaper accused the company of paying its staff at the Shirebrook warehouse in Derbyshire below the legal minimum wage. In fact, while the staff were nominally receiving the statutory minimum, the company made them wait through lengthy security checks on entering and exiting the site and deducted pay for that time. If these security checks were counted as part of the working day (which they should have been, since people weren't standing in them for fun), the hourly wage averaged out to less than the minimum.

Here the problem of low pay was caught out by a particular technical and legal calculation, but it is important to stress that concealed behind this calculation are many other qualitative issues. By staging these security checks the organisation demonstrated that it distrusted its employees. It made a public show of the fact that it could subject them to invasions of personal space on a daily basis.[4] Workers could be singled out by name and shouted at, like a primary school teacher with a naughty child, if a supervisor judged them not to be working fast enough.

Upon starting the job, workers were welcomed with a letter containing the lines: 'your performance on-site will be monitored and if you do not meet the expectations of Sports Direct then your assignment will be terminated'. This kind of text is one of those things that, to those accustomed to living in the system we live in, sounds 'harsh but fair', like something Alan Sugar would say. How unreasonable it would be to expect someone who doesn't 'meet expectations' *not* to be fired. But what are these expectations? In this case they were defined unilaterally by management, and so became more like an autocratic system of laws over which the worker has no say, but which they have to follow for fear of losing their livelihood. As the *Guardian* reported, at Sports Direct, falling short of expectations could involve spending too long on the toilet, clocking in one minute late, or the perennial 'horseplay'. For this reason, the reporters also found that the children of Sports Direct workers needed to stay at school despite illnesses, because their parents were afraid of management punishment if they left work to look after them.

The employers' initial response to the *Guardian*'s exposé was that many of these practices are standard for UK warehousing work. It is easy to sneer at this but perhaps we should take them at their word. Some years ago I worked for a labour rights organisation in the United States where we uncovered very similar practices at a warehouse in the Deep South. There, the employers also used a 'strike' system whereby workers reported losing their jobs after leaving early to provide emergency care for their children, or coming back one minute late after lunch. In this sense Sports Direct has merely been engaging in the transatlantic diffusion of cutting-edge management techniques.

Warehouse workers at UK Amazon sites encounter similar methods. They were asked to walk up to eleven miles over a night shift, and were expected to collect an order every 33 seconds. Enforcing this required no human contact: they were monitored by a wearable device which bleeped if their pace slackened. According to the undercover reporter who worked at the plant: 'We are machines, we are robots, we plug our scanner in, we're holding it, but we might as well be plugging it into ourselves … We don't think for ourselves, maybe they don't trust us to think for ourselves as human beings.'[5]

It is unlikely that this kind of highly intense and dehumanising monitoring is unique to retail industry warehousing. Managers across the economy have begun to take control over work time much more seriously in recent years, and in this they have been egged on by media exaggerations about the supposed costs to the economy of people being off sick. They have intensified the surveillance of ill workers, through measures such as the now-ubiquitous 'return to work interview', where people are required to explain periods of sickness in intrusive discussions about their health. There are also attempts to link sickness absence to disciplinary procedures (as illustrated by Sports Direct's 'strikes' system) which have proliferated much more widely.[6] Surveys show that British workers are becoming more conscious of managerial intervention around their health and feel increasingly pressured to attend work when ill.[7]

Beyond these threats relating to absences from work, the Amazon case in particular shows the intensive monitoring of workers' actions while they are clocked in. Employees had to perform repetitive and uninteresting tasks for many hours at a time, watched over by an electronic handset that would berate them if they slowed down. Here, the machine becomes a relentlessly pedantic overseer which is programmed to tut-tut at its human victim incessantly.

In manufacturing, one of the major themes of management literature over the last 40 years has been lean production, which has often been assumed to make the labour process less alienating for workers and reverse various 'Taylorist' methods. Lean production as a concept originates in Japan, particularly with the car company Toyota. Lean at Toyota and other Japanese manufacturers was a shift away from the Taylorist workplace, towards a more flexible and team-based model of production. It emphasised 'quality teams', where groups of workers had greater 'functional flexibility'. In other words, they were supposed to collaborate in understanding and performing a wider range of tasks, taking part in quality control as well as suggesting new ideas for the production process.

But despite these kinds of trends, there are inevitably limits to how far control can really be loosened in the capitalist workplace. The efforts to transpose 'lean' methods to Western workplaces shows this. We need to note a general observation: the fact that workers are sorted into teams with some greater degree of autonomy does not necessarily mean control is loosened. In some respects, it can become tighter. In Barker's[8] famous study of US telecommunications workplaces, the shift to autonomous teamworking appeared, counter-intuitively, to lead to much tighter restrictions. Previously, while a lot of power was concentrated in a more dictatorial manager figure, the fact that one manager can never be omni-present meant workers could find ample scope to regulate their own pace of work and covertly find time to talk with colleagues. But once their 'self-managed teams' were established, free to set their own processes and targets, individuals found they were under a much more relentless kind of surveillance. Co-workers with whom they would once have been co-conspirators against management were suddenly responsible for ensuring targets were met, creating a whole new set of monitoring eyes. However autonomous the team, the fact that it became bound up in the process of surplus value extraction and realisation means these pressures are inevitable.

The more humane aspects of lean production were lost in transit from East Asia. In Japan, lean production was bolstered by the 'three pillars' system of employment relations, which implied very strong job security and intensive worker training as well as an active trade union role (not universal, but applied to a large segment of the workforce). These were seen as necessary to enable workers to take part in quality control. Only some of these features made it into Western manufacturing: while functional flexibility and quality teams have been adopted to some degree, job security and stronger trade unionism have not. Control remains very intense. In the US, a lean manufacturing worker-turned-academic Darius Mehri found that, much like in Barker's study, quality teams fostered a culture of informal peer-to-peer surveillance and intense pressure to meet targets.[9] The snazzy new office designs intended to support teamworking also served these ends:

The open office space ... facilitates both monitoring and bullying. It is important that the employee who is the subject of harassment be humiliated in front of the other members of his group ... at times the rules are vague, allowing managers the flexibility to blame the workers at will ... The most powerful rules are unwritten and can only be learned by observation.[10]

In the UK, Rick Delbridge's research also shows that workers in lean manufacturing remained under a culture of surveillance, with decision-making powers only devolved very slightly to employees.[11] Managers were stricter in holding them responsible for problems, but they did not have significant autonomy to address these problems. This meant an intensified culture of blame as workers sought to shift responsibility on to colleagues for faults that once would have lain with management. The consequence was work intensification rather than empowerment.[12] Wayne Lewchuk et al. have also shown that lean production in the British car industry has done little to reduce the arduousness of manufacturing work.[13] Under capitalism, a workplace with genuine individual freedom is unthinkable.

Misanthropic Boredom and Surveillance

At two points on the script, workers are encouraged to try joking with the customer. The first is during the confirmation of details. There are two eligibility questions where the customer is asked to confirm 'that you spend seven out of 12 months a year in the UK?' and 'that this is where you pay your taxes?' These questions respectively open the door to two jokes: 'So no long holidays planned this year then?' And 'no escaping that, is there?' (On a couple of occasions I tried adding to the second question 'unless you are Vodafone', but this was quickly discouraged by the supervisors). The second point … is later in the script, during the communication of the exclusion 'that you won't be covered for death as a result of … participation in any illegal acts', to which almost every worker adds, with feigned laughter, 'so if you were planning to rob a bank we wouldn't be able to pay out!' While this is presumably a new joke for the customer, the workers will get to enjoy it over and over again throughout the day.[14]

[H]e did another return, again the math squared and there were no itemizations on 34A and the printout's numbers for W-2 and 1099 and Forms 2440 and 2441 appeared to square and he filled out his codes for the middle tray's 402 and signed his name and ID number that some part of him still refused to quite get memorised so he had to unclip his badge and check it each time and then stapled the 402 to the return and put the file in the top tier's rightmost tray for 402s Out and refused to let himself count the number in the trays yet, and then unbidden came the thought that *boring* also meant something that drilled in and made a hole … Then he looked up despite all best prior intentions. In four minutes it would be another hour, a half hour after that was the fifteen minute break. Lane Dean imagined himself running around on the break waving his arms and shouting gibberish and holding ten cigarettes at once in his mouth like a panpipe ... He knew what he'd really do on the break was sit facing the wall clock in the lounge and despite prayers and effort sit counting the seconds tick off until he had to come back and do this again.[15]

Huge numbers of British people are bored by their jobs, and this is by no means limited to low-skilled or repetitive work.[16] Management surveillance can make this boredom very hard to cope with. One of the UK's major growth industries is call centre work, the grimness of which has been very well-documented by others.[17] When I did this kind of job, we were told by supervisors to lie to the (usually old) people that answered the phone, telling them our long and dreary list of questions would only take ten minutes (it could take 45). This was quite spirit-crushing, especially given that supervisors were often listening in to check you were following the script. I found that the time spent at the phone on a shift stretched out into seeming infinity: despite the shifts being relatively short, the end of the working day seemed like an inconceivable utopia right up to the moment you were actually allowed to leave.

This tedium and repetition, combined with the embarrassment and guilt of lying to people, made me look for any way I could to reclaim control over my own time. In one call centre, they (very unusually) had a hot chocolate machine which was free for staff to use. I would drink six or seven cups over a four-hour shift, not for the drink (this was unhealthy), but for the time you could spend just waiting for it to pour. Thirty seconds or so where you can think your own thoughts. At most call centres nowadays you would not get away with this, so I was evidently lucky, though I did eventually end up getting fired. At another job, you would be shouted at by supervisors for standing up without permission, making drink or toilet breaks out of the question. So to reclaim time I was reduced to just dialling the phone numbers in my list as slowly as I could, and carefully redialling unrecognised numbers two or three times 'just to be sure'. Nowadays, though, in most outgoing call centres computers dial the numbers for staff, affording no means of escape; auto-dialling technology imposes a machine's suffocating rhythm on the worker. A friend of mine found the only way of breaking this sadistic rhythm was to spend a few minutes just immediately hanging up on people that answered, though he fairly quickly got sacked for this.

Managers like to pretend they are humanising this intensely anti-human activity, though whether they really believe this, or just see it as a useful human resource facade, probably depends on the manager. For example, they encourage their underlings to 'be yourself', i.e. appear fun and authentic, as a means of coping with the ridiculousness of what they are doing, as well as the relentless hostility they receive from the people they have to call.[18] This authenticity is somewhat undermined by the wholly synthetic interactions with call receivers, sometimes vulnerable older people. As one journalist puts it:

> When someone tells you about the rising price of their weekly shop, or how their husband was recently diagnosed with bowel cancer, or how they're on their own now, alone in an empty house, continuing to flick through your objection handling booklet makes you feel like a sociopath.[19]

Nonetheless, you have to be careful because, as in many other workplaces, call centre managers survey staff without telling them. Someone can finish a call and then have a manager walk over to tell them they were listening and describe where they went wrong. For instance, I was told off for jiggling my leg too much, which made me self-conscious for a while. There was also something weirdly oppressive about the 'incentives' management dished out. Incentives are a standby of management science; in a call centre you might get a voucher or something if you get the most positive responses in a day. I used to wonder whether there was something wrong with me for not being enthused by this. But apparently it works, or at least managers think it does: expressions of power which grimly masquerade as fun are characteristic of the modern British workplace, from the recruitment stage onwards. For instance, job interviewees have been forced to dance in exchange for a chance to work at Curry's,[20] and I have spoken to students who have attended job 'assessment centres' which are apparently run by frustrated *X Factor* presenters (who will require people to attend from hundreds of miles away, only to sort them into groups to be sent home halfway through the day).

The surveillance and monitoring of workers is clearly not limited to lower-skilled and lower-paid jobs such as call centre or warehousing work. The nature of the labour–capital relationships suggests that these dynamics will emerge anywhere that people sell their time in exchange for a wage. Consider Bob Carter et al.'s studies of relatively profession-alised white-collar jobs in the tax office.[21] Following shifts towards teamworking (intended as a means of reducing public sector bureau-cracy) in 2005, they show how the role of the line manager in HMRC (Her Majesty's Revenue and Customs) changed. Previously, as we might expect given the professional setting, line management's role had involved expert knowledge and various staff support functions, enabling them to cultivate interpersonal relationships with those under them. 'Lean' policies ended up shifting this relationship to something much closer to a labour–capital one. Line managers were made more tightly responsible for monitoring team productivity. Quantitative targets were increased, and their relationship with staff became more impersonal and, importantly, more oriented towards monitoring performance rather than support. This led to friction with employees, and it also signalled a reduction in the status of line management itself. Their position as experts was diminished, since their job now involved simply keeping tabs on targets set from above. Their 'tacit knowledge' – the subtle under-standings both workers and managers have which influence how they do their work – was usurped by codification and management 'science'.

It is no good to oversimplify here. The general point is that any labour–capital relationship requires control, but clearly the way in which this control is exercised varies greatly in different types of work. Martha Crowley's[22] research in the US has shown that whereas service and manual workers tend to experience 'coercive control', like in the examples described above, professionals appear to have greater autonomy. But even so, their performance is just as likely as the warehouse operative's to be continually monitored against company objectives. In this situation true autonomy is surely a mirage. Professional workers may live in fear of the consequences of disappointing their managers and falling behind. They typically have to impose intense self-control in order to meet organisational expectations – in particular, they are pushed to furnish 'an enormous amount of "voluntary" effort', which breaks down boundaries between work and personal life. Thus arise phenomena like the politics of out-of-hours emailing: people feel the need to respond to emails at two in the morning, not because the issue is actually urgent, but because whoever replies quickest and at the most inconvenient times seems the most dedicated.* As researchers such as Christopher Grey have shown, high-status organisational cultures such as those found in accountancy impose huge pressures on workers to monitor themselves and conform to the correct image.[23] They play golf on weekends even though they don't like golf, and they marry people who look like they'll fit in socially with the bosses' partners.

For a particularly extreme example of control methods in ostensibly high-status white-collar work, look no further than Amazon – a company that evidently excels at worker discipline from top to bottom. This is from another press exposé, this time of work in their offices conducted in the US by the *New York Times*:

At Amazon, workers are encouraged to tear apart one another's ideas in meetings, toil long and late (emails arrive past midnight, followed by text messages asking why they were not answered), and held to standards that the company boasts are 'unreasonably high.' The internal phone directory instructs colleagues on how to send secret feedback to one another's bosses. Employees say it is frequently used to sabotage others. (The tool offers sample texts, including this: 'I felt concerned about his inflexibility and openly complaining about minor tasks.')[24]

The UK is not far behind these pioneering methods. Broadsheet journalists, ostensibly one of the most elite and glamorous occupations, are feeling the tightening of organisational control as their industry goes down the pan. *The Telegraph*, for instance, attempted to install electronic sensors at staff desks to monitor their attendance, though the staff made such a fuss it only lasted a day.[25] They probably got the idea from previous reports they had written themselves about increases in the use of electronic technology to monitor workers in 2008,[26] and again in 2015.[27] In the last case, the subject was wearable technology, another US import, which can record whether or not workers go to the gym in their free time. This apparently makes them 'fitter, happier and more productive', though it is not immediately clear why the middle adjective necessarily follows from the first and last.

---

* For this point I am grateful to Sarah McCann, a talented undergraduate student with whom I worked in 2016.

Journalism, incidentally, is a new frontier in the conflict between worker autonomy and management control in other ways as well. Up-and-coming prospective journalists may now find themselves working at websites where they are paid per click. This imposes a fundamental change in the nature of the job: the aim is to compete according to a computer-generated metric. There is reduced scope to act on what the journalists themselves believe is important or worthwhile; instead the incentive is to produce contentious bullshit with misleading-but-outrageous titles.[28] In this sense, the widely discussed phenomena of 'fake news' probably has as much to do with new forms of management incentive in the industry rather than the world's population simply becoming more gullible, as is the standard diagnosis.*

The point underpinning all these varied examples is as follows: it is natural for capital to try, over time, to find ways of codifying and monitoring what labour does. In doing so, it can find better ways of manipulating, incentivising and punishing. Obviously, this plays out very differently in different contexts and can only go so far. A news website can impose quantifiable criteria on a journalist (as in pay per click) but it would be perverse and counterproductive actually to dictate what they write. This would be going too far, and would count as 'eating the elbows and armpits', to refer back to the Thomas Ligotti quotation with which I began this chapter. Instead, the worker's creativity is not completely removed, but forced into a straitjacket of constraints and incentives. Their job becomes more and more about servicing the demands of someone else's system, even if they can sometimes make their own decisions about *how* they do so.

This is evident in the growth of online workflow management systems which proliferate in many professional jobs. Clive Trusson and Donald Hislop[†] have looked at how IT support workers experience 'deprofessionalisation via control' through this kind of software infrastructure. Theirs is a job based around technical understanding and problem solving. But the researchers found that a lot of the initiative was sucked out of their research participants' work by online systems which allocated tasks and prescribed particular methods and processes for resolving them. When they did find an unconventional way of fixing an issue,

---

* You'll Never Guess Which Supposedly Elite Profession Is Being Deskilled by the Combination of the Profit Imperative and New Technology!.

† I saw these authors presenting their findings at the International Labour Process Conference, University of Sheffield, April 2017.

they were supposed to input it into this system, so that it could then be prescribed to others in turn. The worker's 'tacit knowledge' is continually being codified and turned into a management asset.

I will come back to technology in more depth in Chapter 7, but for now it is important to stress the potential of the Internet in extending workplace control among professionals and 'knowledge workers'. As researchers in North Carolina put it, 'monitoring and surveillance' technologies can be

> used to measure, shape, and/or control the behaviour of employees. Details of sales, deliveries, contact with customers, phone calls, time taken to complete tasks are routinely logged onto computer systems and the information used by bosses to evaluate their staff and make sure performance targets are hit … Employee surveillance is so pervasive in the workplace that one study found managers in a fifth of British workplaces admit to monitoring their employees using computer-based systems.[29]

Hence, while the so-called 'knowledge economy' is often considered incompatible with Taylorist/'scientific management' principles, it is amazing what can be achieved with a can-do attitude. In more traditional industrial settings, the effort management needs to extract might be more easily quantifiable. The difficulties in quantifying work in, say, the creative industries, or highly skilled white-collar professions, of course means that workers are likely to have more discretion and independence. But the fact that this is difficult does not mean capitalists do not try: in fact, the theory outlined in Chapter 2 suggests that they *have to* try.

Between the 1980s and mid-2000s, while the average skill requirement for jobs in Britain increased, the average level of job discretion decreased.[30] This suggests that there is no simple relationship between being more skilled and having more autonomy at work. Francis Green also found a decline in average levels of job discretion between the 1980s and 2000.[31] This went along with accelerating work intensification, with surveys of employees showing that they were experiencing more frequent periods of having to work at high speed, and more frequent periods of working under tension. After the 2008 crisis, work intensity increased again, as did organisational skill demands, but without the corresponding increase in job discretion that the latter might suppose.[32]

Control and the Reserve Army in the 'Creative Industries'

The cutting edge of the British knowledge economy are the so-called 'creative industries': an odd, vague term which encompasses everything from interpretive dance through to marketing and software design. It is here that the rhetoric of the inspired autonomous worker comes into its own. The stereotypical creative worker is the dreamer of revolutionary ideas, who views his or her work as a labour of love, and who requires absolute freedom from management interference.

In music and the performing arts, the creative core of the creative industries, many people clearly do not easily fit the definition of 'labour' that I have been using so far. Often, people working in this context are essentially own-account artisans. In other words, they trade directly with customers without selling their labour to a capitalist in exchange for a wage, and any 'profit' made they keep for themselves. Albeit on a small scale, they usually own their 'means of production' (their instruments or materials, for instance). They certainly have more autonomy in their work than most people could dream of, albeit usually purchased at the expense of financial security.

But on closer inspection it is clear that the theme of control is still important, because these kinds of jobs do not simply exist independently of the wider capitalist system. Robert Hewison has shown how British governments (most enthusiastically, New Labour ones) have sought to integrate the arts much more closely as a cog within the economy as a whole.[33] For instance, they have sought to use artistic activity as a means of creating a 'buzz' which can enthuse capital into investing in deprived post-industrial communities. In other words, to appropriate it as aphrodisiac mood music for the continuation of the M-C-M' cycle. They have encouraged venerable funding organisations such as arts councils to change their priorities to support these efforts. In this sense, 'culture-led regeneration' policies have seen the arts being converted into a kind of supportive prop for further capitalist development.*

The result is that government has sought to increase its direct control over what goes on in arts and culture much more forcefully than it had in the past. There has been the imposition of extensive quantitative indicators which seek to codify a measurable set of achievements (such as levels of audience 'engagement', or numbers of people encouraged to

---

* This has been the aim, anyway. Its success is debatable.

visit a museum) to which funding recipients in the arts are expected to work.[34] Arts councils, over time, have followed this shift, moving from a somewhat stuffy panel of artistic elites making judgements about artistic quality, to a more technocratic role in charge of totting up measurables defined by politicians.[35]

The point here is not that artists end up being completely controlled by state and capital – this would be a ridiculous overstatement. In practice, of course, they end up finding ways of doing what they want while fobbing off requests for bureaucratic form-filling as best they can. Nor am I particularly lamenting the demise of 'art for art's sake' in the face of political 'instrumentalism'.[36] It is simply to observe that as soon as any sphere of activity starts to become more closely bound up into capitalist processes, it is inevitable that someone will at least try to find new ways of codifying, measuring and controlling the labour contained within it.

Look, for instance, at video games design. Paul Thompson et al., in their study of the Australian games industry, found that, among the designers and creators of computer games, the quality of jobs degraded as companies matured.[37] Games companies would have highly developed divisions of labour, so that junior staff could find themselves on quality control duty, which could mean simply opening the same door in a computer game several hundred times a day. And designers themselves would rapidly become pigeonholed to a specific role as if on an assembly line, such as making imp heads out of pixels. Particularly in the larger firms, where the marketing of the console is most important, 'work was more technical, more driven by the hardware and therefore less creative'.

Games testers – people who are paid to play games – get the worst of both worlds. Their actual job epitomises the 'degradation of fun', as their enjoyment of gaming gets ruined through repetition. But on the other hand, the fact that it *sounds* like a dream job creates a sizeable reserve army of people who are desperate to do it themselves, reducing their job security and bargaining power.[38] Indeed, the creative industries are a very good illustration of the reserve army concept: so many people are desperate to do 'creative' jobs, drifting around the edges of the labour market, that employers have no difficulty at all in arguing down labour costs.[39] The fact that so many people want to pursue careers where they can escape the 9.00–5.00 routine and actually spend their life doing something they find interesting means that workers' bargaining power has fallen through the floor. It is common to find prospective 'buyers' in the arts and creative industries expecting people to work for nothing at all.*

I said earlier that many artists resemble independent artisans rather than *labour*, as defined in Chapter 2. The latter may be applied to someone working in a games studio, but what about in areas such as music and the performing arts? While in some respects, people doing these things carry on in much the same artisanal way as they have ever done, there are also examples where a labour–capital relationship starts to become more evident. Particularly so in the wake of new technology.

For instance, in Britain, many working musicians who have not reached 'big name' status earn a living through doing 'function' work; i.e. playing at private parties or weddings, or providing background music at hotels or corporate events. Typically, the workers involved here might follow a small-scale artisanal model, working on their own or with their bands, cultivating direct relationships with customers and selling a product they largely develop themselves. In some cases, agents might be involved, representing musicians and using their insider contact networks to get them more work. By limiting who gets on their books, agents also limit the competitiveness of the marketplace.

However, with the Internet, a rapid process of socialisation is underway, and the agent business model is changing. Now, most people when booking function bands are less likely to go via the esoteric 'old-school' agent, and more likely to type something like 'wedding band north-west' into Google. In doing so, they will find many sites which act essentially as price comparison databases for hundreds of acts, where the buyer can compare prices instantaneously. The site takes a cut when the buyer selects and pays a band.

While the bands themselves may still work in an 'artisanal' way, exercising great autonomy over the services they provide and the way they divide up gig fees, they are nonetheless integrated into these extensive computerised systems alongside thousands of other people. Price competition becomes the order of the day, pushing fees lower and furnishing profit for intermediaries. The tacit knowledge of the traditional agent is replaced by the algorithmic resources of the online agency. Procedures become standardised and streamlined: while many such agencies still take a percentage commission, which, in theory, gives them an incentive

---

* For constantly updated real-life examples, see the Facebook group 'Stop Working for Free', or the Twitter account @forexposure_txt.

to negotiate on the musician's behalf, they tend not to do this, because it involves three or four emails rather than one. Speed is of the essence in capitalist circulation.

Competition means downwards pressure on fees; if musicians join one of these agencies and struggle to find work, the agent will warn them that it's because they are charging more than others on the site. And because agents have access to such a wide range of artists, musicians are often afraid of challenging problems such as low fees, late payments or the extraction of extortionate commissions. In many of these cases, agents may request that the musicians they represent do not hand out their own business cards at gigs, instead dispersing only those of the agent. This is interesting because, while the musician is nominally a freelancer who interacts with many clients, the agency tries to exert some control over who they transact with, making them resemble a quasi-employee. The result is a reserve army of people which is at least partially dependent on the agent, and integrated into a system which is under their control.

This short sketch of developments in the market for function musicians is, of course, a niche example. Nonetheless, it illustrates an important point. A particular job, like music, ostensibly seems very remote from the experience of providing labour under capitalism, as defined in Chapter 2. But those people doing it can still become a source of labour and consequently a source of profit for capital. It's just that this depends on the capitalist finding some way of separating the worker from the things they need in order to sell their time and effort. Internet technology has enabled intermediaries to emerge who control the channels through which workers access jobs, and this leads to a relationship which starts more closely to resemble a labour–capital one.

CONFLICT, RESISTANCE AND CLASS POWER

Some observers are hyperbolic about how far surveillance and control at work can go. One such refers to his friend, Mara, who works in retail, and I will quote his evocative article at length:

What is Mara's job like? Her sales figures are monitored ... by the microsecond. By hidden cameras and mics. They listen to her every word; they capture her every movement; that track and stalk her as if she were an animal; or a prisoner; or both. She's jacked into a headset that literally barks algorithmic, programmed 'orders' at her, parroting her own 'performance' back to her, telling her how she compares with quotas calculated ... down to the second ... for all the hundreds of items in the store ...

Mara's boss sits in the back. Monitoring all twelve, or fifteen, or twenty people that work in the store. On a set of screens. Half camera displays, half spreadsheets; numbers blinking in real-time. Glued to it like a zombie. Chewing slowly with her mouth open. Jacked into a headset. A drone-pilot ... piloting a fleet of human drones ...

The whole scene is like a maximum-security mental asylum designed by sadomasochists in a sci-fi movie. If Jeffrey Dahmer, Rasputin, and Michael Bay designed a 'store' together, they couldn't do any better. Her 'job' will begin to drive her crazy – paranoid, depressed, deluded – in a matter of years if she continues doing it. No human psyche can bear that kind of relentless, systematic abuse.[40]

An arguably even more dystopian picture is given by another journalist, writing about technology which can enable managers to monitor the moods of their staff. An innovator is quoted: 'Conducting weekly one-on-ones when you have 20 or more people in your team is impractical. Therefore, we designed Vibe as a tool to help managers follow the morale of their team, see what causes the team vibe to rise, but also be notified when the morale drops.'[41]

These kinds of depictions of total surveillance can make us forget a couple of important insights. One: the all-encompassing power of technology is often overhyped. This is something I will return to in Chapter 7. Two: workers are not simply passive victims of managerial control. Admittedly, when we look at the precipitous declines in things like strike rates over the last 40 years, Marx's prediction that capitalist class relations inevitably lead to conflict and resistance seems wrong. But there probably is a lot more 'resistance' to management control in British workplaces than we might realise, albeit manifested in more unexpected ways. Researchers who have spent time in call centres, for instance, have documented in sometimes gruesome detail the way in which workers found ways to undermine and even humiliate managers with their use of in-jokes and pranks.[42] Workers may find subtle ways of derailing or obstructing change initiatives imposed by management,[43] or of injecting their own agency and skill into the creation of products that management is trying to standardise.[44]

The point, from a Marxist perspective, is not so much that all workers will be forced to toil on an assembly line until the revolution, but that in any workplace there is a tension which never really goes away, even if it is manifested very differently from one context to another. This tension is between, on the one hand, a worker's entirely human desire to control their own activity and use their own initiative, and on the other, the need for capital to make a profit which is dictated by the alien power of competition. This does not mean that all workplaces are always under intense control, but it does mean that new attempts at extending control will always be lurking around the corner.

Remember that there is a power imbalance between labour and capital because the latter controls the resources that the former needs to access in order to obtain a wage. It follows from this that capital is able to withhold, or threaten to withhold, access to these things – ultimately the most important kind of control is the threat that if things do not go capital's way it will deprive labour of its living. In other words, it could close or scale down operations at a given site, or outsource, or invest in labour-saving technology. This means that insufficiently profitable or compliant workers can be rendered disposable.

The fear of losing one's job is extremely powerful. Even setting aside welfare policy, which has successfully made unemployment much scarier over the last 20 years, this fear has been exacerbated by other facets of government policy, notably legal policy relating to unfair dismissal. One of the Coalition government's sourest achievements – albeit a temporary one that backfired* – was the introduction of fees to bring employment tribunals against employers in the event of unfair dismissal, which resulted in a 70 per cent drop in the number of claims.[45] It also extended probationary periods, effectively meaning that new employees could be dropped under any pretext during their first two years of work (New Labour had reduced this 'qualifying' period to one year in 1999 before the Coalition restored it to two). While the manufactured image of the chancer frivolously suing their innocent employer was used to justify these changes, it is far more likely that many more workers had legitimate grievances that were not aired for fear of the legal apparatuses ranged against them.[46]

---

* It was later overturned by the Supreme Court in July 2017.

Capitalists and Labour Discipline: Strikes

The right of capital to shed labour is accepted as common sense in our society. When a company announces potential redundancies, and if they are sufficiently high-profile, they may send someone to be interviewed on the news. These interviews are typically conducted in the 'business segment' of current affairs shows, where critical thinking faculties tend to be suspended. In them, the agency of capital in the discussion is not made explicit: nobody voices that what is really happening is a decision by a small group of wealthy people to destroy the livelihoods of much less wealthy people because they judge they are not making enough profits. Instead, the danger of redundancies is talked about very much in the terms people use to talk about bad weather, with the interviewee from the company acting as the weatherman: we hope there don't have to be redundancies, but sometimes that's just what happens, like snow disruption.

Certainly, as I argued in Chapter 2, when capitalists take actions that damage workers' interests, this is generally not because they are horrible individuals, but because they are forced to come to terms with an alien power known as the marketplace. But it is still important to understand the various means through which management get its way. We need to ask some important questions: why, at the current juncture, is it so difficult for trade unions to extract meaningful concessions from employers? Why have they been unable to challenge the extension of control and the stagnation of wages? Why are strikes so much less likely to be successful than they were a few decades ago? In short, why are the representatives of labour as a class so weak?

There were some obvious answers sketched out in Chapter 3: international competition and economic restructuring, the pressures of financialisation and restrictive government policy. But these factors just exacerbate the underpinning point: since capital owns the means of production, it can decide who can work and who can't. This places some very powerful tools at its disposal, such as 'whipsawing'. This is where employers create competition for jobs between groups of workers in order to extract concessions from them. This could take various forms. There may be explicit threats ('if our demands aren't met, we are moving production to a different plant'), frameworks and rules put in place for competition ('we want to make a new investment, so all potential sites need to show us their best deal to receive it') or a more informal understanding (the awareness among workers that, if they don't make life easy for capital, investments may move).[47]

It hardly needs mentioning how much easier globalisation has made these sorts of techniques: on the one hand it opens up new labour sources to be played off against each other. On the other, international competition makes managers feel a more intense need to extract these concessions in the first place. These kinds of 'coercive comparison' strategies have been very explicitly employed in heavy industry in European countries, notably the automotive sector, particularly as the expansion of the EU has led to a much wider variation in national wage levels.[48]

In Britain, the strongholds of trade union strength are becoming much more scattered, but they are still likely to be the site of flashpoints of tension between labour and capital. The 2013 dispute over the future of the Grangemouth oil refinery, between the union Unite and the chemicals multinational Ineos, is an important recent episode. Here, the director of Ineos threatened to shut down the plant unless a series of demands were met by workers, including less generous pensions, a wage freeze and some job cuts – things which had actually been staved off in 2008 by strike tactics from Unite. This time, it was the employer who went on strike: Ineos staged a lock-out of workers to threaten Unite into agreeing terms. By then it was clear that the threat of closure was too powerful for Unite and the workers to resist: capital's wish list was imposed in full.

This dispute was also politically important. During their unsuccessful campaign, Unite members pulled a stunt in which they erected an inflatable rat on a company director's street (rats being a labour movement symbol for people who are screwing over a trade union). The Coalition government of the time leapt on this as an example of union 'intimidation', evidently believing that inflatable rats are a scarier prospect than the threat to create 800 redundancies. This was used as a pretext for further anti-union legislation, which I talk more about below.

Another important conflict was the dispute at the Lyndsey oil refinery in 2009 – another situation in which management threats to worker job security assumed important and quite ugly political overtones. These were 'wildcat' strikes – in other words, strikes called by workers themselves without the say-so of the official union – and included walkouts by other workers at different energy sites in support of the Lyndsey strikers, after many of them were sacked. The dispute was started when the refinery hired in an Italian contractor to provide work at the plant, using the EU's

Posted Worker's Directive to bring in workers from abroad to get round the conditions agreed nationally with the union.

Since the Lyndsey strikers used the phrase 'British jobs for British workers', aping a slogan the then Prime Minister Gordon Brown had adopted, it became very easy for them to be presented as xenophobes. Brown leapt at the opportunity to criticise them, just as far-right political parties rushed to offer insincere support. This dispute crystallises the disorientation of labour under globalisation. As Theresa May might observe, it was capital that was acting as a citizen of the world, and that was using its world citizenship to disorganise the workforce. The strikers clearly saw little other hope than to try and throw Brown's words back at him, and he condemned them for it with no little amount of hypocrisy. These are cases where capital's superior command of space (i.e. its capacity to either go elsewhere itself, or bring other workers to it) has forced labour into impossible situations with seemingly no appropriate way out.

In these kinds of disputes, capital can invariably rely on outside help. Specifically, from government.* A good example here would be the Unite–British Airways dispute of 2011. Unite members voted to strike in late 2009 in response to management plans to freeze pay, alter working practices and cut jobs. The interesting thing about this dispute is what happened next. These strikes had a huge effect on the company's bottom line, but came to be heavily disrupted by legal injunctions which the employer sought against the union. This was on the grounds that strike ballots were conducted improperly, including violations of technical balloting procedure. Some observers attributed this to union incompetence, musing that 'members required to pay an annual membership fee of more than £130 could now question how the union had repeatedly failed to conduct legally-binding ballots, with all the resources at their disposal'.[49]

The problem with this argument, though, is that the injunctions in question rested on spurious legal technicalities. For instance, the court found that 'Unite failed to carry out its statutory duties by making sure that everyone balloted was told the result', despite employers not being able to find a single employee who didn't know about it.[50] This injunction was later overturned. Similar injunctions have been repeatedly used against unions representing London Underground workers. Still, it

---

* And, it goes without saying, from the media, though we return to this in Chapter 8.

makes a change to hear about cases where business finds itself on the side of bureaucratic pedantry and idiotic restrictions: if these kinds of arbitrary obstacles were applied to anyone other than labour, they would be described as the worst sort of 'red tape'.

So we need to be realistic in recognising the problems facing trade unionism. They are, clearly, severe. So far, I have not even mentioned another important factor: shifts in workplace cultures. In the service industry, people often work in smaller units with less regular shift patterns, and they may spend a lot more time in relative isolation (as with the warehouse staff walking round with only a bleeping electronic tag for company). For all the misery of working in a coal mine, it evidently tended to produce a sense of community and shared adversity that you simply cannot find in a call centre. This is bad news for unions, resulting in torturous internal debates around whether they can really make a worthwhile effort to recruit new members in emerging industries, or whether their future depends on trying to defend those they still retain.

They can still, sometimes, win. Particularly in the service industries, if workers can successfully build unions, they may be able to make positive gains rather than desperately defending themselves against management threats. Staff working for Picturehouse Cinemas in London, for instance, based their campaign, which has seen a series of strikes over a two-year period, around demands for the London Living Wage. In this case management had threatened to undertake mass firings in response to the action at the Ritzy Cinema in Brixton, but these were stamped on by its parent company for fear of bad publicity. Such cases benefitted from high-profile campaigns which could capitalise on their fairly bohemian localities in order to embarrass managers.[51]

Evidently, workers in industries that are typically outsourced have an even harder time. Indeed, part of the reason for outsourcing is to disorganise: where unions might have managed to secure an agreement over conditions for a particular large company, it is unusual that these conditions will apply to the outsourced staff as well. John Lewis, for instance, receives a lot of liberal kudos for its 'partnership' approach to employment, but it does not apply this to everyone. Its cleaners are outsourced and so the company has no obligation to afford them the same privileges: 'Worse still is that the annual bonus is publicly announced every year in store. This means the cleaners are forced to watch everyone celebrate and then sweep up the confetti and mop up the spilt champagne as a cruel reminder of their second class status within John Lewis.'[52]

Service workers in some cases have joined insurgent unions rather than established ones, though examples of this are rare. Probably the most important recent case is the Deliveroo strikes of 2016. Deliveroo is part of the 'gig economy', where workers pick up jobs via mobile app platforms and are typically considered 'self-employed'. For this reason there is often an assumption that these workers are difficult to organise – or even that they are disorganised by definition, given their status. Nonetheless, in 2016 they went on strike against Deliveroo's plans to shift them from an hourly rate into a more unreliable 'per drop' rate. They had some success, deterring the company from the plan, after another highly visible campaign which was supported by a crowd-funding initiative. There is some evidence that workers at comparable companies such as UberEATS are taking note, though it is early days.[53] In such cases, workers in service industries go on the offensive rather than the defensive – typically through more radical emerging unions and potentially through wildcat activity. The really big test here, which is only just emerging at time of writing, is the formation of an unofficial pilot's union in Ryanair, whose model is based, in part, on union avoidance, but who have apparently pushed their own workforce a little bit too far to be sustainable.[54]

These are success stories, but they are not widespread. In general, the climate for trade unionism is becoming harsher. Unions in the public sector – their current stronghold – have seemingly had little response to austerity measures targeting public sector staff. There have been various strikes, but these have typically been isolated one-day affairs, asking members to sacrifice pay in exchange for a largely symbolic gesture.

More on the Trade Union Act

I referred to the Trade Union Act (2015) in passing in Chapter 3, but it is worth looking at in a little more depth here, since it tells us a lot about the way in which the British government intervenes in labour–capital relations. It was pushed through with overwhelming support from the right-wing press in the UK, as well as the indirect support of the liberal press who, while they opposed the bill itself, have paved the ground for it by tut-tutting in editorial columns every time workers go on strike. It was also welcomed by pro-business lobbying groups such as the Confederation of British Industry and the Institute of Directors. Admittedly, some business bodies such as the Chartered Institute for Personnel and Development did criticise it as a somewhat passé and uncalled-for rehashing of Thatcherite legislation from the 1980s.[55] But the problem with these kinds of well-meaning critiques was that they were a bit too logical. They were asking: if there is no evidence that strikes are damaging the economy, why put new restrictions on them? This seems to miss the underlying point, which is that the Act is not about solving a problem but about making labour scared of capital.

The headline measure of the Act was to introduce new turnout thresholds for valid strike ballots – 50 per cent of eligible voters must take part in any strike ballot or the action will be deemed illegal. There are more stringent requirements for public service jobs. By these measures, around half of the strikes in Britain since 1997 would have been disallowed.[56] Further provisions, several of which were eventually dropped, purported to be about preventing 'intimidation' in the course of industrial disputes. To this effect the original bill tried to push through tighter police monitoring of strikers with the potential criminalisation of those picketing incorrectly. The justification for this was the widely hyped case of the inflatable rat in the Ineos dispute, but the government was frustrated in its attempts to gather any more shocking examples.[57] This will not be surprising for anyone who has actually been involved in a strike in Britain in the twenty-first century, which are often friendly and community-oriented events populated by very mild-mannered people.

It is important to point out the hypocrisy behind these kinds of policies, because they seem like common sense to so many people who don't follow these issues closely. Of course higher turnouts in strike ballots are a good thing, of course strikers shouldn't intimidate people, and so on. But if turnout thresholds are genuinely important in safe-guarding democratic processes, why only apply them to union ballots rather than, say, referenda on EU membership? Or indeed the election of MPs. Talking of common sense, it also seems obvious that, to try and address the problem of low turnout, unions should be allowed to ballot members about strike action electronically, but the government has ruled this out, saying they have to stick to posting out ballot papers. So the Trade Union Act was sold as a 'modernisation' of industrial relations, but it was modernisation of a very particular kind that did not, apparently, extend to trade unionists being allowed to use the Internet. Of course, from capital's perspective there is no point in imposing restrictions on strikes on the basis of low turnouts if you don't then take steps to make sure turnout stays low.

Similarly, as the government was consulting over the development of the Act, it was striking how relentlessly one-way the issue of 'intimidation' became. It has apparently been accepted as self-evident that the only intimidation that goes on in industrial disputes is strikers intimidating non-strikers (despite the lack of evidence that this really happens at all).* People just seem to assume that strikers are intimidating by definition, no matter how little support can be found for this claim.

On the other hand, the Act contained nothing to stop the intimidation of strikers by management, which is something that actually happens in reality as well as in people's minds. It is common for human resource managers to send emails to the entire staff at organisations where a strike is planned. They often, particularly in white-collar jobs, adopt a collegial tone, warmly addressing those employees who don't plan to strike, before making the request, which is always presented as entirely reasonable and practical, that those who do plan to strike inform management in advance. They cannot say workers are obliged to do this since (for now) they cannot be, but it is clear that pressure is exerted, especially on those not fully aware of their rights.

The nervousness this can cause is compounded by the harder language that often seeps in subtly. Workers that take strike action will be in 'breach of contract': three words that conjure the idea in many people's minds that management will be justified in doing whatever they want to them by way of reprisal. This perception is exacerbated by the knowledge that managers have indeed sacked strikers in cases such as the Lyndsey dispute of 2009. The superior legal and organisational resources wielded by human resources, and the threat of job loss, mean that this kind of thing is several orders of magnitude more intimidating than pretty much anything strikers can muster.

It is interesting how social media may open up new routes for management action against strikers, though so far attempts to do so have been apt to fall flat on their face. For instance, during one of the strikes arising as part of a long-running dispute between Southern Rail and its workforce, the company tried to use Twitter to recruit members of the public into criticising union members. They sent out a tweet encouraging inconvenienced travellers to contact the RMT (the National Union

---

* Beyond the now thrice-mentioned inflatable rat of Grangemouth.

of Rail, Maritime and Transport Workers) directly to express their frustrations, under the banner 'Let's strike back', as if they too were innocent victims just like the passengers. However, they generally received more abuse than support, from people who were old-fashioned enough to believe that employers should not be encouraging people to attack their staff publicly.[58]

Anyway, more obvious than the hypocrisy are the holes in the reasoning offered in support of the Act. The Regulatory Policy Committee – a watchdog tagged with evaluating the costs and savings of new legislation – roundly judged the proposals as 'not fit for purpose'.[59] They noted a variety of problems with the legislation, including the weak definition of the problem (where are these supposed mobs of violent and intimidating strikers? Why bother with more anti-strike legislation when there are already so few strikes anyway?) and the questionable wisdom of hiring temp agency workers as strike-breaking labour (another proposal of the bill that got ditched along the way).

Ultimately, this is the point. Despite its hype, the Act was not actually about fairness, modernisation, preventing intimidation or indeed even efficiency and good practice in industrial relations. If it had really been about any of these things it would have been a spectacular failure. Moreover, the Act is not about preventing strikes that have 'weak mandates'; it is about preventing strikes full stop. It is about showing workers that it is going to become more and more difficult for them to take industrial action, and that if they try to, they will be bogged down in costly legal battles. Furthermore, should a strike get through, it is also about making strikers aware that the law is not on their side, and that if they do take part they will be vulnerable to legally sanctioned reprisals. In this sense it is a nice official complement to other, more sinister examples of the surveillance of trade unionists, most notably the blacklisting of construction workers which has been going on for decades, apparently with state collusion, and which is at last beginning to blow up in the faces of its perpetrators.[60]

We can't understand the wider political picture here without recalling the discussion from Chapter 1, about the way 'class' is used in contemporary politics. There is an effort to ensure that 'working class' no longer refers to the people who do the striking, but to the 'victims' of strikes; i.e. the inconvenienced public. Some right-wing voices, such as the columnist Leo McKinstry, are quite lurid in their attempts to drive a wedge between trade unionists and other workers: 'Once trade unions

were the authentic voice of the British working class.* Now they are
noisy pressure groups for a narrow part of the national workforce ...
Something has to be done to emasculate these evangelists for failure
and conflict'.[61] As the party of the working class, the Conservatives have
even considered setting up their own trade unions for 'moderate' workers
to join.[62,†]

One thing I have barely discussed in this chapter is work in the
public sector. There is a lot to say about this. Interestingly, it is in the
public sector that government attempts to marginalise unions are most
obvious and evident. Government was always supposed to act as a 'model
employer', with the best equality and diversity policies, the most progressive attitude towards training and so on. While this remains the case in
some respects, it has emerged as a model employer in a different sense
too. I will talk about this in Chapter 5.

---

*   As a general rule, people who say that trade unionists used to be on the side of workers,
but aren't any more, are the kind of people that have always hated them anyway.

†   The man responsible for this scheme is cryptic about the target 'moderate' demographic:
presumably people who are happy to see their own working conditions decline without a
fight, so long as they know disabled welfare recipients are also being hounded to suicide.

5

Government

The economy is the central, critical, irreducible core of this election. Everything depends on a strong economy. Every job; every pay packet; every business; every teacher's salary in our schools; every heart operation in our NHS; every kind of help we can give the elderly and frail.[1]

The basic argument in Chapters 1 and 2 was that class is not just a means of categorising people into different groups. Instead, I argued that it is most important to focus on the economic functions of labour and capital: the imperatives that act on them, and the way in which they interact with each other. Once this is recognised, it quickly becomes clear that class has much wider-ranging implications for society as a whole than is usually recognised.

This is most obvious and important when it comes to the question of government. In capitalist societies, the prospects for economic growth depends on the successful extraction and profitable reinvestment of surplus value. David Cameron was right to say that, under capitalism, 'everything depends on a strong economy', but the question is what actually *is* a strong economy? In capitalist terms 'a strong economy' can only ever be one in which the M-C-M' cycle is running smoothly. If it is interrupted or blocked, then we have crisis, unemployment, possibly recession or depression. So the role of government has to, inevitably, involve finding ways to ensure this process can continue. This is often very difficult, particularly when you consider that governments have to balance various other priorities (demands for improving standards of living, for acceptable public services and so on). So politicians are subject to competing and confusing pressures which they have to navigate.

In Britain, as in many other developed countries, the widespread perception that liberal parliamentary democracy is by far the 'least worst' form of government appears to have weakened. Survey research suggests that, across a range of wealthy democracies, the number of people who believe it is essential to live in a democratic system is declining, and the number of people who think it would be 'good' or 'very good' to live under a military dictatorship is increasing (albeit from a low base).[2] Until the 2017 general election saw a bounce in youth turnout, young people were clearly becoming less interested in joining political parties and in voting than previous generations.

For now, suffice to say that it seems as though democratic governments in Western countries have weakening legitimacy. In other words, people appear to be less and less convinced that elected ruling parties, whatever their alignment, are capable of acting in the interests of national populations as a whole.

This situation is manifested in various different ways. There is a growing fear among many commentators (and excitement among others) that the British people are devolving back into a pitchfork-wielding mob. For many moderates and liberals, the unusually high youth turnout in 2017 was a confirmation of this rather than a refutation.[3] The paradigmatic villain in this respect is Michael Gove, who became notorious for a sound bite during the Brexit campaign. When challenged with the argument that the majority of academic commentators believed that leaving the EU would have negative consequences, he said that 'I think people in this country have had enough of experts'. This caused much dismay in many quarters[4] as exemplifying the intellectual degeneration of British democracy. Brexit became, of course, the focal point for this worrying, with the default narrative among centre-left 'Remainers' being one of a gullible population being sold obvious snake oil. Indeed, much excitement was generated in this demographic at the imminent possibility of being able to say 'I told you so'.[5]

Clearly this is more than a British phenomenon. Donald Trump turned not knowing very much into a campaign-winning advantage, and in doing so became the great symbol of so-called 'post-truth politics'[6] – the idea that it has become more useful for political leaders to regurgitate inaccurate bullshit that reinforces people's existing prejudices than develop an accurate understanding of a situation.* From this perspective, the simplest response to Brexit/Trump is to look with furrowed-but-

---

* My problem with this idea is not so much that there isn't a lot of this kind of thing going on; more that it is wrong to present it as a new development. People who are familiar with British newspapers, upon being told about the 'post-truth era', will wonder when the 'truth era' was and how they managed to miss it.

caring brow upon the non-expert and easily led mentality of voters on the opposing side.

Certainly, it is possible that the narrative of 'the world is being hi-jacked by yokels who revel in their own ignorance' has become a very powerful one, and may yet form the basis for renewed interest in liberal-left politics if the right figureheads can be found to articulate it. But it is not my aim to help in these efforts. We are better off looking in a much less superficial way at the relationship between expertise, government and class. In this sense, complaining that people should listen more carefully to experts overlooks some very important things: it ignores the extent to which 'expertise' can be appropriated in the service of capital (think of the 'scientific management' expounded by Taylor as discussed in Chapter 4); and it also ignores the high-profile failures of 'experts' themselves, particularly in the economic domain. It is not anti-intellectualism to say that European economic experts failed to avoid the financial disasters of the last decade, and have likewise failed to find an adequate solution to the crisis that doesn't involve the inhumane and destructive 'financial waterboarding' of countries such as Greece, Spain, Portugal and Ireland.

Something that goes hand in hand with distrust of democracy and distrust of experts is conspiracy theory. The idea that everyone's problems are attributable to a shady and malevolent clique has graduated from fringe obsession to the centre of the political agenda. This is reflected in the proliferation of increasingly vague nouns which serve as media punching bags: 'elites', 'the establishment', 'globalists', 'Brussels bureaucrats' (or, in the US, 'Washington insiders'), and sometimes just pronouns ('they'). The vagueness of these accusations means they can be brought out at almost any juncture and sound plausible.

But, again, it is short-sighted to say that ordinary voters have simply become more gullible, and more prone to demagogic political leaders who use this sort of rhetoric. Capitalism's elite institutions are themselves becoming vaguer, as shown in Moretti and Pestre's study of the grammar and syntax used in World Bank publications.[7] These documents talk recurrently about what is supposed to happen in any given country to aid its development, while becoming increasingly fuzzy on the question of who is supposed to do it and how. We could also look at the way no expert commentator interviewed on the news is able to reliably anticipate how 'the markets' will react to political circumstances, instead limiting themselves to providing *post hoc* rationalisations of up-or-downswings. In other words, the apparent fact that fewer people now trust experts is not as worrying as the state of expertise itself under financialised capitalism, which has managed to produce a world of opaque confusion in which many people, including governments, feel powerless and uncertain about how to act.

ADEQUATE FORMS AND ALIEN POWERS

Before looking at government in Britain today, I will offer a short theoretical detour. How have Marxists historically thought about the role of government and politics? The first Marxist 'theory of the State' is expressed, albeit very briefly, in the *Communist Manifesto*, where governments in capitalist societies are described as 'but a committee for managing the common affairs of the bourgeoisie'. In other words, government is ultimately a means of organising society to achieve the best results for capital. Taken out of context, this could resemble the kind of conspiracy theories discussed previously, with government and capital in cahoots behind the machinery of power.

But elsewhere, while retaining this general gist, Marx adds many subtleties to his analysis of political power. In *Capital*, he discusses the role of the British government in introducing the Factory Acts, which imposed limits on the working day. This was to some degree a response to pressure from radicals and reformers, and was pushed through in spite of opposition from capital. However, Marx argues, the government sought to ensure that this legislation did not, in practice, impose much of a burden, creating various loopholes and providing for very weak enforcement: 'parliament passed five labour Laws between 1802 and 1833, but was shrewd enough not to vote a penny for their carrying out, for the requisite officials, etc'.[8]

This reading sets a pattern: ostensibly progressive reforming legislation is generally viewed warily by Marxists, since they suspect it is more likely to be a way of keeping labour quiet while ultimately doing little harm to capital's interests. Indeed, if it defuses potentially damaging class conflict on relatively non-threatening terms, it has done capital a big favour.

In *Grundrisse*, Marx writes repeatedly of the need for political institutions to be set up in a way that is 'adequate to the needs' of capital. There is something Darwinian about this view of politics: institutions and laws that obstruct the M-C-M' cycle will either be forced to change or become obsolete over time, like the ancestors of giraffes whose necks were not long enough to reach leaves. For instance, in the legal system: laws that facilitate public access to common resources were phased out as capitalism developed, whereas laws that ensured transparent private contracting and the protection of private property have proliferated. In the Marxist view, it is not that these laws are introduced and then capitalist society comes about as a result. Rather, the M-C-M' process forces political, social and legal institutions to adapt or die.

So it is far too simple to say that capitalists *control* government. Government makes its own decisions, but it has to do so with the question of 'how will this affect capital?' constantly in mind. As a result, things like 'business confidence' become unreadable and remote forces that terrify governments into pursuing capital-friendly policies. There are thousands of individual investors controlling vast quantities of massed capital, looking for somewhere to put it. Governments know they have to get their 'confidence', but since capital is the collective product of countless individuals all competing with each other, rather than something which speaks with one unified voice, it often does not know how. Consequently, 'business confidence' becomes an *alien power*: a disembodied collective entity whose terms must be met, except that there is no way of knowing, generally, what these terms actually are. Usually, the UK government has responded to this situation by point-lessly but extravagantly punching labour in the face as hard as it thinks it can get away with (metaphorically speaking).

We can apply the idea of searching for 'adequate forms' to various important political questions. While, for instance, the motivations of many Brexit voters were of a decidedly capital-unfriendly kind (worries about socio-economic insecurity, deteriorating community, anti-globalism), this is almost certainly not how the political architects of the project see it. For the latter, the real motivation has been the belief that the regulations entailed by EU membership obstruct British capital. Even highly Europhile British politicians have implicitly accepted this premise and had sought to reshape the EU in a more capital-friendly way until Brexit made this a moot point. I return to this later. But as the Brexit episode shows, finding these adequate forms can be a highly conflicted and confusing process – many British businesses are deeply worried at the prospect of leaving the EU and see it as a gamble gone horribly awry. So governments try to do what is best for capital, but there is usually intense disagreement over what this means in practice.

Miliband and 'Common Sense'

Various later Marxists sought to sketch out a more complete 'theory of the State', and in doing so tended to minimise the chaotic and Darwinian reading of government implied in the idea of 'adequate forms'. The most influential exchange on the topic was the debate between Ralph Miliband and Nicos Poulantzas, which occupied the pages of the journal *New Left Review* in the 1960s and 1970s,[9] and which is incisively analysed by Theda Skocpol.[10]

Miliband was an influential Marxist academic at the London School of Economics (among other places), who is now better known as the father of Ed and David. In fact, on the right, he is most notorious as 'the man who hated Britain', following a famous newspaper article which broke the news that he wrote a sniffy diary entry about English nationalism when he was 17.[11] The article in question was part of an attack on his son, back when he looked like having a credible chance of being the next prime minister. Consequently, Ed was forced to respond by talking solemnly about how much his dad, contrary to reports, actually thought Britain was great. At the time, this episode summed up the narcissistic spirit of the age: it seems a bit much to blame the gullible public for the advent of 'post-truth' politics when the country's most influential newspaper is arguing with one of its leading politicians about so twee and pointless a question as whether or not a dead academic 'loved Britain'.

Whether he loved or hated Britain, Miliband was a major innovator in the Marxist analysis of government. The motivation for his classic book *The State and Capitalist Society* was his annoyance at the 'polyarchy' argument held by influential academics such as Robert Dahl, which remains highly influential today. Polyarchy theorists believed that different groups (be they manufacturing lobbies, trade unionists, consumer organisations, agricultural interests, banks, religious groups and so on) competed with each other to influence government. They also believed that in the long term a democratic polyarchy would mean that no one group could decisively dominate all the others; 'all the active and legitimate groups in the population can make themselves heard at some stage in the process of decision'.[12] Governments, then, mediate and balance between different interests, and do so depending on various factors, including things like ideology.

Miliband was contemptuous of this argument. He believed that one particular force (i.e. *capital*) was not simply one of many competing influences on government, but was the *decisive influence*. Parliamentary democracy, while ostensibly giving voice to everyone, in fact reinforced this influence, for various reasons. One reason, in his view, was that business and state elites tended to be drawn from wealthier backgrounds, and therefore had a shared interest in maintaining the status quo. Because they share similar backgrounds and tight personal interconnections, capital is far more likely to have the ear of government than those representing labour (such as unions). Miliband does not, of course, rule out that people from more humble backgrounds could penetrate these circles, but he does think that those who enter government from the outside will always come under irresistible pressure to remain within the confines of 'respectable' opinion. So Miliband is not interested in 'meritocracy' per se; it's more about the way in which proximity to power makes everyone more conservative irrespective of background or views.

For Miliband this has very important ideological consequences. It means that business elites can establish their own values as the point from which all 'sensible' political debate must begin, and from which people cannot stray too far without being considered unacceptably extreme. The voice of 'business' therefore appears as the only one able to talk in good faith, as a kind of neutral arbiter that is able to give a down-to-earth view of what the economy needs, away from the political fray:

> Businessmen themselves have often tended to stress their remoteness from, even their distaste for, 'politics'; and they have also tended to have a poor view of politicians as men who, in the hallowed phrase, have never had to meet a payroll, and who therefore do not know what the world is about. What this means is that businessmen, like administrators, wish to 'depoliticise' highly contentious issues and to have these issues judged according to the criteria favoured by business. This may look like an avoidance of politics and ideology: it is in fact their clandestine importation into public affairs.[13]

This false 'depoliticisation' of business means that the interests of business come to be seen as synonymous with the *national* interest. Therefore, according to Miliband, the very idea of the 'national interest' is a biased and ideological one, since 'common sense' always constructs it with reference to what is best for business. This point is very important and I come back to it in later chapters.

Such a view is reinforced through what he calls *indoctrination*; in other words, the rigging of 'ideological competition' towards one side. He refers to various institutions – most obviously the media, but also education among others, which he says narrow down the limits of acceptable discussion. From leaving the nursery, he believes that a 'pot pourri'[14] of conservative ideology is presented to people as simply common sense: for instance, that what is good for business is good for everyone, and that there is such a thing as the 'national interest' which must be pursued by anyone in public life.

In this sense Miliband gave quite a 'personalised' analysis: business elites have power because they have direct interpersonal ties to government. They essentially *control* the state in their capacity as influential individuals. But it quickly becomes apparent that the situation is a lot more wayward than this in reality.

Poulantzas and the Functionalist State

Miliband's highest-profile critic (within Marxism) was the philosopher Poulantzas, who vehemently rejected Miliband's person-centric analysis. He disliked the idea that there is a particular group of people who have an iron control over the apparatus of government. For him, the state* is a kind of institutional crystallisation of class relations. In other words, a network of institutions and relationships that is not in the hands of any one group, but which acts in a 'relatively autonomous' way to stabilise the capitalist system.

What might this mean? By its very existence, the state creates a 'political' arena where social conflicts are fought out, without ever needing to spill over into the realm of production. So, for instance, rather than workers making direct demands of capitalists in the workplace itself (quite a scary prospect for capital), there are representative organisations (such as the Labour Party) who are supposed to fight their cause in a more indirect and restrained way in the House of Commons. The conflict between labour and capital is diverted into the world of parlia-

---

* There is a danger of conflating the terms 'state' and 'government'. The difference is usually that 'the state' is a broader term, comprising all sorts of things like the police and military, the judiciary and so on, whereas government refers to the specific people elected (or not) to make policy decisions.

mentary procedure before it can pose a serious threat to the basic power relationship between labour and capital.

Likewise, according to Poulantzas, the state has to intervene in the interests of stability when capitalism is in trouble. So, for instance, Martin Carnoy and Manuel Castells use Poulantzas's ideas to explain the initial steps of globalisation.[15] They argue that it was engineered by governments as a means of rectifying the destabilising problems of the 1970s: declining profits, trade union strength and fewer opportunities for profitable investment. 'Globalization was, in fact, induced by the state, as a way out of the crisis. Not under the command of corporations, but certainly with corporate interests as a fundamental concern: this is the kind of policy that Poulantzas could have characterised as an expression of the relative autonomy of the state.'[16]

Poulantzas's view of the state is therefore a 'functionalist' one,[17] meaning that the state is defined and understood according to the specific role it has to fulfil (rather than being seen as, say, one entity with its own agenda which does not necessarily fit easily with a wider 'system'). It is a stabilising influence which has a defined purpose: binding a potentially conflict-riddled and crisis-prone system into a sustainable whole. Hence, although coming from different angles, both Miliband and Poulantzas assign a kind of 'managerial' role to government. This is made more explicit still in Fred Block's work,[18] which presents government as the long-term 'manager' in contrast with the short-termist energies of capital. So the state may do various things that capital might dislike in the short term, like levying taxes in order to pay for services or infrastructure, but which are necessary for the sustainability of the system. When I talked about globalisation and financialisation Chapter 3, I suggested that it is becoming harder for states to 'manage' capitalist economies in this way. I will return to this point in more depth towards the end of this chapter.

Following on from these arguments, it is obvious that, in the Marxist view, things like socialised health and education systems are not created in capitalist societies for humanitarian reasons. They appear because they have a necessary role in supporting capital accumulation, providing ways of training or maintaining a workforce without individual capitalists having to pay for these things themselves. This creates interesting tensions. While the 'welfare state' has become a major rallying point for the political left in recent years, historically many Marxists have tended to distrust it, seeing it as a means of giving people a bare minimum to prevent them from demanding any more. Welfare systems may benefit labour in many respects but they do so as a by-product rather than an end. The end is to maintain an environment in which capital can go on extracting and reinvesting surplus value. We might ask: if public services get delivered all the same, why does this matter? This becomes more evident when we look at the subject in more depth.

PUBLIC SERVICES AND CAPITAL

Public services are important in supporting the M-C-M' process. Without the provision of healthcare or education, for instance, the quality of the workforce would deteriorate, and capitalists would be stuck. In this sense, public service provision by the state is an indirect way of subsidising the creation of surplus value. By socialising the costs of health, training, even (sometimes) things like housing, government pays for things that individual capitalists would otherwise have to pay for from their own profits (since they can't manage if their workers are perpetually ill, or completely unskilled, or cannot find anywhere to live near their workplace). It does this either through taxation, which spreads around the burden of funding these things, or just by going into debt.

This means, importantly, that public sector workers are bound up into the same system of extraction as private sector workers. Capital extracts value from them just as it does from anyone else, it's just that this happens in a more indirect way. This may just sound like quibbling over terminology, but it helps us recognise some very important things. The NHS, for instance, is widely revered and romanticised on the left in Britain as an example of a 'socialist' holdout in a capitalist system. There is *some* truth in this, but it is a socialist system which must inevitably always be adapting itself to capitalist needs. The NHS must try to find forms adequate to the system it inhabits, with important practical consequences. This observation is particularly significant in a period of austerity. Under austerity policies, where government is actively trying to lessen the burden placed on the capitalist class as a whole (i.e. by reducing taxes levied to pay for public services), there emerges an urgent need to shrink public services *which clearly outweighs the objective of improving or maintaining the quality of service provided*. It could never be the other way around.

It is also clear that public service provision is a site of class struggle. Evidently, wage levels must enable workers to pursue a sustainable standard of living, but what this actually means depends on social attitudes about what constitute tolerable living conditions. The stronger the voice of labour, the higher the expectations that must be met. The same thing can be said of public services. It may be that the state wants to reduce the tax burden on capital, but its ability to do this by cutting public services will depend on how prepared people are to fight. Hence under post-2008 austerity, one of the most important political stakes has been the extent to which government can get away with shrinking the socialised burden of public services, without social tensions getting too inflamed. I will return to this below.

Public services could well also be a more direct source of profit for capital. Capital has an existential need to find profitable sources of investment. This could involve geographical expansion – finding new markets and new sources of labour in different countries. However, it could also involve opening up areas that already exist within a given territory, including public services. David Harvey uses the term 'accumulation by dispossession' to get at this idea of capital trying to convert common resources into commodities that can be bought and sold for profit. Various Marx-influenced researchers have applied this idea to privatisations of public property, notably of natural resources like water supply.[19] In what follows, I will apply these general points to public services in the UK, in particularly health and education.

Education, Training, 'Employability'

To some extent capital assumes different forms, and behaves in different ways, from country to country. Writers on political economy have tended to classify Britain (alongside the US) as a more 'liberal' system than other developed countries such as Germany, France, Japan or the Scandinavian economies. Capital is generally more 'impatient', demanding higher levels of managerial control with less legal or regulatory interference, particularly from unions, along with an expectation of greater flexibility and shorter-term returns on investment.[20] I discussed the implications of this specifically for UK labour markets in Chapter 3, and considered how various trends such as financialisation have affected things.

But what about other aspects of society? If public services are shaped by the interests of capital, then the nature of capital clearly matters. Influential writers such as Peter Hall and David Soskice and the 'varieties of capitalism' school see British capitalism as depending on a particular form of education and skills system, namely a low-skills equilibrium.[21]

Because capital moves around quickly and demands high levels of flex-ibility, there needs to be a steady supply of workers who have a highly generalised set of basic and 'portable' (i.e. non-industry-specific) skills. For this reason, things like vocational apprenticeships have typically been less developed in Britain compared to so-called 'coordinated market economies' such as Germany or Japan. These kinds of things require organisation and mutual commitment between public training providers, worker representatives and private employers. If a worker is to dedicate time to take very specific vocational training, there needs to be a stable job in industry at the end (otherwise it's a waste of time and effort). These kinds of mutual commitments between labour, state and capital do not really exist in Britain.*

International orthodoxy in education policy is that training and skills systems have to become more 'employer-led'.[22] In other words, there is a growing awareness of the need to make sure that people come through education more adequately adapted to the needs of capital. This preoccupation, however, does not always fit with other political objectives. Since the crisis, and particularly when Vince Cable was at the Department for Business, Information and Skills, British politicians have been desperate to show they were taking the 'high road' to recovery. There was a well-meaning desire to encourage longer-term investment in skills on the part of employers. The hope was that, by doing so, the economy could be rebalanced away from finance and towards manufac-turing, along with improved prospects for workers to upskill themselves to job security.

The problem is that this kind of approach is not adequate to the needs of British capital, and hence has not materialised. In the UK, once employees enter the labour force, training and upskilling become highly voluntaristic, and dependent on the employer's buy-in. Successive UK governments have seen little scope to challenge this: they agonise about why employers don't bother to invest more in training, despite presumably also being aware that vast swathes of the UK labour market (call centre work, many service and retail jobs, highly routinised manu-facturing or logistics) only really require low skills.[23] There is, evidently, an antagonism between what is seen politically as a Good Thing (training people) and what suits the needs of capital (a generally low-skilled, easily

---

* It is important to note that countries like Germany or Japan no longer look as 'coordinated' as they used to, but that is the subject for a different book.

moulded workforce, and training systems that don't require much from individual employers).

Consequently, in the UK apprenticeship schemes, long presented as a panacea which ties together the obsession with improving skills and the sense that we need to stimulate 'good' manufacture (as opposed to 'bad' finance), have evolved in a disappointing way. They frequently provide low-skilled and low-prospect positions, essentially renamed in a way that sounds social democratic and virtuous.[24] Historically, significant damage had already been done to apprenticeships schemes in Britain since the 1980s, owing to factors such as the public sector withdrawing from fields like construction, and the acceleration of vertical disintegration (i.e. subcontracting).[25]

The mismatch between what capital wants and the desire to improve skills is also obvious in relation to higher education. This sector has been expanding, in part fuelled by successive governments' belief that Britain is becoming a 'knowledge economy'. There is some truth to this, in the sense that work in Britain is becoming more polarised, with growth in the highest- and lowest-paid jobs but middle-earning ones being stripped away.[26] This might, on the face of things, imply the need for more people with graduate-level skills as opportunities for reliable work in non-graduate jobs decline. But the knowledge economy rhetoric has obscured the extent to which the British economy still relies on highly routine and dull work, and as a result the push in this direction has led to a rising problem of overqualification.[27] There is an emerging generation of graduates who have skills which British capitalism is simply not equipped to put to good use. 'The number of graduates [has] now "significantly outstripped" the creation of high-skilled jobs'.[28] Many graduates find themselves working in low-skilled jobs for extended periods while waiting for a graduate job to come along.[29]

Once again, observe the mismatch between what governments think is good (more highly skilled graduates) and what actually suits capital. In practice, the ideology of 'employability' has evolved as an increasingly important concern in British education, as a means of defusing this tension – or at least of making students believe it is their own fault, which amounts to the same thing. Employability – in other words, how well-adapted graduates are to what employers want – is something that increasingly concerns British universities. More prestigious universities perhaps a little less, since their graduates are presumed to have a stamp of approval that helps them on the job market anyway. But where graduate

employment rates are a worry, courses may be designed and reshaped
with the question constantly lurking: 'how will this programme of study
fit with what employers want?'

Hence 'employability' is refracted through a fairly vague set of
assumptions – either university staff inferring what they think employers might want, or the pontifications of employers themselves voiced
through various committees and business 'engagement' panels. This
'employer-higher education interface'[30] is now accepted as common
sense in many universities, particularly as league tables have taken off
and universities are increasingly judged on what their graduates end up
earning. When surveys of employers reveal they are unhappy with the
level of skills of UK graduates (as they do very frequently), this is always
taken as a pronouncement of doom from some unimpeachable authority. But what role the UK's 'employer-driven' skills system may play in
the problem is rarely, if ever, questioned. Hence, while it is very obvious
that access to differing levels of social, cultural and economic 'capital'
give more affluent students a vast head start in 'playing the game',[31] it is
equally important to recognise the way in which the terms of this 'game'
are set by the demands of capital.

Health

One thing I did not mention in relation to education was the idea of
public services as a source of profitable investment for capital. While
this does happen in education, it is arguably more sensitive in the case
of health. Obviously, there are a lot of capitalists who would love to
exercise some 'accumulation by dispossession' on the British health
system. In theory, delivering healthcare can be very profitable. But from
capital's perspective, the last three decades in British health policy have
been characterised by raised hopes and continuing frustration, because
making money from the NHS is not always easy and often encounters
resistance on the ground.

There have been various waves of efforts to extend private profit-
making in front-line health services, particularly in England, with the
most important tool being the purchaser–provider split, which has
progressed through various different guises. This is where local health
institutions (such as general practitioner (GP) consortia or hospital
trusts) are re-envisioned as commissioning organisations who buy in
care on behalf of the public, potentially from private companies. The

Coalition government's Health and Social Care Act was the most significant recent manifestation of this idea, pushing large chunks of NHS money on to Clinical Commissioning Groups (CCGs) – groups of GPs responsible for commissioning services in their area from any willing provider. This has led to an urgent discussion on the left about the possibility of wholesale privatisation of NHS services.

Proportionately, the amount of NHS services transferred to for-profit companies is comparatively small. Privatisation has been 'gradual and inexorable' rather than a rapid 'explosion'; the amount of NHS money in private hands has gone from about 4 per cent in 2009–10 to about 8 per cent in 2015–16.[32] It may well be that the government has had a premeditated strategy to privatise large sections of the NHS, but they have gone about it in a fairly blundering fashion. As Nick Krachler and Ian Greer show,[33] the Health and Social Care Act encountered various obstacles which proved very difficult to overcome. For one thing, it was imposed at a time of austerity: the fact that there was so little money about meant a lot of private companies felt it wasn't worth the trouble of taking over NHS services. For another, the institutions on the front line of privatisation (i.e. the CCGs) appear to be somewhat brittle and in many cases may not have the stomach to push through controversial privatisations in the face of public opposition. Government has generally failed to depoliticise the NHS and many retain a strong sentimental attachment to it, and consequently CCGs are very susceptible to pressure on the part of motivated and organised local campaign groups.[34] If one wants to force through highly sensitive privatisations, you really need the iron fist of central government rather than little consortia of local doctors. This may help explain why Jeremy Hunt sought new legal powers to unilaterally shut down or restructure public hospitals.[35]

This latter point hints at a much wider issue, which is to do with capital as a whole rather than specific capitalists wanting to profit from healthcare. Above, I argued that socialised health spending serves a particular purpose in a capitalist economy: to relieve the burden of maintaining a functioning workforce from individual capitalists. We might dismiss this observation as just a difference in terminology, so long as the result is something which benefits everyone – and, of course, there are also extensive political pressures at work which have extended and preserved the scope of the NHS. But looking at things this way helps us to understand a fact that is so widely accepted as common sense that its strangeness is rarely recognised: the extent and resources of the NHS, like that of any health service, are ultimately limited and conditioned by what is tolerable to capital. This is particularly salient given that, as argued in Chapter 3, British capital has become much less indulgent of taxation and regulation since the 1970s, meaning budget pressures have intensified.

The human costs of this in the NHS are very extensively documented on a regular basis in the news and do not need to be repeated here. Expanding waiting times, people being treated in a corridor rather than a ward, relentless attacks on the terms and conditions of health workers and so on. But the real point of interest here is a simple one: the NHS is not this bastion of socialist independence in a sea of capitalism. It is on a tight leash. There is no independent entity that evaluates what resources are required to meet the population's health needs, and which demands that government adapt the wider economy so that these can be provided (which might make sense, given that healthcare is arguably the most important thing for any society to provide). It is the other way round: health has to adapt to the economy. To this end, its budgets are set by central government, and the health secretary has extensive and increasing powers to reorganise it as s/he sees fit.

So, for people on the left, it is politically useful to sentimentalise 'our' NHS (recall the tribute to it in the 2012 Olympics opening ceremony), but this sentimentality can also be a problem – as, arguably, is the left-wing fixation on what percentage of the NHS is being outsourced to the private sector. Quasi-privatisation has been a priority of successive governments, but it only benefits small segments of capital. The bigger issue, and the more important thing from capital's perspective, is the need to apply intense budget pressure so as to lower the costs of the system as a whole.

The need to find a health system adequate to twenty-first-century British capital defined New Labour's NHS policy during their years in power. Growing, and increasingly complex, public need demanded greater investment, but this had to be done in such a way that 'tax and spend' policies were avoided. The 'Third Way' ideology that talked in grand terms about revolutionising the manning and planning of health services was arguably just a *post hoc* rationalisation of this basic reality.[36] The main effect of the policy obsession with 'competition' and the market was not so much crony capitalism – i.e. a nefarious scheme to hand NHS services to mates in the private sector – but just plain capitalism: growing pressure on NHS workers themselves to produce more and more indirect surplus value to capital as a whole. This meant extracting more work for less, and it is this obsession that defines working life in the NHS today as much as in Sports Direct or Amazon. NHS staff are harder to bully than those warehouse workers in some respects (since they are typically higher-skilled and more likely to be unionised). But in other ways they are easier to push around, since they tend to be very squeamish about making too much of a fuss in the workplace because of their sense of duty.

Hence 'our' NHS has become a very bad employer. Front-line work in hospitals is being more intensively monitored by an increasingly distinct managerial layer, imposing targets on staff to acccleiate treatment times and other targets, though many workers have evidently been quite effective in retaining their professional autonomy in spite of these measures.[37] Hannah Cooke interviewed nursing staff and found an infestation of what they called 'seagull managers': people who 'fly in from a great height, make a lot of noise, drop a lot of crap, then they fly off again'.[38] Her research shows 'flexibilisation' has been used to justify changes that intensify managerial control over nurses: increased training was promised (which would 'release [their] untapped potential'), but this turned out to mean they were expected to do more things faster. Managers remained distant and unsupportive in this process, circling round to administer aggressive and punitive public 'bollockings' to those who were not keeping up. The proportion (a quarter) of NHS staff who say they have been bullied at work is extraordinarily high.[39] The fact that this work intensification has *not* been accompanied by corresponding increases in staffing levels has had very serious consequences, as cases such as the Mid Staffs hospital trust show.[40]

Real-terms NHS pay has stagnated, as in the rest of the public sector.[41] Job insecurity has increased, resulting in a fear-driven culture of longer hours.[42] The increasing unilateralism of central government in the NHS is also evident in the case of staff working conditions, most notably the junior doctors' dispute of 2016. Many observers were taken aback at the bluntness of the tools used by Jeremy Hunt in this conflict, which appear to make a mockery of the 'respect' and 'partnership' language which is all-pervading when the NHS talks publicly about its staff. Hunt essentially imposed changes without consultation once negotiations did not produce the result he wanted.

But this is merely the most high-profile manifestation of something that is common across the public sector: increasing unilateralism on the part of government as employer. In areas such as teaching, local government and the police, negotiation structures in pay-setting have been weakened and the union role as a negotiating partner has been marginalised.[43] One of the key innovations of academy schools, for instance, has been to get around national-level bargaining with unions,[44] thus disorganising the teacher's labour market. Across the civil service, trends are towards work intensification, targetisation, deskilling and the weakening of individual staff's decision-making capacities.[45] Government, in other words, is asserting itself with some force in its capacity as employer, in order to boost the indirect surplus value created in the public sector.

More on Public Functions

Talking about health and education can only give a very narrow view of public services in Britain. It is obviously impossible to talk about everything here, but some other issues need to be mentioned. For instance, housing in Britain is another case where the need for systems to evolve in a manner that is adequate to the requirements of capital has completely steamrollered social need, with some strange and jarring consequences. Given that housing has emerged as a rock-solid investment for capitalists with more money than they know what to do with, buying up properties in cities like London is a very useful way to store up excess capital. Referring to a flat development exclusively for the global super-rich in Vauxhall, John Lanchester writes:

> Look at it from a Vauxhall local's point of view. 1. Housing is in crisis and desperately needs fixing; 2. The single biggest thing to be happening in the local economy in decades is a housing development; and yet 2 has nothing to do with 1, will not alleviate it in any respect, and may (if it succeeds in flooding the London market with yet more foreign capital) make it worse.[46]

There can be no clearer example of the way in which questions of social need spiral off into almost surreal territory when subordinated to the needs of capital.

It is important to note that, as I argued in the case of the NHS, austerity policies are not really about 'shrinking the state', strictly speaking. They generally involve the state reducing the extent of the services it provides. But in order to push through this objective it tends to require the reinforcement of central government authority. In the arts, attempts to make money go further in the sector have involved the rapid extension of centrally imposed accountability bureaucracy.[47] In local government, the centre has used its iron control over the allocation of resources to force local authorities to cut back on service provision massively. In the past this has involved quite brutal clampdowns on local authorities (such as the militant Labour councils of the Thatcher era) who have sought to retain greater influence over local taxing and spending. One of Tony Blair's maxims was: 'if you want to drive through systemic change, you've got to drive it from the centre'.[48]

Bureaucratically speaking, this assertion of central power often happens through channels that are popularly assumed to have the opposite effect. The 'marketisation' of public service delivery – i.e. putting particular functions out to competitive tender so potential providers can bid to be awarded contracts – does not diminish central government power. Instead, it creates a new institutional relationship between purchaser (i.e. government) and provider that is largely sealed off from outside influences (such as public participation in the planning of service delivery),[49] meaning that cost-cutting objectives can continue with fewer obstacles. This (rather than the questionable assumption that for-profit private suppliers are better value than in-house public services) may be why the contracting out of public services is so important in forcing through austerity measures.

The point here is therefore a very simple one. Public services are ultimately structured and limited by the need to assume a form which is adequate to the requirements of capital accumulation. This basic requirement can lead to the failure of key strategic initiatives, such as apprenticeship schemes, or the turning over of things like housing to 'market forces' with surreal consequences. More fundamentally, though, in recent years it means government using its power to force down costs in the public sector to contribute more effectively to the indirect accumulation of surplus value.

But where does this leave the idea of government as the 'manager' of capital? Looking at British public services that characterisation doesn't seem to fit. Consider developments like the Health and Social Care Act. This was not about 'stabilisation' or 'long-term management': it was simultaneously highly radical and *destabilising* (as an attempt to marketise healthcare provision), but also very badly thought through (for instance, in the way in which this objective conflicted with austerity priorities, as described above). The government has often appeared utterly clueless in its efforts to cut costs, such as when it fired 4,000 public sector staff only to find it couldn't manage without them.[50] Or when David Cameron became confused about why his government's 'savings' were actually having negative effects on public services in his constituency, rather than merely affecting 'back room bureaucrats' who may only have existed in his own head.* In this context I want to revisit some of the Marxist ideas around government introduced earlier.

BLOOD SACRIFICES TO ALIEN POWERS

Though the human sacrifice is the most talked about, there were actually many types of sacrifices in the empire. The people believed that they owed a blood-debt to the gods. They wanted to avert disaster by paying the endless debt. Blood was a common theme – the sacrifice that the gods required. So, animals would be sacrificed, as well as humans. Also, there was ritual blood-letting, where people would cut themselves to offer their blood to the gods.[51]

In Chapter 3, I wrote about the more short-termist and compromise-averse sides to capital that have come to the fore under financialisation, and discussed its effects on the British labour market. But what does it mean for government policy? Mainly, it makes it much harder for them to fulfil the 'managerial' role often assigned to them in Marxist theory. Above I quoted Carnoy and Castells, who emphasised the role of governments in initiating globalisation as a fix for the crises of the 1970s. However, 'once the progress of globalisation was set in motion, it slipped largely out of the control of states'.[52] In other words, they unleashed a force and then found they weren't sure how to deal with it. The 'functionalist' state becomes a dysfunctional one. Government essentially needs to assume a form which it hopes can guarantee that

---

* He wrote to the head of Witney council: 'I was disappointed at the long list of suggestions floated in the briefing note to make up significant cuts to frontline services – from elderly day centres, to libraries, to museums. This is in addition to the unwelcome and counter-productive proposals to close children's centres across the county. I would have hoped that Oxfordshire would instead be following the best practice of Conservative councils from across the country in making back office savings and protecting the frontline' (quoted in Crewe, see note 48).

financial actors across the economy can make sustainable profits. Cédric Durand writes:

> The austerity measures running down public services and impinging upon social rights seek to guarantee continuity in the interest payments that administrations pay out. Meanwhile, structural reforms have the goal of supporting firms' profitability – and thus their capacity to pay dividends and interest and generate gains on the stock markets – by reducing the price of labour and opening up new spaces for their operations.[53]

Nonetheless, the policies needed to assume an 'adequate form' under financialised globalisation are difficult for governments to identify. It is obvious that states across Europe are finding it harder to develop ways of regulating their economies which are conducive to stable growth. The post-war system that lasted until the 1970s was stabilised by a mutually reinforcing series of factors: rapid wage growth, new technology, 'class compromise' and an economy dominated by large, vertically integrated firms. However, as Matt Vidal argues, there is no combination on display in developed capitalist economies today that appears capable of generating the same growth rates or similar rates of profit.[54] Instability is the norm in Europe.

Financialisation exacerbates this dysfunction for government policy. The fast-moving and self-referential character of financial markets (in other words, the fact that they respond primarily to their own price signals rather than to what is actually going on in the 'concrete' world of production) makes it harder for governments to understand and plan in advance how their economies will develop in the longer term.[55] It is no use establishing durable institutions for training, collective bargaining or industrial policy if capital wants to move about more and more quickly across sectors and borders in pursuit of value. It has therefore long been theorised that, since the 1980s, state policies have been pushed towards greater short-termism, relinquishing various tools that could foster institutional stability.[56]

It is too simple to say that national governments have simply lost power. This is the case in some respects, but I have also argued that we have seen a reassertion of central authority in others. Chris Howell shows how, across the developed world, governments have been highly proactive in reshaping regulatory institutions in order to give more freedom to employers, and push aside other actors that may act as a counterweight.[57] I illustrated this previously with regard to employment relations in the NHS, but it has been a similar story in the public sectors of most European countries.[58] While different countries present different contexts, the main contrasts seem to be in the pace of change rather than the direction.

The problem is that, while these kinds of measures may be adequate to financialised capitalism, this does not mean they can produce stability in the longer term. Various macroeconomists have shown how shifting more power away from labour and towards capital can have destabilising effects.[59] However, these policies continue to be pursued despite poor results. The need to gain the 'confidence' of financial markets has acted as an alien power over successive British governments, pressurising them to become more and more 'market facing' at any cost. This means squeezing out any impediments to the free movement of capital and to the fluctuation of market prices, whatever the consequences.[60] As one of the most financialised economies, the UK must therefore also be an archetypal 'competition state':[61] in other words, one in which the government competes against others to impose the fewest burdens on capital, and to support it proactively wherever possible. The bottom line is this: shifting the balance of power from labour to capital has become more important to British governments than the objective of stable growth in the longer term.

This situation is reinforced at a global level by an arcane superstructure of arbitrary judgement, as exemplified by organisations such as credit ratings agencies (CRAs), which set themselves up as the voice of capital. Timothy Sinclair's work is important here.[62] As investors have become less patient and less tied to individual productive businesses, the amount of concrete knowledge they have about potential credit recipients diminishes. CRAs have emerged as a highly flawed response to these knowledge gaps, as they assign 'scores' to countries' creditworthiness. But Sinclair shows how the variables involved in these kinds of scores are opaque, speculative and highly subjective; inevitably so given the vast complexity of the social systems which are supposed to be encapsulated within it. Credit scores are thus a means of imposing a reassuring (but possibly delusional) sense of order on to a volatile and unknowable economic environment.

Preserving Britain's 'AAA' credit rating and thus the confidence of capital was one of the primary goals of austerity as envisioned by

George Osborne.* In this sense, a lot of the damage done to public services since 2010 come to look like fairly arbitrary sacrifices designed to appease an alien power ('the markets') which is fundamentally vague and unknowable. Certainly, financial markets are often invoked in a reverential, quasi-mystical way. Their judgements are rarely predicted accurately by expert media commentators, and rationalisations for why they have reacted to a given situation are almost always *post hoc*. In this context, it seems quite legitimate to doubt the credibility of 'experts', since they appear to serve the same process as a high priest in theocratic societies; finding after-the-fact explanations for bad (or good) things that have happened, rather than having any real powers of prediction.[63] The problem here is exacerbated by the way in which CRA judgements have become increasingly politically motivated over the last decade, with a growing propensity to punish insufficiently right-wing governments. Previously, this outlook only really applied to weaker economies, but since 2008 has increasingly been levelled at the most economically stable countries as well.[64]

The main source of blood sacrifices was, as we have seen, labour, whose position relative to capital has been hammered via restrictive legislation, increasingly coercive welfare systems, severe restraint over wages and the undermining of job security. British politicians have shown an almost religious devotion to undermining the working conditions of British labour. Since the 1970s the most coherent trend is that of class discipline: rendering workers more malleable from capital's perspective, and reducing their opportunities to engage and negotiate with their employers. This was the story told in Chapter 3.

This dynamic is also evident in the attitude of British governments (Conservative, Coalition and Labour) towards the European Union. One likely prospect of Brexit is a reintensification of competition with the rest of Europe for trade and investment. There is a strong possibility that Britain will cut taxes and spending in an effort to attract capital away from the EU,[65] and seek to exert even greater pressure on labour. This indicates an important (if hardly well-concealed) tension that is likely to weigh heavily on British politics in coming years: many who voted to leave the EU did so as a rejection of the consequences of intense international competition, which is likely the exact opposite motivation from that of the real architects of Brexit. For the latter, the attraction

---

* Though under his chancellorship the UK's credit rating was indeed downgraded.

is precisely the hope that through Brexit Britain will be liberated to compete more fiercely.

As such, the confrontation between Brexiters and Remainers generates a lot of heat and noise but overlooks the extent to which even the most enthusiastic Europhiles in British politics have had an ingrained Euroscepticism in many respects. This is particularly so regarding efforts to harmonise social regulations. New Labour sought to water down and wriggle out of key pieces of European legislation that were designed to mitigate the effects of international economic competition on working conditions. With the Working Time Directive, which imposed a Europe-wide 48-hour limit to the working week, among other stipulations, New Labour bargained for an 'opt-out' clause for individual businesses. The effects of this opt-out are ambiguous: it initially appeared to have completely defeated the object of the legislation,[66] though more recent studies suggest that by placing modest limits on working time it has, to some extent, limited surplus value extraction and even made workers a bit happier.[67] For this reason it is one of the most hated of all EU inventions in the eyes of leading Brexiters.

Another area where New Labour opted out of European employment legislation is in worker participation and representation. One of the ways British companies respond to more diffuse and fast-moving patterns of share ownership is through centralising more power in company CEOs. This way they can respond more quickly to market pressures without having to involve their workforce, and the UK government has tried very hard to render company law adequate to this situation. Along with Ireland, it was the UK government that lobbied to water down the 2002 Information and Consultation Directive which sought to limit companies' ability to make strategic decisions without prior consultation with their workforce. Such provisions are arguably quite meagre and inoffensive, while giving the impression of being sufficiently fuzzy and consensus-driven, which may be why Theresa May made a song and dance of promising 'workers on company boards', before swiftly retracting when placed face to face with actual business leaders.[68] While UK governments have adopted the Agency Workers' Directive, which stipulates that agency workers should be hired on the same pay and conditions as directly employed workers, they have been happy to allow UK employers to make full use of the so-called 'Swedish derogation' (aka the 'German derogation'), in which this stipulation is not applied to pay.[69] Indeed the British government has actively pounced on these sorts of technical compromises at European level in order to reduce protections for agency workers and increase the freedoms of employers.[70]

The point, then, is that the British government has always done what it can to minimise the burden British workers impose on capital. This has defined its approach to regulating the labour market, in a whole range of areas including Europe. Often, these measures have been chaotic and poorly thought through, seemingly designed to cause suffering as an end in itself. Changes to the benefits system are the ultimate paragon of scattergun irrationality in the service of labour force discipline. A system that pushes people towards homelessness or malnutrition through baroque punishments administered for spurious reasons, which forces disabled and ill people to apply for jobs they cannot do leading thousands of them to premature deaths,[71] and a culture of mandatory 'volunteering' on labour schemes that have no educational value whatsoever, all without any discernible positive effect on labour market statistics.[72] Here, there has not simply been a wild rush to force vulnerable people into work regardless of the consequences, but a willing recognition that even where these measures fail in reducing unemployment, they serve a useful purpose in piling extra pressure on people who use (or who might need to use) the benefits system. The assumption is that it is primarily about changing the behaviour of welfare recipients, but the actual intended audience for such schemes is something else: politicians want to demonstrate to capital that they are serious about making workers afraid.

6

Class and Equality

CLASS, 'IDENTITY POLITICS' AND COSMOPOLITANS

One of the recurrent themes of previous chapters has been the profound failures of the mainstream centre-left in Britain, as well as in Europe and the US. While any number of examples could be chosen, the two major humiliations for the left that most interested British people throughout 2016 were the Brexit referendum and Donald Trump's election in the United States. The main reason these events are humiliations is not simply because of the results per se, but because in both cases it was the right that successfully deployed the language of class, and the left that tried to frame this language as divisive. It was the latter, as a result, that was more easily presented as the out-of-touch elite.

This was discussed at length in Chapter 1. But the language around class politics has inevitably become closely entangled with other debates around identity and diversity, often in counterproductive or self-serving ways. A narrative has proliferated which basically runs as follows: it is now the political right that speaks for those that have been left behind by global capitalism, while the political left is mainly concerned with 'identity politics'. 'Left behind' is a euphemism used to refer to people in communities rendered insecure and/or impoverished by globalisation.* 'Identity politics' is used to denote political movements seeking to secure greater inclusion in public life for particular population groups that have previously been marginalised – often related to sexuality, race or gender. It is now mainly used as a pejorative phrase in more or less the same way as 'political correctness' always has been – its meaning is largely equivalent but has the advantage of making its user sound less like Alan Partridge. A comedian, in character as an angry left-wing journalist, encapsulates an explanation for Donald Trump's victory which is apparently accepted as gospel by many people from a range of political backgrounds:

---

* See also the 'just-about managing' in Theresa May-speak.

If I see, fuck me, one more tweet containing a '#TrumpWins' next to a '#EverydaySexism' I'm going to drop a *inaudible* ... Most people didn't vote for [Clinton] not because she's a women, but because she offered no palpable change whatsoever ... People can't admit what they think, the left don't allow them to ... every time someone on the left says 'you mustn't say that' they are contributing to this culture ... if my mansplaining is triggering you, you can fuck off to your safe space.

This is the right-wing class warrior's argument repurposed as liberal self-flagellation. The story goes that the 'working class' has been alienated by anti-racism or anti-sexism campaigns. The latter are basically minority concerns voiced by cosmopolitans who have no connection to the real 'left behind', who have quite justifiably embraced right-wing nationalism as a result. It is very important to note that, in these kinds of arguments, the idea of the 'working class' is employed in a way that is obviously very different to the category of 'labour' as I have been using it in this book.

Evidently, global financial capitalism has created insecurity, power-lessness and a sense of diminished community among many people. The failure of the centre-left in Britain and elsewhere has been their inability to find alternative means of coping with this problem which are more compelling than those proposed by the nationalist right. It has been the shift to a more radical approach that has seen the Labour Party take some tentative steps to addressing this, a point to which I return in the Conclusion. On the international centre-left, by contrast, the tone of debate is not particularly encouraging. Take the US, whose left-leaning political talk-show scene is thriving in inverse proportion to its ability to get its agenda implemented. Some commentators therein have basically accepted the right-wing class warrior narrative, deciding that the left's response to Trump should be a period of remorse for having spent too much time worrying about the use of racist and sexist language. According to the comedian/talk-show host Bill Maher, the left has gone from 'protecting people to protecting feelings'. This kind of material is highly reliant on some dubious generalisations about how easily offended college students are, enabling the speaker to present himself as the tough-but-rational left-winger in a culture of 'PC gone mad'.

There are two main problems with this wearyingly trendy argument. First, because it accepts a very flimsy premise: the intolerant and unrea-sonable practitioner of politically correct identity politics looms much larger in conservative imagination than in empirical reality. For instance, even if there was not a single person that had ever wanted to disinvite a 'mens' rights activist' from a university debate, the same people would still print news stories about how left-wing students are stifling free speech on campuses, and the same audience would still believe these stories. Hence, fixating on this as 'the reason for Trump/Brexit' becomes nothing more than a self-fulfilling prophecy. Second, it misses a much bigger and more important truth, which is that Trump and Brexit were decisive *victories* of 'identity politics', just identity politics practised by very different demographics. There is no more perfect distillation of identity politics than Nigel Farage wearing tweed, drinking in a pub and talking about 'real Britons'.

There is an alternative response which, once again, is expressed more loudly and explicitly in the US. This is to take pride in the 'identity politics' label and double down on it. Another liberal comedian/talk-show host, Samantha Bee, responds to arguments such as those advanced by Bill Maher as follows:

> Democrats, I know you're having a rough time, you hate being lost in the wilderness ... but if your panic over a loss makes you abandon both your principles and the people who actually vote for you, then you'll be in the wilderness for a decade ... By all means invite working class white people to the party, just don't let them take over the DJ table.*

Here, it is made explicit that the Democrats, as a centre-left party, should see its natural base as open-minded cosmopolitans, and be fighting primarily on their behalf. According to this line, the conservative class warrior is not the sad result of the mainstream left abandoning its historic constituencies, but the natural enemy it should have been fighting all along. This is the kind of argument that ends up with people like the bosses of Amazon or Apple being held up as the vanguard of anti-Trump sentiment whenever they express queasiness about travel bans and the like. They may heap misery and degradation on their workers, but at least they believe in *openness*.

Rebecca Solnit has written a powerful attack on the idea that Clinton lost because of her identity politics, making various points: most notably,

---

* See the *Full Frontal with Samantha Bee* segment entitled 'Democrats in the Wilderness', uploaded onto YouTube on 12 December 2016, and available to view here: www.youtube. com/watch?v=CH7GCMm1ngA.

that Trump is in reality a far more practised exponent, and the reason that Clinton was labelled the identity politics candidate is more to do with her gender than her politics (in this sense, the attack on identity politics demonstrates the need for it).[1] This is almost certainly true, but Solnit also protests that Clinton actually mentioned jobs significantly more frequently than she did issues such as abortion or racism. This, she suggests, indicates that any female candidate, unless they were explicitly running on an anti-abortion platform, would probably be accused of only caring about 'women's issues'.

This is highly likely, but it reveals another problem. It is one thing to mention the word 'jobs' frequently, but this was generally done in a highly abstract way: jobs are good things in themselves, and if business is confident, the economy will grow and there will be more jobs, and so on. But evidently there was a level of emotion and rage in her opponent's language that resonated far more deeply among the 'left behind'.* It is not enough to talk about jobs, it also depends what you say about them. Lots of blue-collar Trump voters have jobs, but they are (often) very unrewarding ones. Dylan Riley writes that 'the basic problems to which Trump points are demonstrably real'. Much of his support was drawn from areas where many people have 'uncertain prospects' and where the most highly routinised jobs are disproportionately common. 'But this class-based revolt was supercharged by racist and patriarchal resentment. This issue is not whether class, race or gender was the decisive factor, but rather how they combined'.[2]

Hopefully I can be forgiven for this short detour into US politics, since it has some lessons for what is happening in the UK. In both countries, the goals of increased inequality and inclusion on the grounds of gender, race or sexuality are jeopardised by the shifting balance of class power, and particularly of the complicity of centre-left politicians in this shift. Insecurity, class discipline and the hollowing-out of post-industrial areas produces anger, which the centre-left has done nothing to harness; if anything, it has tried to hush it up, and it has done this because it's scared of capital. The fact that the same parties have, over the same period, been comparatively more sympathetic on issues relating to gender, race and sexuality has made it very easy for 'identity politics' to be made the scapegoat for class-related failures. The root problem for

---

* We need to be careful here, because in the end Clinton still got more votes than Trump. But it is still clear that defeat was snatched from the jaws of victory by the Democrats' failures with groups that were traditionally supportive of them.

centre-left parties is thus not that 'identity politics' is incompatible with 'representing the working class', but that their manifest failure to do the latter has tarnished their entire project, setting the stage for right-wing nationalism to appropriate the language of class.

As such, this chapter is concerned with looking in more depth at the way in which the concept of class (by which, of course, I mean the relationship between labour and capital) interacts with other issues that connect with the broader idea of 'equality' and identity, beginning with the subject of gender.

MARXISM AND FEMINISM

There is clearly at least one common thread between Marxist theory and feminism: both are 'theories of power and its distribution: inequality. They provide accounts of how social arrangements ... can be internally rational yet unjust.'[3] In other words, both bodies of thought identify *systems* within society which impose a particular set of rules around the way resources and power are distributed, and argue that these systems lead to the subordination of a particular group. However, because they emphasise the subordination of different groups (women or labour), there is also a lot of room for tension.

There is, potentially, a fairly crude version of Marxism which dislikes feminism on the grounds that it is not sufficiently focused on class differences (which, of course, exist between women as well as men). Likewise feminists have also criticised Marxism for failing to differentiate between the experiences of men and women *within* classes. It is also true that, historically, labour movements have often undervalued or marginalised women's perspectives. Marxist and feminist arguments have clashed quite directly at some points. See, for instance, Rosa Luxemburg's criticisms of suffragette campaigners in the early twentieth century: 'most of these bourgeois women who act like lionesses in the struggle against "male prerogatives" would trot like docile lambs in the camp of conservative and clerical reaction if they had the suffrage'.[4] In other words, campaigners from wealthy backgrounds, however worthy the cause, can never be trusted when it comes to the real conflict between labour and capital.

There is a lot of common ground concerning the concept of 'social reproduction'. This term refers to the perpetual need for the creation and socialisation of a new labour force to replace the old one, which is clearly essential to capitalism if it wants to go on for more than a generation or so. This includes functions like childbirth, childrearing and all those other factors (education, health and so on) which prepare the next generation of human beings to become a labour input.

Some of these social reproduction functions are provided by government (see Chapter 5) but much of it is done in the home, and it is still, mostly, done on an unpaid basis by women. In this sense, the family has a dual significance under capitalism. It is a private space, but one with a critical social function. For those within such a space it is usually a place of very intense interpersonal relationships, be these loving, supportive, authoritarian or perhaps abusive. But it also has a critical role in supporting capitalist systems, and in this sense it is something capital and state have always needed to administer and account for, in varying ways. For instance, in some countries governments try to incentivise families to have more children, in others less, depending on the status of the economy; in some countries they recognise childcare responsibilities within benefits systems, in others they discourage them.

In this sense, the historical subordination of women in the home, under a male breadwinner patriarch, is by no means inconvenient from capital's perspective, because in such an arrangement women end up doing an important job for free. Silvia Federici shows how capitalist governments throughout history have frequently taken various measures to entrench the status of women in domestic life: through imposing rules around contraception, limiting their access to jobs or even, in extreme cases, through hunting down difficult women as witches.[5]

Women's subordination in domestic life may also be increased as a by-product of other processes. The retrenching of the public sector, which I discussed extensively in previous chapters, has had particularly important implications for women since it pushes many of the jobs that could have been done by public services back into the home.[6] Ultimately, the 'traditional' family (i.e. one with a breadwinner and a housewife) is a hierarchical structure in itself, because the (waged) *job* of the former generally confers power over the unremunerated *work* of the latter.

Here, I am of course talking about 'the family' as an institution rather than women as a gender. Sometimes men do more domestic work than their female partners, but this is still comparatively unusual and so it remains the case that family structures are more likely to put women into a subordinate position. Conservative thought has often inferred from this that the family is the foundation for social order, worrying that women's increasing labour market participation could lead to social breakdown and the emergence of a new generation that is not sufficiently disciplined to take its place in the labour force. They may become hoodie-wearing rioters rather than neatly turned-out sources of surplus value. So there is an interesting parallel with Marxism: both see the family as the bedrock of capitalist social order, but disagree on whether this is a good or bad thing.

But things are, of course, more complicated than this, because these 'social reproduction' dynamics do not just *support* capitalist processes. They are also profoundly affected by them. While the conservative view worries about the decline of the traditional family unit, it is generally less keen to recognise the way in which increasing insecurity at work can lead to familial dysfunction and breakdown.[7] A system defined by the conflictual relationship between two forces within society (i.e. labour and capital) is likely to be unstable, chewing up and spitting out the things upon which it once relied.

The increase in women's labour market participation which Britain has seen over the last 50 years has various causes: women's own efforts to resist being confined to the home, increased access to birth control and legalisation of abortion,[8] alongside broader economic factors including the growth of the service industry and part-time work, as well as the threat of insecurity and wage stagnation in typical 'male breadwinner' jobs. 'Breadwinners' secured solid wage growth under the post-war economic order, but as we have seen, this 'consensus' has faltered, necessitating more dual-earner families.

British policy has wrestled with some contradictions in this respect. On one hand, it has sought to encourage women's labour market participation, seeing this as a means of increasing productivity.[9] Hence it has formulated legislation relating to gender equality in the workplace, and sought to shift the impetus of the benefits system to provide weaker support for childcare responsibilities.[10] But on the other, the imperatives of post-2007 austerity have worked against these efforts. The difficulty for British governments has been to facilitate the labour market experience of women while ensuring that policy evolves in a way that is *adequate to capital's needs*. The next section looks at this tension in more depth.

EQUALITY AND CAPITAL

For Marx, the form of 'equality' that was adequate from capital's perspective was a highly legalistic one: citizens should have 'equality' in the sense that there should be an independent legal system which enforces property rights without discrimination and in which everyone has the same rights as a private individual. This, clearly, says nothing about (in fact, it obscures) the imbalances of power that emerge in the workplace and in wider society as a result of capitalist processes. This pattern has been replicated in the way British governments have approached the issue of discrimination.

Legislation against discriminatory treatment at work has dripped through bit by bit since the 1970s, gradually widening the number of characteristics protected against discrimination as well as the forms of discrimination which are recognised (beginning with rudimentary pro tections against unequal pay levels, shifting towards a more proactive push to 'promote equality'). As Linda Dickens argues, these develop-ments were sometimes prompted by major shocks, such as eruptions of social unrest directed against racist policing methods in Brixton and Toxteth in the early 1980s, or the aftermath of Stephen Lawrence's murder in 1993.[11] It has also been catalysed by the need to comply with EU-level directives (something Labour governments have generally been more receptive to than Conservative ones, though with some important limits – see Chapter 5).

This development has involved the creation of new agencies, such as the Advisory, Conciliation and Arbitration Service, and new mechanisms, such as employment tribunals, intended to enshrine equalities legislation in a legal framework. In Britain, these new legal resources have tended to provide little or no scope for the involvement of collective actors such as trade unions, meaning that they focus solely on righting wrongs against individuals rather than using collective force to push employers to make positive adjustments.[12] In addition, claimants are often at a disadvantage, given imbalances in access to legal support and expertise. Consequently, as Dickens argues, there is the perpetual danger that equality 'becomes subordinated to the goal of efficiency',[13] with various 'business reasons' provided for in the legislation that can be invoked to justify unfair treatment as necessary for the smooth functioning of capital.

This kind of equalities legislation was a key agenda of New Labour throughout their period in office. The Equality Act of 2010, one of their final actions before losing power, sought to expand *positive* duties towards the 'mainstreaming' of equality in public sector organisations, as well as imposing greater responsibilities on private employers to monitor and adjust their equality provisions. The emphasis on 'positive' duties is important here: organisations were not supposed to just react when individuals sue them over something that has affected them, they are supposed to try to iron out barriers to equality in a more proactive way. So, for instance, organisations should consider and implement policies to prevent homophobic bullying, rather than waiting for an individual to make a complaint after experiencing it.[14] 'Should', here, is of course ambiguous: the Act provided no definite instruction for organisations to do this, it just requires them to give 'due regard' to equality concerns. This voluntaristic approach and softly-softly language is typical of the British approach: capital is like a field of wild horses liable to get spooked and stampede if you do anything that it might actually notice.

The 'equality agenda', while generally non-threatening to capital, still ran up against economic crisis and austerity. There can only be one winner in such a collision. George Osborne's 'emergency budget' of 2010 was challenged legally by the Fawcett Society.[15] They argued that austerity looked likely to violate equality legislation by disproportionately impacting women. Women rely more on public services, and are more likely to work in public sector employment, for instance. They said that the government should have done a 'gender impact assessment' to consider the consequences of their policies for women's jobs and pay. Nonetheless, the challenge was rejected, for reasons Hazel Conley paraphrases as follows: 'the budget was complex and needed to be done to a tight timetable and therefore an overview of the gender impact would have been difficult'.[16] In other words, who in their right mind would bother? Later, Conley adds that

> a compelling case for a judicial review seems to have been eclipsed by a desire to maintain political stability in the face of the economic crisis. Another view of the events is that the State, in the form of the government and the judiciary, moved to express the interests of capital at the expense of working women.[17]

In various respects the Cameron government did seek to run with the New Labour equalities agenda, since it is a very good way of burnishing progressive credentials while posing little genuine threat to the balance of power between labour and capital. Equalities legislation had developed in a relatively benign environment where voluntaristic attempts to prod capital towards a 'positive duty' on equality were quite tolerable. But under the Coalition's austerity programme the range of tolerability narrowed sharply with key provisions that emphasised the positive duties of employers being scrapped on the grounds that it constituted 'red tape', obstructing the reduction of public expenditure.[18]

It is fairly obvious why women, in particular, should be disproportionately affected by public expenditure cuts. Public services are particularly important to women because 'they free women from unpaid care in the family, provide substantial opportunities for paid caring work and provide safer environments for women to work and live in'.[19] When public provision withdraws, social reproduction functions are pushed back into the home, on to the unpaid labour of (usually) women. The loss of public sector jobs and their replacement with private sector ones (as was Coalition policy) disadvantages women, who are more likely to work in caring professions.[20] As Conley also points out, many services which provide vital lifelines to particularly vulnerable women, such as domestic abuse support services, suffered heavy cuts.[21] Austerity has thus undermined women's access to services, their incomes and job security, and their own personal security.[22]

Austerity has also caused comparable problems for people from ethnic minorities. Ethnic minority groups are generally likely to be in lower-paid work with higher risks of in-work poverty, as well as in more routinised work with lower levels of control over their labour process.[23] Nabil Khattab et al. find that, while religious and ethnic minorities fared about the same as 'Christian White British' ones in terms of unemployment since the 2008 recession, they did proportionately worse in terms of other factors, notably in income levels, part-time employment, and rates of overqualification.[24] Discrimination against these groups is obviously not a new phenomenon, though it has arguably increased over recent decades.[25] However, as I argued when discussing women's labour market participation, it appears that UK legislation remains relatively weakly adapted to tackling these kinds of problems. The most extreme case of the reversal of progress in terms of equality and 'inclusion' during the austerity period is the one inflicted on disabled people. The welfare system's treatment of the sick and disabled has been mentioned previously, has greatly intensified since 2010 and has been considered a violation of basic human rights by the United Nations.[26]

These indicators are often seen as pointing to higher rates of 'social exclusion' among these kinds of groups, a situation exacerbated by austerity policies which have dismantled public initiatives aimed at 'including' people from minority backgrounds, such as 'inclusion-through-sport' schemes.[27] From a Marxist perspective, there are problems with the term social exclusion. It generally refers to groups of people who do not have access to jobs, skills or community support networks. Given what I said earlier, it seems strange to define these kinds of people as 'excluded' from British capitalism, since the creation of a large population of people who do not have access to the means of supporting themselves is an integral feature of capitalist economies.*

Still, there is evidently a tension in British capitalism, between the aspiration for so-called 'social inclusion' (since 'exclusion' can create labour market frictions and burdens on the welfare state) and the evident desire not to impose too much on capital (which has been greatly heightened by crisis and austerity). In this context, an extensive ideological industry has emerged seeking to reconcile these things. This revolves around the concept of the 'business case for diversity', which has now become dominant in mainstream attempts to promote the interests of under-represented groups in the workplace.

This 'business case' is the idea that equality and diversity is good, not necessarily as an end in itself, but because it can benefit capital. Networking events and conferences are built around encouraging women to advocate for fairer treatment on the basis that it can improve things for their employers, with a particular focus on how to avoid spooking the boss with too much equality talk.[28] This may be why Harriet Harman was among the Blairite politicians most demonised by the right: she seemed like she actually wanted women's equality for its own sake rather than just in pursuit of the higher goal of the M-C-M' cycle. The acceptable feminist icons of the day must simultaneously be capitalist icons: for example Sheryl Sandberg, whose advice for women focuses on ways of conducting oneself assertively in high-powered business situations rather than raising any more systematic questions about the relationship between labour and capital and its effect on women.[29] The business case for diversity also has unexpected disadvantages: some clever statistician can always come along and demonstrate that, in certain circumstances, a more diverse workforce is actually a problem for business.[30]

A more productive approach for advancing demographic equality is to think about how it relates to wider labour–capital conflicts. Equalities,

---

* At the risk of seeming glib, I should add that, under capitalism, pretty much by definition anyone who acts as *labour* is 'socially excluded', since they are excluded from owning the means of production and all the forms of power this entails.

for instance, have become more and more central to trade union work. This is partly because members themselves have become more diverse, notably as the public sector, rather than mining and heavy industry, has become the spine of union membership. The highly legalistic and individualistic approach to equality legislation is a problem for unions since it creates fairly shallow ways of addressing these kinds of problems, avoiding any kind of collective power for labour. There is some evidence that a legal framework for equalities has strengthened trade unions' hand in many cases, lending more gravitas to their wider attempts to negotiate better conditions.[31] But this remains a more unreliable and limited model for representing labour's interests than real collective bargaining, which has of course continued to decline over the same period.[32] On a rhetorical level, it is hard to argue for unions when the 'business case' for equality is all-pervading.

But collective action on labour's part can get at problems that are far beyond the scope of legalistic approaches, because they can be proactive and independent rather than simply following governmental rules. Dickens writes, with regard to gender equality, that

> collective bargaining permits the needs and interests of women – and men – as they perceive them to be ascertained and acted on. Collective bargaining, resting on representative structures, provides a way of giving women a voice; an ability to define their own needs and concerns and to set their own priorities for action.[33]

In this sense, it would be a bad mistake for class politics to buy into the pejorative rhetoric around 'identity politics' and so forth. Trade unions lose their purpose if they cannot plausibly claim to represent the wider workforce rather than small sections of it. The perception of British trade unionism as a highly macho environment has not done it any good. Conversely, demographic equality has often been contained within limits that are acceptable to capital, which may explain its slow progress. If it is to go beyond being tolerated, and more substantive gains are to be made, then it requires collective action on the part of labour, actively pushing for better pay claims that address discrepancies, and demanding positive action from organisations even (or, especially) where this is inconvenient for capital.

CAPITAL AND IMMIGRATION

There has emerged a widespread belief in British politics that immigration is a taboo subject that is always hushed up in political discourse. This is manufactured. In reality, anyone in their thirties that follows the news will have spent their entire adult life with an almost constant stream of 'debate' about immigration being sluiced into their ears and eyes, generally of a highly strung and sensationalist type. But this is a useful fiction for people with an unhealthy fixation on the topic, because it lets them present themselves as the forthright slayer of sacred cows rather than just people who say the same irrelevant things over and over again.

Politicians, particularly those on the centre-left, have fallen for this gambit embarrassingly easily. Now, one of the most common sights in British politics is the social democratic politician declaring with faux self-righteousness that 'the time has come for a frank debate around immigration', or some variant thereof. Over the years, this dismal cliché has been perpetuated by various Labour luminaries such as Andy Burnham (in 2016), Yvette Cooper (in 2017), Gordon Brown (in 2010), and Ed Miliband, who even printed it on a mug in 2015. Of all potential dystopian futures that could befall the British people, one of the most plausible is one in which there is no news available except the sound of centre-left politicians calling for a 'frank debate about immigration', beamed out on a continuous loop across a desolate landscape ravaged by economic decline and environmental chaos. These luminaries appear unaware that this debate continues quite happily without them, increasingly assuming an explicitly racist aspect, as (to pluck one example out of thin air) when one newspaper complained bitterly about how NHS resources had been spent trying to keep alive the children of a Nigerian visitor to the UK.[34]

In this context it has been very easy to make an anti-immigration argument that is rooted in the language of class; even one with slightly mangled Marxist overtones. There is some intuitive sense in the idea that migration works in favour of capital and against labour, since it creates a cheap and easily bullied labour supply. So, this logic continues, immigration is a tool of capital, just like outsourcing or union-busting. It is increasingly common to hear this even on the radical left now. This line of reasoning also fits very nicely with the superstition that nobody is allowed to talk about immigration, since it conjures the idea of an elite conspiracy. Hence the increasingly popular conflation between being 'working class' and being a right-wing nationalist – this was the starting point in Chapter 1.

The more pessimistic arguments about the material consequences of migration in Britain – that migrants deplete the supply of jobs and undermine wages – tend to be either inaccurate or half-truths. Migrants obviously increase the supply of labour but they also increase the demand for it, since while working they also consume products and services. Once the latter part of the equation is taken into account, there is little obvious reason why the overall effect should be negative. There is little evidence that migration has much of an effect on overall employment rates.[35] With regard to wages, findings are ambiguous and do not suggest a strong connection on a wider societal. Stephen Nickell and Jumana Saleheen estimate a very slight negative impact on British wages from immigration, but note that this effect is extremely small overall and is concentrated in one particular context: low-skilled service work.[36] This concentration at the lower end of the service sector is compounded by the fact that migrants tend to end up doing work of a much lower skill level than they are qualified for.[37] The effects of immigration on 'native' wages is further dampened by the way in which recent migrants tend to end up doing jobs that were already being done by previous migrants already in the country[38] – notably highly precarious and transient jobs like temporary seasonal work.[39] Overall, the idea of a migrant-led collapse in British wages is unconvincing because the labour market is so segmented.

This point about segmentation was illustrated by a particular furore concerning the sandwich chain Pret a Manger, when it emerged in 2017 that only a very tiny proportion of the people that apply for work there are 'native' British. The reaction to this kind of story is interesting, because it tends to lead to some fairly triumphalist responses from liberals (e.g. 'See? I told you immigrants aren't the problem – British people don't want these jobs anyway'), which then hardens into a much nastier rhetoric around the supposed laziness of British youth. On the subject of UK applicants to Pret, one observer ponders 'What is that about? These are hard jobs, potentially physically demanding. I'm not sure we prepare people very well. They are paid national living wage. We need to work on attitudes to work, that's a challenge for employers.'

Why don't teenagers recognise that it counts as 'a success' to be a young person who '[comes] to work at somewhere like *Pret*'?[40] This encapsulates the mainstream prescription for British young people:

worried about the future? Simply lower your expectations for what you can get from working life. It is also a fairly transparent divide-and-rule tactic which capital has used on labour for centuries: saying to British workers 'why don't you work as hard as the immigrants?' and saying to the immigrants 'why don't you work as hard as British workers?' The end result is everybody working harder to the exclusive benefit of capital.

However, focusing on these kinds of statistical debates misses a much more important point. I have, so far, been talking about how migration affects *labour market competition*: in other words, what consequences does it have for the dynamics of supply and demand? But we should know by now that this is the wrong question. Instead, we should ask: why should labour be subject to these dynamics in the first place?

We saw earlier that 'supply and demand' are not natural laws with the same status as gravity; they are products of decisions made by capital (and potentially others). In Chapter 3, I argued that one of the key characteristics of post-war British capitalism was the way in which collective bargaining and the welfare state, at least partially, took wages out of competition, rendering workers less vulnerable to fluctuations in supply and demand. As we have seen, the decline of these kinds of mechanisms is not something that simply happened; it was engineered by state and capital over recent decades and has intensified under austerity. Research[41] shows that even where the migrant effect on wages was at its most negative (-2 per cent in low-skilled service work), this pales in comparison to the -8 per cent impact of the financial crisis across the economy as a whole.[42] In this sense, migrants become a personalised scapegoat (based on evidence which is always assumed rather than actually provided) for much more impersonal class imperatives.

The *conflictual* relationship between labour and capital needs to be applied to understanding migrant labour just as much as to any other kind, and this implies at least some form of resistance on labour's part. Against the stereotype of the cowed and docile migrant under total control by employers, it is important to recognise how many migrant workers seek to escape degrading jobs, often by moving on to find better conditions elsewhere.[43] Many of the agencies that bring migrant workers from countries in Central and Eastern Europe shamelessly inflate the prestige and value of getting a job in Britain, creating a jarring disconnect between migrant workers' own sense of self-worth and the bullshit jobs they may end up doing.[44]

In Chapter 2 I described how Marx, in the first volume of *Capital*, made remarks about migration controls that initially seem to contrast with the situation today (or at least the media presentation of 'uncontrolled immigration'): capitalist governments were seeking to *restrict* the movement of labour for fear of workers' 'mobility power' making things difficult for employers. On one level this just shows that the context has changed, but it also illustrates how control over a person's legal status in a country, and their ability to move around, is inevitably a labour–capital issue (even if it is driven by sentimental nationalist pressures). The more restrictions are placed on an individual's movement and access to services, the more their status is differentiated from the 'native' population, the more they come to resemble the powerless victim of capital evoked by the right-wing class warrior. This is why people are wrong to scoff at David Davis when he says that Brexit might not lead to overall declines in the levels of immigration: even if migration itself does not decline after Brexit, the power of migrant labour in relation to capital certainly will.[45]

There is a relatively simple and straightforward Marxist line on immigration, which has fallen chronically out of fashion but which is no less true for that: labour is labour, whether conducted by 'native' workers or migrants. Anyone who acts as labour has a shared interest in standing up to capital and suppressing the destructive consequences of labour market competition. In this respect, improving the rights and earning power of migrant workers is clearly also good for *all* workers. Marx used to write letters to Friedrich Engels fretting about the way in which Irish migrant workers were seen as rivals rather than allies by English ones, facilitating capital's very simple divide-and-rule tactics.

Overcoming these divisions is, of course, much easier said than done. Many migrants are clustered in the more 'precarious' ends of the labour market, in which trade union representation is highly unusual. Trade unions themselves have often been paralysed by these kinds of questions. Unions continually have to navigate contradictory pressures to include and exclude:[46] include, because every worker that does not have union representation is one that may be disorganising the labour market by undercutting union-agreed conditions; exclude, because workforces are easier to organise if entry to them can be restricted. Given that the latter course is not usually sustainable in the long term, there seems to be a bleak future for British trade unionism unless it can organise more migrant workers.

This is very obvious in specific sectors such as construction where capital has, indeed, sought to use migrant labour as an industrial 'reserve army' to disorganise the labour market.[47] In such cases, given that if migrants weren't there employers would just find other means of disorganising their workforce anyway (perhaps through subcontracting chains or dubious 'self-employment'), it seems perverse to blame migrants themselves for this. The way to counter these problems is surely to try and recruit and represent those migrants themselves, even if various officials and members need to be persuaded of the benefits of doing so.[48]

There is, of course, a bigger historical issue here for labour. The disorganisation of the labour market has beaten back many of the institutional arrangements that enabled workers to punch above their weight. While many workers still have union representation and access to collective bargaining, these things will ultimately be harder and harder to retain if highly insecure and disorganised labour markets become the norm. It is increasingly obvious that labour cannot rely on state institutions and regulation to advance its interests, and it needs to start organising as a class, rather than as a series of segments each with differentiated access to rights and representation.[49] This means solidarity with migrants as an urgent priority.

A common observation, when talking about migration, is that the figures regarding wages and employment rates are beside the point, and what actually matters is this deeper cultural malaise that comes from people seeing their local areas transformed. There are various academics now building a lucrative media profile from saying this kind of thing. In the right hands this is the most high-minded, and arguably the most persuasive, form of anti-immigrant argument. Many British towns and regions have suffered not simply from increased insecurity, but also from a weakened sense of shared purpose. Regardless of how grim the work itself may have been, the community ties and identities that built up around Britain's heavy industry heartlands are very different to those that emerge when those areas shift towards an identikit service economy.

It has to be said that this sense of absent community is by no means limited to deprived post-industrial areas, as anyone who has lived in a white-collar suburb will know. Growing up, I used to watch the Australian soap opera *Neighbours* every day. Looking back, by far the most implausible thing about this show was not the plot twists (people coming back from the dead, getting divorced and remarried several times a year, and so on), but the fact that here was a suburban street populated by people who were fairly affluent except when the plot demanded otherwise, in which people living in adjacent houses actually appeared to know and care about each other, and have some kind of meaningful role in each other's lives. This is not normal. And the fact that I grew up in a culturally homogeneous area with very little immigration did not make me feel any closer to this vision (probably the reverse).

The answer to this problem is to observe that community is built through struggle. Standing on picket lines together during a strike is the best way to make people feel like they have something in common. Obviously, this is a kind of community that specifically excludes capitalists, but then the whole point of Chapter 1 was to criticise the idea of a harmonious social whole where 'the economy works for everyone'. A good society, ultimately, has to exclude capital. And so, rather than restrictions on freedom of movement, rather than family values, or whatever else, class struggle is the true source of social cohesion.

7

Technology

[W]hen they look up from their spreadsheets, they see automation high and low – robots in the operating room and behind the fast-food counter. They imagine self-driving cars snaking through the streets and Amazon drones dotting the sky, replacing millions of drivers, warehouse stockers, and retail workers. They observe that the capabilities of machines – already formidable – continue to expand exponentially, while our own remain the same. And they wonder: *Is any job truly safe?*[1]

This quote from *The Atlantic* is deliberately hyperbolic, but it leads us to ask the question: would it be a bad thing if the vast majority of jobs currently done by humans were replaced by robots?

The short answer to this is that yes, it obviously would be. It would (at least in the short term) lead to mass unemployment, precipitating all manner of social and economic problems. The longer answer forces us to consider why this is the case. How have human beings managed to create a situation in which the elimination of huge amounts of work – much of which is tedious, depressing or back-breaking – becomes a prospect to be feared rather than one to be celebrated? Enthusiasts for capitalism like to talk about its capacity for technological innovation. But the most innovative, and the strangest, thing that capitalists have achieved with regard to technological progress is the way they have converted it from an unambiguous good to a source of anxiety and social neurosis.

You would think labour-saving technological advances should be embraced without reservation. By reducing the amount of time spent working, people can have greater freedom to do things from which they or others may actually benefit:[2] spending time with friends and family, pursuing things that interest them, looking after the sick or old, or whatever else.

It is, of course, the specific rules of capitalist economies that convert technological progress from a way of solving problems into a way of creating them. Here are two basic facts about capitalism: first, since they are separated from the means of production, workers require a job in order to afford a decent standard of living; second, since labour is the source of surplus value, capitalists can only be making a profit if they are employing human beings. This means that the well-being of any capitalist society depends on technological advance remaining within strict limits. No human workers equals no profits (in the long run).

Intuitively we might think that surely, being able to avoid having to employ anybody is a dream situation for the capitalist. There would be no need to pay wages, thus increasing profits. But capital needs labour as much as vice versa. Imagine a situation in which all human needs and wants can be produced by machines with barely any input from human beings. These machines are self-sustaining and require virtually no maintenance. Imagine also that these machines remain, as now, under the control of capital (rather than under the democratic control of society as a whole). Various problems quickly become apparent. First, there is the obvious issue that, if nobody has a job, nobody can afford to buy the things capital wants to sell.

But imagine that we could still retain an extensive welfare state which would allow people to continue buying things. In that case, there would appear to be an even more fundamental problem. Commodities only have value because work has gone into producing them. If things can be produced without any effort, they have no value. So capital would be producing things which, irrespective of their usefulness, have no exchange value. Even setting aside people's ability to pay, prices would be on a terminal downwards trend.

What would happen in such a situation (which, for the foreseeable future, remains purely a fantasy)? At least two outcomes can be imagined. Government might have to step in on capital's side, either using its power to protect artificially high prices, while presumably finding some way of ensuring people can continue spending. Alternatively, it may be that the system of producing commodities for sale in exchange for private profit breaks down; machines could be taken away from capitalists, and used to produce things that correspond to the needs and wants of society as a whole (communism, in other words).

This dilemma, evidently, remains a very distant one. The prospect of a jobless world will likely keep getting postponed, and the technological progress of recent decades has not led to massive increases in unemployment. As some jobs become obsolete, new ones have emerged. In addition, for the reasons I have just mentioned, just because an industry can be radically automated, doesn't mean it will be. In industries such as textiles and footwear, for instance, many companies prefer to relocate manufacturing operations to parts of the world where technology is much less developed, but where more surplus value can be extracted from labour.[3] In such cases the search for profits slows or even reverses technical progress in the workplace. Meek, in his reporting on Cadbury plants relocating to Poland, writes:

> Because workers in Poland were so much cheaper, automation took a step backward when production moved; the honeycombed sugar in Crunchie bars, which at Somerdale had been automatically cut with high-speed jets of oil, reverted in Poland to being cut the old labour-intensive way with saws.[4]

Despite this, it is also obvious that technology has an important effect on employment in Britain, as elsewhere. The likelihood of having your job automated out of existence is not simply related to the ostensible 'status' of the job (i.e. its rates of pay and the qualifications it demands). There have been attempts to rank the kinds of people that are most, or least, likely to be replaced by robots in the near future. It is not the lowest-paid jobs that are most at risk (although many of the worst-paid jobs are among the most vulnerable, for instance the call centre worker). The most endangered are generally those that are highly routinised and executed according to standardised procedures – things like bookkeeping and many other mid-ranking administrative positions[5] as well as, of course, much manufacturing employment. Jobs which in other respects are often lower paid and more insecure, such as front-line service industry work or cleaning jobs, require more of an intuitive human touch. They demand more 'emotional labour' – a term proposed by Arlie Hochschild to capture the often draining work that many service workers have to put in so that their outward mood comes to resemble what managers and customers expect, rather than how they are really feeling.[6] Consequently, they fare better against robot competition. Nonetheless, as technology advances, there is no reason to assume that much less routinisable tasks will not also be automated.[7] University staff, for instance, might render themselves superfluous by dispersing PowerPoint slides and recorded lectures to paying learners across the globe.

As I argued in Chapter 3, when we talk about insecurity (or 'precarity') in the British labour market, we have to be somewhat careful, since there is no clear evidence that contingent employment is expanding in the same way as it is in some other countries. The fact that capital is dependent on labour for profits makes the mass ejection of workers from the labour force highly unlikely. Just as with government policy and regulatory institutions, the forms of technological development that occur under capitalism need to be adequate to capital's needs. In the long run, this means the most important forms of innovation are not so much those that get rid of labour, but those which enable greater control over it. Those which remove the technical expertise, creativity and knowledge from labour as far as possible and transfer it to capital.

As ever, for Marx, this process is afflicted by internal contradictions. As this machinery develops and becomes more oppressive, it also creates the potential for a very different use of technology. If the means of production are under workers' control, he writes, they genuinely could be used to lessen the drudgery of human labour, and produce enough goods to support societies while abolishing the labour–capital relationship. The sophistication of the machine could liberate individuals rather than subordinate them.

Later, in the mid-twentieth century, the development of labour process theory, notably following the American Marxist Harry Braverman, expanded these ideas around technology.[8] Braverman was concerned with what he saw as the 'degradation of work' in advanced capitalist societies. New technology, he argued, should be something that can benefit humanity greatly, but the fact that it develops under the initiative and control of capital means this is not the case. 'Machinery comes into the world not as the servant of "humanity", but as the instrument of those to whom the accumulation of capital gives the *ownership* of machines'.[9] So there is a distant vision of a better way of doing things which seems unreachable:

> An automatic system of machinery opens up the possibility of the true control over a highly productive factory by a relatively small corps of workers, provided these workers attain the level of mastery over the machinery offered by engineering knowledge, and providing they share out among themselves the routines of the operation, from the most technically advanced to the most routine.[10]

In other words, smaller groups of more highly skilled workers who assume control of factories, dividing stimulating and boring tasks alike among themselves and who have genuine mastery over productive machinery. Combine this with some means of distributing the proceeds according to human need rather than the market, and you have, basically, the communist utopia. But for Braverman, one of the great problems of capitalism was that it prevented machinery ever being used in this way.

Instead, Braverman argued that, deep down, capital is not really that interested in genuinely exciting technological progress. Certainly, increasing productivity and saving labour is one advantage, though a short-sighted one. But the true agenda was to use technology to create more effective labour discipline. Thus, Braverman suggested, machinery under capitalism led to the *degradation*, not the improvement, of work. It devalued and alienated the worker by taking their decision-making power and initiative away, and breaking their jobs down into simple, repetitive and easily quantifiable tasks (here, the paradigm is of course the industrial assembly line). Thus,

> Machinery offers to management the opportunity to do by wholly mechanical means that which it had previously attempted to do by organisational and disciplinary means. The fact that many machines may be paced and controlled according to centralized decisions, and that these controls may thus be in the hands of management, removed from the site of production to the office – these technical possibilities are of just as great interest to management as the fact that the machine multiplies the productivity of labour.[11]

To this end he quotes Charles Babbage, the pioneer of the mechanical computer: 'one great advantage which we may derive from machinery is from the check which it affords against the inattention, the idleness, or the dishonesty of humans'.[12] And so, he argues grimly, workers themselves *regress* under the influence of machines: 'workers in each industry today are far less capable of operating that industry than were the workers of a half-century ago, and even less than those of a hundred years ago'.[13] This is a profoundly pessimistic vision, foreseeing not just the degradation of work but the degradation of human capabilities.

THE MEANS OF EVALUATION

We do not need to be quite this downbeat, but nor should we get consumed by false optimism. The idea of the 'knowledge economy' and the 'creative industries' as the core of British industry could easily be presented as a rebuttal to predictions of the kind made by Braverman. However, as I argued in Chapter 4, we still see the use of technology and new organisational methods as a means of, if not negating, at least controlling worker initiative, even in high-status jobs. I also argued that workers tend to resist this, so it is not that there is an ever-increasing cage of control encircling labour, but rather that in any job there is inevitably a tension between the ability of the worker to exercise their own initiative and the imperative for capital to control. In more 'knowledge'-centric jobs, such as education, healthcare or creative industries, this may be done less through the implementation of assembly line-type technology, and more through the creation of a 'system' with rigidly quantified parameters and 'metrics'. These metrics – manifested in things like evaluation forms, relentless requests for 'customer feedback', reporting on time usage – are attempts to quantify things that were previously considered too difficult to quantify (the process of caring for someone, the process of thinking up a lecture or research paper, the process of developing an artistic project).

New information systems are important in this respect. Chapter 4 discussed how the controlling possibilities of new technology extend way beyond the bleeped-at warehouse worker: journalists monitored at their desks, live musicians orchestrated by search algorithms and so on. Some writers have been led towards the metaphor of the 'electronic panopticon' – in other words, a system of electronic control which means workers can be monitored with an intensity way beyond anything an old-fashioned factory foreman could dream of. However, such systems are inevitably imperfect, since people try to find ways of resisting this control.[14]

French researchers have examined the use of information systems to monitor workers at a consultancy firm.[15] Mobile information systems, where workers can be updating records and communicating with management well outside the walls of the firm, mean that 'management is no longer confined to company premises but potentially can exert influence anywhere, anytime, even in unexpected contexts'. In their study, workers were encouraged to work from home using mobile devices they bought themselves, so as to make the organisation more 'agile and flexible'. They thus spent their own money to be able to respond to work obligations at any time and any place. Some of the researchers' interviewees thought this was alright. One staff member, for instance, said: 'I don't regret at all to have bought personally this equipment, in the sense that it enables me to be more productive and satisfy my manager.' One manager rejoiced that 'I know what consultants in my team do without seeing them ... even if they are alone, they are never alone, we follow each other from a distance.' Here is one of corporate culture's great triumphs: the ability to make creepy surveillance seem like inspiring 'work hard play hard' camaraderie.

The main casualty of this triumph was any semblance of control the up-and-coming management consultants might have had over their 'free time':

> Our observation revealed that no one wanted to be considered a 'weak link' ... so that mobile technologies were used at their maximum, even beyond the company's implicit expectations ... For example, some junior consultants used mobile information systems as 'proof' to show their involvement with and loyalty to the company, by working at a distance on shared files beyond the classical workday hours to finish projects earlier than expected, or by showing managers they remained on call in the evenings and on holidays. Our observations revealed hidden but intense competition among consultants, which mobile information systems helped create and continuously reinforce through shared behaviours and emulation ... 'I'm working at home and I can't afford not being always connected. Reactivity is an integral part of my job, and I don't want people to think that I'm not working if I don't reply immediately when someone sends an email or calls me'.[16]

In this case, in a very highly skilled and sought-after professional job, technology produces control just as effectively as on the assembly line. But rather than transferring knowledge away from the worker, it imposes a form of 'connectedness' (a modern euphemism for being perpetually at the beck and call of capital) which compels knowledge workers to make themselves open for extraction in perpetuity.

Technology also creates new ways of exercising control over the reserve army of labour. I talked about this a little with regard to live musicians in Chapter 4, but it could equally be said of labour in more cutting-edge industries. Crowdsourcing the development of apps has enabled software companies to switch from employing salaried workers to getting their material from a vast 'reserve army' of semi-volunteers.[17] The latter, while serving the purpose of a highly casualised labour force, are presented as small-scale 'entrepreneurs'. In such cases, control over labour is delegated to workers themselves. They are not under surveillance, but in order to survive and keep getting work they have to impose strict self-discipline. They have to force themselves to learn new things continually, on their own time and money (as opposed to in-house training that a 'responsible' employer might provide). The apps they produce as a result then become a cash cow for the company.

Likewise, in the so-called 'gig economy', new platforms enable new ways of monitoring and evaluating workers where data are inputted by customers themselves rather than managers – such as the star ratings assigned to drivers on platforms like Uber, or the micro-workers operating on online crowdworking sites. For workers, these things have a big impact: the knowledge that they can be subject to continual anonymous judgement (and will lose work if their star rating drops) can regularly lead to them offering more work for less.[18] As Trebor Scholz points out, 'platform capitalists' tend to retain control over the data on these ranking systems, refusing to allow crowdworkers to use positive customer ratings accrued on one platform to be transferred to their records on another.[19] This is capital exercising its ownership of the 'means of evaluation'.

Aside from direct control over the labour process and worker surveillance, there is the much broader control that comes with the worker knowing they are expendable. I argued in Chapter 2 that Marx does not accept the way in which mainstream economists invoke 'supply and demand' as natural laws with the same status as gravity. Instead, they are things which are constantly manipulated by capital. One of the key ways in which this happens is through technology. Capital's control over the nature and pace of the implementation of new technology enables it to manipulate the industrial reserve army.

Consider here one of the most ubiquitous of modern innovations, the automated self-checkout. On first appearances this is a fairly standard example of the use of computing technology to replace the work done by a human. But on closer inspection this isn't quite true, since self-checkouts involve the same amount of human labour as staffed checkouts do: it's just that this labour is supplied for free by the customer, rather than a paid worker. Wages are saved, but work isn't. As one American observer describes it: 'so it's 2011 and I'm waiting in line … I see an attorney that I know is on $300,000 plus. She's swiping her own groceries and getting nothing for it. Not even minimum wage.'[20] For the customer, time is rarely saved, and the 'experience' is no better (probably the reverse, due to the stripping out of human contact). But for the staff, there is a sense that their expendability is ratcheted up another notch, and this has consequences. Evidence from Australia, for instance, suggests self-checkout to be a significant cause of declining wages and increasing profits for retail firms.[21] Self-checkout technology doesn't just affect checkout workers, but also supervisory staff: Charles Koeber[22] refers to the little electronic screens that you find at security checks in airports, among other places, where the 'customer' has to press a smiley or sad face depending on how much they enjoyed their time going through security (or whatever). Here, technology again outsources the job of evaluating and criticising front-line workers to customers.

So, despite raising the *threat* of unemployment and probably hindering new employment growth, self-checkout often does not result in significant lay-offs, because people tend to be bumped into a different function rather than sacked. For one thing, they have to be constantly on guard to deal with the various unexpected items in bagging areas, and so on.[23] In this sense, the front-line service job is transferred to the customer, and the job of supervising the new front-line service worker (i.e. the customer) is transferred to the old front-line service worker. Technology in this case is thus an aide to complicated managerial hi-jinks, with seemingly no purpose other than, presumably, increasing profits somehow. All of this suggests that technological progress *in and of itself* does not need to have negative consequences for job quality. As Gallie points out, declining job quality in the UK is not necessarily replicated in other countries such as Germany, which uses comparable technology in comparable ways.[24] The problem is not so much to do with technology per se but the British context: a general rise in (at least perceived) insecurity, and an increasingly disciplined labour force.

CAPITALISM AND THE WASTING OF RESOURCES

While many worry about technology and the labour market, others are optimistic about technology's capacity to save the world from the existential problem of climate change. For the most part, Marxism has been comparatively slow to engage with the issue of climate. It is relatively easy to use Marxist thought to draw some fairly glib conclusions: given that capitalism needs to keep expanding and consuming more resources, and given that we have already seen the weakness of governments to interfere in this process, we might surmise that capitalism dooms the world to climate disaster.

Jason Moore coins the term 'capitalocene' as a twist on the trendy (in academic circles) 'anthropocene'.[25] The latter term is intended to indicate that we have now entered a period of history in which human activity, rather than anything out of our control – such as continental drifts or colliding asteroids – exerts a decisive influence on the world's climate. Moore does not like this term because it imposes a vague collective responsibility on *all* humans, whereas in fact fossil fuel consumption is overwhelmingly conducted by the world's elite businesses. So the 'anthropocene', from a Marxist perspective, is a bit of a sick joke, since it implies guilt shared across an entire species when in fact the vast majority of that species are completely shut out from any say over how fossil fuels are used and consumed.

It is usually assumed that action on climate change can only function if it is conducted 'at the international level'. This is, evidently, because there is no incentive for individual countries to regulate over issues like carbon emissions on their own, especially in the 'competition state' described in Chapter 4. Because international cooperation weakens the pressures on states to compete by slashing environmental regulations or strengthening labour discipline, it is worrying to capital.[26] But the problem is that, precisely because of these competitive pressures acting on states, it is dubious to what extent a proper 'international level' actually exists. Any international institution is a product of its constituent parts, i.e. national-level governments, and the urgent need for national governments to push the agendas that will best benefit capital accumulation in their particular territories presents powerful obstacles to genuine transnational cooperation. The 'structural power of capital' inclines national governments to compete, not cooperate.[27]

Consequently (particularly following the US's withdrawal from the Paris Agreement), there is pessimism about the prospects of governments intervening effectively around climate change. Some have responded with wishful thinking about the prospects of 'new' forms of 'socially responsible' capitalism emerging. This kind of thing usually involves a seemingly bottomless faith in 'the market' and the supposed human ingenuity it conjures: why not just rely on capitalists' desire for profit to prompt them to invent some new commodity that can solve the problem of climate change?[28] In this sense, the world being saved depends on the brilliant whims of telegenic entrepreneurs like Elon Musk. Maybe some form of new technology will be invented that saves the world from these terrible problems, without us having to make any significant changes to our economic system.

In Marxist terms, there is little value in speculating about the transformative power of technology unless we also consider how this technology may affect the kind of social and economic structures we have (and vice versa). This is difficult to do. Steven Shaviro, for instance, has criticised science fiction authors for the way they have imagined 'post-Singularity' worlds[29] – in other words, worlds where technology has progressed to such an extent that human existence is totally transformed and all needs can be fulfilled more or less instantly. He notices that many authors that write about this sort of thing seem unable to imagine how this might actually affect human society, and tend to assume that various things – 'private property, capital accumulation, branding and advertising, stringent copyright enforcement and, above all "business models"' – would largely still exist in the same forms as they do today. The point here is that just as it is strange to imagine technological change without considering how that effects society, it is equally bizarre to suppose that technology alone can save the world from ecological disaster without corresponding changes to the way society is organised.

This obsession with technological change as the main motor of human advancement, has, for some people, become a ridiculous and pitiful cult. Consider the following account of an Apple product launch, which illustrates the perfect intersection between smoke-and-mirrors bullshit and hard-line control freakery on the part of capital:

> [Steve] Jobs's demonstration of the new phone … was a tremendous piece of salesmanship. It's all the more impressive in retrospect, because we now know that the iPhone was nowhere near ready. The music player had a tendency to conk out mid-song, the battery died at random, it would let a user send an email and surf the net in that order but the reverse sequence would crash it. Phone reception was a weak point (it still is) so AT&T set up a special tower to boost the signal; also the phone Jobs used on stage was rigged to display five full bars of signal at all times. He had done what seemed like a hundred rehearsals and things kept going wrong. During this process he was, according to one of the engineers present, relatively restrained. 'Mostly he just looked at you and very directly said in a very loud and stern voice, "you are fucking up my company" or "if we fail, it will be because of you"'.[30]

All this bullshit for what is essentially a slightly zazzed-up mobile phone. As David Graeber points out, it is hardly the flying cars and robots with laser eyes that sci-fi writers from the 1950s liked to imagine we'd have by now.[31] There is a significant gap between the kind of technological revolutions capitalists praise themselves for, and the actual extent of progress that capitalism as a system can tolerate.

8
Media and Ideology

It has become an accepted cliché on the radical left that people find it easier to imagine the end of all life on earth than to imagine the end of capitalism. Frightening predictions about climate change and its consequences are by now familiar, to the extent that many people would not be particularly surprised if a visitor from the future were to appear and tell them that the earth had become an uninhabitable wasteland. On the other hand, the mantra when it comes to our economic and political system has, for several decades now, been the relentless dirge of 'There Is No Alternative'. As things stand, the prospect of environmental catastrophe is probably a less remote one than the prospect of a different kind of economy.

When I talked about Marxist views on government in Chapter 5, I referred to 'common sense'. This is a highly loaded term which has been used very intelligently on the political right. It is most commonly used to express the idea that there is an intuitive wisdom possessed by ordinary people (or 'real people') that can get to the truth of the matter in ways that rarefied expertise cannot. This of course brings us back to Michael Gove and his experts. Nobody wants to feel like they don't have common sense, and so it becomes very easy to use the term to flatter potential voters, readers or social media followers.

This kind of language, in its own way, has an obvious 'class' element to it since it is ostensibly an anti-elite discourse. The fact that many of its main figureheads (Michael Gove, Nigel Farage, Donald Trump, etc.) are themselves elites is not particularly relevant here, and is almost an advantage; they are the insiders who are revealing to the outsiders how corrupt the world really is. It is a highly effective line of argument which has proved very convenient for conservatives because of various looming issues (most obviously climate change) where formal and technical expertise is very much weighted against their arguments. As such, it has been very expedient to play on the idea of common sense as a legitimate alternative to actual sense.

On one level, the idea of common sense is useful for political opportunists looking for a nice way of fobbing off unhelpful evidence, from whatever perspective. But there are deeper reasons why the idea of common sense has been so much more effectively wielded in conservative hands in recent decades. Most left projects tend to be about disrupting established hierarchies and the proactive creation of a more equal society, which may appear to conflict with the 'natural order' of things. For example, very few people actually like the idea that the rich can buy much better access to essential services such as health and education, but this has been so obviously the case for such a long time that it seems strange to think you can change it. While many people may be sympathetic to the objective, common sense dictates that these things are basically inevitable and therefore it is utopian meddling to make too much of a fuss about it.

As we saw previously, writers such as Ralph Miliband saw common sense as a set of assumptions about the way things are and must always be, like it or not. He also observed that the nature of these assumptions takes a particular form which is, of course, *adequate to capital's needs*. For instance, for Miliband it is an unshakeable article of common sense that what is good for business is basically good for society. People are not necessarily expected to be enthused about the business world, and in fact many find great enjoyment in ridiculing those who appear to take it too seriously, as the success of TV freak shows like *The Apprentice* indicates. However, there is also a widespread assumption that people should not do things that unduly upset 'business', however much one might like to.

But, of course, various caveats are required here. Brexit was one sign that this form of common sense is losing some traction, given that at the time of the vote it was widely supposed that it would be bad for business (and maybe this perception even encouraged many Brexit supporters). In this respect, the unfortunate fact is that the nationalist right has often done a far better job of playing on people's desire to break out of this way of thinking than the left.

Nonetheless, the point remains. The mainstream political right, which has dominated British politics for most of the time since the 1970s, has been successful because it recognises that it doesn't actually need to enthuse people about the pro-capital policies it has pursued. The important thing is to tell people what is unrealistic and utopian; common sense is defined by the 'limitations it imposes upon our collective imag-ination'.[1] You might want policies that support labour's interests against those of capital, and that's fine, but in an economy which is entirely dependent on capital's ability to make and reinvest profits, these are basically off-limits.

So the true enemy of this kind of common sense is not so much the 'expert' per se (this is a fairly recent development) but the more demo-cratic figure of the meddler. Because common sense is about defining what is off-limits, most invocations of it need to be directed against some individual or group that is tinkering too much with things beyond these limits, often in a utopian quest to further the cause of equality. Through-out much of the 1990 and 2000s, it appeared that large segments of the newspaper industry were entirely based on stories which played on one particular juxtaposition: between good old British (i.e. English) tradi-tions on the one hand, and the meddling Politically Correct Brigade, who were always trying to ban things so as to further the cause of various disadvantaged groups. It's all very well, so the argument went, wanting to create more equality, but actually to interfere with anything that currently exists in order to do so violates principles of common sense.

As a consequence, in various influential papers there has been a constant series of stories about how these people wanted to ban a long list of treasured cultural hallmarks such as Baa Baa Black Sheep, Thomas the Tank Engine, James Bond, piggy banks and Christmas. One might comment that, as of 2017, all these things apparently continue to exist. But this is somewhat missing the point: through the sheer volume of bullshit, there has emerged a widespread sense of a profound tension between the common sense possessed by the normal 'man or woman on the street' and efforts to include disadvantaged groups more in public life. This argument has fermented into the darker and more explicitly racist and misogynistic language which currently occupies a prominent place in the politics of Britain, Europe, America and elsewhere.

THE NEWS MEDIA

This idea of politically correct meddlers violating common sense has become grimly ironic when applied to Britain's most important news source, the BBC.* Looking at its role tells us a lot about ideology in

---

* I realise that in talking about this I am inevitably going to be in the shadow of Tom Mills's excellent book, *The BBC: Myth of a Public Service*.

Britain and its relationship to capital. The BBC has long been carica-
tured on the right as an archetypal meddler, when in fact it is impeccably
in tune with the common sense of the day when it comes to economic
and political reporting. The proposition that the BBC is biased to the left
has become forcibly established as fact in many quarters through sheer
weight of hearsay, often centring on the somewhat implausible claim
that anti-immigrant voices receive no BBC airtime.[2] Indeed, right-wing
researchers have attempted to 'prove' this bias by showing how the news
stories featured on the BBC website tend to overlap more with those
covered at the (liberal) *Guardian* than at the (conservative) *Telegraph*.[3]
The possibility that this may say more about the oddities who inhabit
the *Telegraph*'s comment pages than it does about the BBC apparently
does not occur to them.

There is a fairly banal 'centrist' defence of the BBC against these kinds
of attacks, which goes roughly as follows: 'the right claims the BBC is
biased to the left, but the left claims it is biased to the right. Therefore
it must be doing its job.' The problem with this argument is, first, that
it assumes there must be equal merit in both sides of an argument, as if
it is biased to give greater airtime to people who believe in the existence
of climate change than to people who don't. But the bigger issue is more
complex than the kind of editorial inflection the BBC might convey on
a given topic, or whether its interviewers are ruder to Labour or Conservative politicians.

More important is the fact that the BBC typically puts itself firmly in
line with common sense in Ralph Miliband's sense: its belief in the unity
of business and national interests. While, on any given issue, the BBC
may scrupulously present different sides of an issue, there is an underpinning assumption that is rarely, if ever, properly questioned – that the
happiness of private business is a necessary condition for the 'economy
that works for everyone'.

This assumption is most obviously manifested in its coverage of
business issues. In the numerous 'business segments' strewn throughout
BBC news output, business figures are typically presented as insider
experts on the economy. They are practitioners who can give us insight
into whether the economy is doing well or not, or whether a particular
policy or development is going to be helpful. By contrast, voices representing labour (mostly trade unions) are more likely to be interviewed
in the same way as a politician would be, i.e. using the oppositional
approach that BBC interviewers have made their trademark. This is not

necessarily conscious bias; it's just the assumption that the interests of British capital are identical with the national interest, and that anyone disrupting the interests of capital had better have a good reason for doing so. They probably sincerely believe this, and hence it is not surprising that business voices, particularly those from the City, are given such a privileged platform as talking heads in BBC news programmes.[4] These are the voices that are assumed to matter most.

Our particular interest here, of course, is what happens in the case of overt conflict between capital and labour, such as strikes. In the event of a strike, we can expect the BBC to present 'both' sides (though there are generally more than two), by interviewing figures from management and union camps. But strikes are often very complicated issues with long and highly specific histories in that workplace, and it may simply be that the BBC lacks the expertise to cover them in much depth. Under John Birt, the BBC began systematically ditching actual industrial correspondents (i.e. journalists trained to report at the coalface of workplace relations) in favour of business correspondents who depend on their ability to schmooze corporate spokespeople.[5] This is particularly worrisome in strike reporting because invariably, in the case of a strike which inconveniences the public, the easiest thing to do is blame the union (since they were the one that actually took the decision to call it). It is only when we look much deeper into cases that we begin to understand workers' grievances and the provocative actions of management, and hence begin to comprehend, even sympathise with, the case for the strike. The BBC does not set out to be biased against strikers but it usually lacks the wherewithal to present their case properly.

This is obviously not a criticism solely of the BBC. In the 1970s, Paul Hartmann found that strikes tended to be presented by the vast majority of news sources as resulting directly from the decisions of unions[6] – a starting assumption from which the rights or wrongs of those decisions could be debated in an 'unbiased' way. But this is wrong because the actions of managers may well initiate or escalate conflicts that end up in a strike, but are much less likely to be reported. The ascendancy of 'business' news (rather than, say, industrial or employment news) compounds this attitude. No matter how politely treated an interviewee representing strikers may be, they are inevitably asked to justify their disruption of the economy.*

---

* And the reporter's sympathy instinctively tends to be with management, since this is where their contacts come from.

Similar remarks can be made regarding the BBC's wider economic reporting, particularly over austerity. It does, of course, try to give pro-austerity politicians just as hard a time as anti-austerity ones. Moreover, it sometimes reports powerfully on the consequences of public spending cuts. Nonetheless, there remains an overall reliance on business voices for expert opinion on economic policy, cementing their position as neutral and technocratic insiders capable of making objective pronouncements free from class interest.[7] As with industrial disputes, economics and financial journalists often do not understand the internal workings of the system as well as their business contributors do, resulting in a deferential attitude even in the midst of a crisis.[8]

Consequently, most news sources, including those like the BBC which are supposed to know better, generally fail to get beyond the most simple narrative about recent economic policy; what the Keynesian economist Simon Wren-Lewis calls 'mediamacro': 'the previous government messed up: they spent too much, and it left the UK economy on the brink of financial meltdown'.[9] As with reporting on strikes, this becomes the 'common sense' line because it is the most readily understandable one; putting labour's case requires more research and more empathy than putting capital's. The BBC's self-conscious agonising about the endless accusations of 'left-wing bias' have probably pushed it into much harder stances which combine with the uglier prejudices of the age, notably its repeated representation of the situations of benefits recipients in order to push a 'welfare state in crisis' narrative.[10]

MARXIST VIEWS ON IDEOLOGY

In Marxist writing, the topic of ideology has often been brought in as a *post hoc* explanation for failure. Since Marx predicted that labour would eventually overthrow capital, we need a story for why this hasn't happened, which discussion of ideology provides. In *The German Ideology*, Marx argues that the ideas that are conducive to the interests of the 'ruling class' (i.e. capital) tend to prevail more widely across society, to the extent that people struggle to see beyond them.

> The ideas of the ruling class are in every epoch the ruling ideas, i.e. the class which is the ruling material force of society, is at the same time its ruling intellectual force. The class which has the means of material production at its disposal, has control at the same time over the means

of mental production, so that thereby, generally speaking, the ideas of those who lack the means of mental production are subject to it.

In other words, capital exerts a disproportionate influence over what people think and what ideas are acceptable in capitalist societies, and it can do this for a fairly straightforward reason. Because, just as it controls the means of (commodity) production, it also controls the 'means of mental production'. Entertainment and cultural industries, the news media and so on.

For later Marxists, such as the Italian philosopher Antonio Gramsci, the situation was more complex than this, although inevitably capitalist ideas still tended to dominate. Gramsci argued that the stability of capitalism was only partly dependent on brutal force (recall he was writing in a time and place – Italy under Mussolini – where Marxist thought was indeed being actively suppressed through violence) but also on consent. Ruling elites are often highly skilled at winning consent for their policies. Gramsci suggested that they tended to use emotionally resonant ideas to create a sense of community and, consequently, shared interest that transcended class boundaries.

Religion is very good at this, providing a historically reliable way of getting people from the poorest to the richest backgrounds to believe that they are basically on the same side. But this could be about much more trivial things. People on the left, for instance, get angry about how Nigel Farage is able to present himself as a man of the people despite his privileged background and personal wealth, simply by being repeatedly photographed drinking beer in pubs. But the idea of drinking beer in pubs has a culturally resonant status as part of many British people's self-identity, so anyone who appears to be at home when doing so has a head start in creating the impression of relatability. A lot of bubbling tensions around national culture and identity are encapsulated in a trivial but resonant image. Obviously not everyone falls for this, but enough do to bestow political influence; that is ideology at work.

Later on, as capitalism's position in the West became stronger, Marxist thought around consent becomes more extensive and complex. Indeed, for Marx-influenced academics such as those of the Frankfurt School, this question became far more interesting than the question of power relations in the realm of production (which, after all, is supposed to be the root of exploitation in capitalist systems). The result of this current of thought was a particularly extensive critique of consumerism as the most effective means of ensuring people's loyalty to capitalist systems. For Theodor Adorno, consumer society basically acted like the Matrix: by buying things, people believe they are cultivating a fulfilling individual identity, when in fact, he argued, their individuality is being stamped out by the capitalist machine.

Adorno's main target in this respect was popular culture, and particularly popular music, which he hated (he himself had studied composition under the twelve-tone serialist composer Arnold Schoenberg). Popular music, he argued, provided the illusion of individuality; you might think that listening exclusively to Deicide and Morbid Angel puts you outside of mainstream society into some form of rebellious counter culture, but basically you are still buying carefully marketed commodities like everyone else, just with different packaging. He believed that popular music was repetitive and formulaic: song structures were highly standardised, the melodies and chord progressions drawn from the same simple harmonic palette, the rhythms were based on simple repetitions (they'd have to be, otherwise you couldn't dance to them). In other words, it could largely be churned out as if in a Taylorised factory according to a standardised template, when true individual expression had to escape from these formulas. He applied this across the entirety of popular music with an admirable lack of nuance, including (notoriously) to jazz, whose improvisatory elements he saw as a fig-leaf for this standardisation.

Because of this it is quite easy to lampoon Adorno today, as a pompous advocate of dry avant-garde music that nobody actually enjoys listening to. It is a profoundly unfashionable argument, in any case, given that culture journalists nowadays often appear to be in thrall to their childhood obsessions with punk or disco and don't like the idea of someone disdaining them for these attachments. However, perhaps people are also scornful of the elitist Adorno because the things that he hated have now become so commonplace. For instance, we could observe the increasing reliance on gift vouchers as a present for friends and relations, or the growing popularity of wedding lists. These kinds of consumer innovations enable a gift-giver to meet their social obligations, without having the inconvenience of acquiring any meaningful knowledge about the other person's personality, or any understanding of the kinds of things they enjoy. Adorno said that such innovations reflect the 'decay of giving … based on the assumption that one does not know what to give because one really does not want to. This merchandise is unrelated like its buyers.'[11]

He had particular disdain for 'connoisseurs' – people who define themselves as experts in particular areas of popular culture. Such people were trying to buy their way to individuality through amassing large record collections. He directed his ire towards 'jitterbugs' – a word used to describe people who were very into dancing to the mainstream jazz music of the 1930s and 1940s. For Adorno, these were

> the enthusiasts who write fan letters to radio stations and orchestras and, at well-managed jazz festivals, produce their own enthusiasm as an advertisement for the wares they consume. They call themselves jitterbugs, as if they simultaneously wanted to affirm and mock their loss of individuality, their transformation into beetles whirring around in fascination. Their only excuse is that the term jitterbug, like all those in the unreal edifice of films and jazz, is hammered into them by the entrepreneurs who make them think that they are on the inside. Their ecstasy is without content.[12]

This is cynical but quite prescient. Adorno's 'connoisseur' has various manifestations today. Consider 'geek culture', which has become a massively profitable industry. When I was growing up the word 'geek' was a mild insult aimed at unfashionable people who liked to play board and/or computer games, whereas now it is a ready-made consumer identity that people can advertise their membership of by buying *Big Bang Theory* merchandise.

Why talk so much about Adorno and the (quasi-)Marxist critique of consumerism here? It is not news that consumerism has been highly effective in helping capitalism win people's support, but it is interesting because it says something about the role of the individual in society. According to Adorno, the consumer's relationship to society is basically a passive one. The consumer, however 'discerning', does not really think for themselves and instead latches on to standardised templates designed by business. This seems unduly harsh and massively overgeneralised, but there is an important insight here that needs to be picked out. For capital, human beings are best when they have this passivity, in all the different aspects of their identity. As a consumer who follows capitalist sugges- tions on what kind of goods they want. As a 'citizen' who votes once every five years but then minds their own business and forgets about politics. As a worker who does what they are told by their boss and has no interest in joining a union. Unfortunately for capital, people are rarely like this, but Adorno's philosophy suggests that consumer culture is one means of pushing them at least a bit further in that direction.

According to the French philosopher Alain Badiou, another thing encouraging people to be passive is a widespread sense of political scepticism, which he sees as the guiding spirit of our age.[13] In other words, he argues, there is a mistrust of ideologically driven change in politics which presents itself as robust realism but which actually becomes a quite a self-indulgent philosophy that celebrates laziness:

> the sceptic worldview has, in effect, led to a pragmatic rallying to the situation as it is at the moment. I would even say: to the satisfaction that we find, in this situation, of not having to raise a little finger for an idea. Scepticism is also the blessed possibility, and even the supreme justification, of only occupying oneself with oneself, since nothing can change in the world as it is.[14]

This is a relatively controversial set of ideas, not least because it could be interpreted as a bit bullying. Maybe people are happy getting on with their own lives and don't want to spend their evenings pursuing utopian political projects. Maybe they like going out and buying things, and certain philosophers are just being jerks by telling them they shouldn't. Maybe, therefore, people like Badiou are simply putting a more radical veneer on the idea of the PC meddler who won't let everyone else get on with their lives. Furthermore, while Badiou might well say this about France, which in 2017 handed unprecedented power to someone who celebrates his own vacuous centrism, what about Britain, where ideological conflict appears to be sharpening again? In the rest of this chapter I will look at three different forms of human activity – being a citizen, being a worker and being a consumer – and consider some ways in which this kind of Marxist philosophising may have a point on the issue of passivity and scepticism.

Voting

I have already talked about government in capitalist societies, suggesting that it is wrong to see them as neutral arbiters between different interest groups, and instead suggesting that they tend to further capital's interests at the expense of labour's. Someone could draw a fairly extreme conclusion from this: i.e. that there is very little point in voting at all, since in a general election you are choosing between a selection of parties that ultimately will not be able to act in labour's interest (even if they wanted to).

This is, indeed, the argument of some Marxists, including Badiou. In his *Meaning of Sarkozy*, Badiou describes gently mocking the students who arrived despondent at one of his seminars the day after the right-wing Nicolas Sarkozy won the French presidential elections in 2007. Why bother getting upset, he wonders, about such a fraudulent process? In this sense, he concurs with the old anarchist slogan, frequently found as lamp-post graffiti in university cities: 'if voting changed anything they'd ban it'.

There are some problems with this argument. First of all, politicians have indeed tried to ban voting, and continue to do so, at least for certain kinds of people. If the slogan was completely correct, they presumably would not bother. In the United States, for instance, Republican-controlled state authorities have been fairly open and unembarrassed about their desire to prevent certain demographics (mainly black people and poor people) from voting (because they assume they will vote Democrat). Conservative governments in Britain may be interested in doing something similar, albeit with students.[15]

Badiou might, admittedly, scoff at this objection, saying that political parties competing for votes is more to do with the internecine squabbling over who gets to act on behalf of capital, than proper change. Even if the Republicans in a given state lose because they can't exclude enough Democrat voters, does this actually pose any kind of threat to capital? Following Chapter 5, we might concede that he has a point. Certainly, unexpected electoral events might throw things off balance. Brexit, or the 2017 UK general election, for instance. But despite the turbulence these kinds of awkward democratic intrusions cause in the short term, capital is very good at reacting to them, and manoeuvring to get the situation back to 'stability' again (i.e. enabling things to continue on its terms). When Syriza was elected in Greece, the forces of European capital closed around them to enforce a suffocating austerity people had supposedly voted against. If Jeremy Corbyn were to be elected in the UK, we would expect a similar move.

But certainly in this country, the kind of voting-sceptic argument Badiou makes is clearly out of fashion, for the obvious reason that the radical left has taken control of the Labour Party. There is a growing sense that there is more genuine choice on offer at the present moment.

We might reasonably speculate that, should the Labour Party under Corbyn get elected, it would be forced to tone down the radical elements of their agenda significantly, but we still need to pay attention to what is happening *now*, with Labour apparently assuming a considerably more leftist stance. It is true that this growth owes much to the unexpectedly high turnout in the 2017 election, particularly (but not exclusively) among younger people. The constructive Marxist response to this development is, first, to celebrate the huge boost the left in this country has received as a result of high voting turnout in the election, while also recognising the vast obstacles that would confront Corbyn's Labour if they were ever to be given a majority in Parliament.

Second, it is also important to note what the enemy is doing at the same time – and this is where we get back to the issue of *passivity*. It is interesting to consider the way the concept of voting has been presented in media sources. Until 2017, there had been a protracted decline in voter turnout, particularly among the young. People who are wedded to the status quo worry about this sort of trend: it raises genuine concerns about the state of civic participation, but it also makes government insecure about their own legitimacy (which is tarnished if only a small number of people bother to take part in the process that gave them their jobs).

Over recent electoral cycles, the response from many quarters was to try to cajole people into voting. Particularly on social media, there has been an escalating glorification of the act of voting itself, as if someone deserves a medal just for doing so – 'It doesn't matter who you vote for, just make sure you vote!' being a common slogan. There is a proliferation of Facebook or Twitter badges users can attach to advertise the fact that they have voted. Generally these symbols do not reveal for whom the user voted; the implication is that they deserve equal recognition whether it was for Labour, Conservatives, the Green Party or the British National Party. Some cynical economists argue that many people are now voting primarily in order to be able to tell others that they have done so.[16]

This kind of empty back-patting is the sickly political equivalent of the 'economy that works for everyone' mantra. Whatever choices you express, you should be happy to take part in this great democratic process where we all come together to find a consensus while respecting each other's opinions. Badiou is justified in attacking the emptiness of this idea, which explicitly chooses to celebrate some overarching number (i.e.

turnout) rather than examine the conflicting interests, values or ideas it conceals. And it is, essentially, passive. People like to say: 'if you didn't vote, you can't complain'. In other words, occasional elections are your only moment to express your view: the rest of the time, make sure you shut up and don't moan. If everyone just patted themselves on the back simply for voting and considered that their civic duty done for the year, without ever getting involved in a union or other kind of campaign, then capital would always have everything its own way.

Worse still, as Badiou argues, the result of an election generally gives an entirely unwarranted and fatuous sense of decisiveness. He talks about this attitude in relation to France: '"The French have decided ... " says the right-minded press. They have not decided anything at all, and moreover, this collective – the French – lacks any existence. Why on earth should 51 per cent of French people be "the French"?' Anyone disillusioned by the way a 52 per cent vote for Brexit has been interpreted as 'the will of the British people' must surely agree that he has a point here.

But things change. Many of the people who were worried about low turnout are currently performing screeching U-turns. Whatever the problems with the celebration of voting *as an end in itself*, once it became obvious that getting more (young) people to vote was an important strategic objective for the left, many people who had once celebrated civic participation were now not so keen. A *Times* columnist writes:

> Last week's election revealed the judgement of many young voters to be as we might expect of those with relatively limited experience: hopelessly naïve. They turned out in their droves for a man who became a kind of millenials' prophet: promising to lead them out of the Badlands of austerity and towards a future where everything is nicer, cheaper, or indeed free. They have voted for a man who would have endangered our economy, the whisper of whose name can send the pound on a swan-dive ... It has been suggested that the great turnout of the youth vote is an argument for lowering the voting age to 16. Given who they voted for *en masse*, I would say it's an argument for raising it to at least 21.[17]

A *Spectator* commentator describes youthful Corbyn supporters as 'the Middle Britain of tomorrow, entitled millennials who can correctly identify the gender pronoun of each Kardashian but think the IRA [Irish Republican Army] were a rough-around-the-edges Amnesty

International'.[18] And *The Sun*, in a sort of 'joking-but-not-joking' kind of way, prints cut-out guides for right-wing middle-aged people on 'how to keep your children from voting'.[19]

There is a lot more where this comes from. When Russell Brand – very much the English Alain Badiou – came out as a non-voter in 2015 he was excoriated as having forfeited his right to play any part in reasonable political discussion. When he started encouraging people to vote for Corbyn, he no doubt found that the same people hate him even more. Generally, I would suggest the following hypothesis: the more upset right-wing columnists get about people turning out to vote, the more likely the vote in question is to precipitate meaningful change, and the more angry capital will get about the result.

Working

> They can laugh, they're no better than me. Just 'cause they're reps who like being reps, and I'm a rep who wants to be something else.
>
> David Brent, in *David Brent: Life on the Road*

Glorifying 'participation' via voting as an end in itself reclassifies people who feel alienated from the British political process as self-exiled outsiders who can have 'no right to complain'. When the topic of work is discussed in Britain, something similar happens, with a strong tendency to distinguish between those who 'contribute' and those who do not. I have already argued that this is a completely bogus distinction in the vast majority of cases, since, as Marx puts it, the 'reserve army' of those outside paid employment 'belongs to capital just as absolutely as if the latter had bred it at its own cost'. The reasons for this were explained in Chapter 2.

Evidently, Marxist philosophy has a very high regard for the idea of work. It suggests that the capacity to design and create things freely is a defining human characteristic, and an important source of individual fulfilment. However, it is important to stress that *work* is very different from a *job*. The former could include unremunerated things people do for their own satisfaction, or else out of care for others, whereas the latter is specifically something people do in order to get a wage. For Marxists, one of the most fundamental problems of capitalist economies is their twisting of the idea of work into the idea of the job; rather than being a source of creative reward for individuals, it becomes something routinised, controlled, boring and alienating.

In Britain today, it is fairly common to find a masochistic obsession with jobs, and whether or not people have them. It is unusual to find critical discussion of what jobs are actually *like* in the national media: the assumption is that higher employment rates are good in themselves. Increasingly, there is severe moral judgement passed on people that do not have jobs, as evidenced by hardening attitudes towards unemployed people in recent years.[20] Many British people today revel masochistically in the latter alternative. For 'just vote!' we can also substitute 'just work!' Don't talk about what jobs are actually like, just obsess over how many people have one.

For a long time, the attitude of politicians on the centre-left has masqueraded as 'realism': political parties like Labour have to mirror this attitude to be in sync with voters (recall the Rachel Reeves quotes in Chapter 1). The problem here is that this interprets 'public opinion' as an independent force of nature which moves according to its own laws and to which anyone purporting to lead needs to attune themselves. But this public opinion shift has been propelled by politicians and various media sources which have worked very hard to strengthen pejorative attitudes towards those out of work. The British media, by international standards, is highly reliant on negative stereotyping of the poor,[21] especially in its prurient and unhealthy spotlighting of the sick and disabled.[22] Hence the other problem with following public opinion: public opinion is often heavily influenced by inaccurate information, particularly so in the benefits system. People routinely and 'wildly' overestimate the levels of benefits many people receive, as well as how benefits compare to sources such as pensions, and the proportion of benefits that are claimed fraudulently.[23] As such, this is an unconventional form of political 'realism': to be realistic, political leaders need to ensure that their positions match the logical conclusions that can be drawn from obvious falsehoods.

One of the most important consequences of a fixation with whether or not people have jobs is that it largely nixes any discussion of the actual content and quality of them. As such, it is a highly convenient ideological buttress for the modern British labour market, which is recurrently labelled a 'success' by people who only look at employment rates. The moral judgement directed towards people who don't have jobs can be quite ghoulish: for instance, in the monstering of a woman who spent some of her welfare money on Prosecco at Christmas time.[24] Such stories epitomise a sweaty newspaper obsession with evaluating the way (usually female) welfare recipients use money, drawing on all the moral certainty of a medieval witch-finder.

This moralising about unemployed people borders on the unhinged. Daytime TV shows will dedicate entire episodes to parading jobless individuals in front of an audience for judgement, usually with the hook that they have some disreputable reason for their lack of work, such as their weight, the number of children they have or (worst of all) because they want to pursue an interest they actually enjoy (stonerish musicians are a good choice here). Inevitably there is another guest or audience member who, let's say, is equally overweight but who does have a job, and who gets a large round of applause for having done so, as the audience revels in this proof of the first guest's fecklessness. This is why the quote at the start of this section pays tribute to David Brent; *Life on the Road* is one of only a few examples of a piece of mainstream culture that presents neglecting a job you hate in order to pursue a passion for music (however deluded) as an understandable and sympathetic way to behave. Sadly, Brent funds this through his own savings and holiday pay rather than welfare entitlements, but still.

This has obviously also been fed by developments at policy level, spearheaded by the sensible 'realists' in both the Labour and Conservative parties. As we have seen, they have shifted welfare policy towards 'work-first' approaches to out-of-work benefits, where the priority is to force someone back into work as quickly as possible irrespective of how unsuitable or depressing the job. While this approach chimes with the common sense of the age, it is also quite a strange phenomenon in the grand sweep of history: the glorification of the existence of large numbers of people doing menial tasks as an end in itself.

The consequences of this are such ideological delusions as the rebranding of capitalists as so-called 'job creators'. It is only in a society where millions of people are severed from common resources and dependent on a wage that 'creating more jobs' is seen as a good thing. A toddler who draws on a wall, an HGV which knocks over a bridge or a highly contagious virus – these are all 'job creators'. Happily, it appears that most British people are more sceptical about the role and motivations of the 'job-creating' class than their political leadership is.[25] This, however, is one of those popular suspicions that is diligently restrained by government and media rather than stoked. The job creator is the true motive force behind society, and the British worker is supposed to be their passive beneficiary.

It is not quite true to say that there is *no* qualitative discussion of working life in the UK today. One topic which does loom large in popular imagination is bureaucracy. 'Red tape' is widely considered one of the great ills of British society. It is interesting to consider how bureaucracy fits into capitalist economies, since one of the most common arguments capital likes to employ against public ownership is that the latter is bureaucratic. A *Telegraph* commentator writes, in a state of high perplexity:

> There is roughly the same number of employees in the Home Civil Service (about 480,000) today as there was in 1979, despite 30 years of supposed rationalisation, value for money blitzes and efficiency drives. Post-Thatcher Britain was meant to have less government, especially after the nationalised industries were privatised, yet we have more than ever with extra tiers in Brussels, Scotland, Wales and London as well as dozens of central agencies, quangos and regional bodies. The cost is stupefying. Figures last week showed that £1 billion is spent on the PR of state-run organisations.[26]

The right-wing supposition is that in any public service there must be vast repositories of bureaucrats with no purpose from which hitherto wasted money can be extracted *ad infinitum*. This has led to some of the greatest feats of naivety of our age, such as the letter David Cameron sent to Witney Council, which I mentioned in Chapter 5.

For the sociologist Max Weber, writing in the early twentieth century, bureaucracy was the hallmark of modern industrial capitalism. Weber was ambivalent about it: bureaucracy is, at root, a system of rules and procedures which everyone has to follow. In other words, one where 'the system' is master, rather than everyone simply doing as some silver-tongued demagogue says. In some respects this is more progressive than systems of tribal or religious authority where power is centred in particular individuals, sometimes for highly mystical reasons, or else accident of birth. However, Weber also described bureaucracy as an 'iron cage'; as modern economies became more and more complex, bureaucratic systems would extend, suppressing individual freedom and creativity.

Weber's pessimism might be widely shared today, and arguably one of the most important and resonant stereotypes we have is that of the 'jobsworth', who pedantically follows bureaucratic procedures much to everyone else's frustration. As Graeber[27] argues, the argument that the public services are bureaucratic but the private sector is not has been an important ideological basis for privatisation and budget cutting. The standard conservative assumption is that bureaucracy is *meddling*: it comes from attempts to impose utopian phantasms such as health and safety measures, diversity regulations or workers' rights upon the world of private business which just wants to get on with competing.

This assumption needs some breaking down. It is very obviously false to imagine a neat distinction between the free and competitive market, and the world of rules and regulations. In the Marxist view, the fact that capital is under competitive pressure creates an urgent need for very intense control within the 'realm of production' (i.e. over the worker). The various examples of workplace control examined in Chapter 4, for instance, meet the popular definition of bureaucracy in that they imply the imposition of a 'system' over and above individual initiative. These kinds of things are rarely described as such because they are bureaucratic measures designed directly by capital. If government were to legislate to *prevent* warehousing companies from monitoring their workers with tracking machines, or to stop them forcing workers to wait at lengthy security queues on their way in and out of work, this would be widely interpreted in conservative eyes as the creation of more bureaucracy, even though the extent to which individual freedom is subordinated to an impersonal system would in fact have been greatly reduced.

This goes to show that 'bureaucracy' is not about meddling per se, but more specifically about *control*. The question is not *whether* we interfere with 'the market' and management, but *who* exercises control and at whose expense. In a highly competitive market, it is not that bureaucratic control doesn't exist, but that capital has the exclusive right to impose it on labour. Richard Walker and Gene Brewer have shown how those lower down in public sector organisations tend to experience vastly greater bureaucratic burdens than those at the top; and more to the point, that senior managers tend to believe that 'the best strategy for reducing red tape is to give themselves more control over the rulemaking process'.[28] Thus where the public sector adopts marketising reforms, this tends to imply the empowerment of management to develop fiercer procedures for controlling their staff.[29]

Bureaucracy protects capital, not just from labour but also from consumers. The overwhelming bureaucracies involved in processing an insurance claim or mortgage application, for instance, are there to protect the *company* from risk, not the consumer. The extensive terms and conditions customers are required to agree to in purchasing almost any service are examples of bureaucracy designed by corporate actors who invariably rest safe in the knowledge that the other party will never properly understand them. Likewise, if we take private utility companies, it may well be that the companies themselves are less bureaucratic than the public enterprises that used to run them, but the weight of bureaucratic responsibility has not disappeared so much as shifted on to the 'customer'. Today, the good energy consumer is expected to spend several hours of their free time on a regular basis perusing data on energy tariffs. If they don't do this, the implication is that they have no right to complain about the profits of energy companies because they aren't participating wholeheartedly enough in the market.

The perception that bureaucracy is only really bureaucracy when it enshrouds capital, rather than workers or consumers, is a further consequence of capitalist common sense. The kind of bureaucracy that emerges as capitalists go about their business is natural and something to be tolerated as an inevitable evil (since what's good for business is good for everyone), and indeed is rarely even labelled as bureaucracy. Conversely, the bad kind of bureaucracy is that which impedes capital, which is perceived as 'red tape' of the most meddlesome variety.

Responsible Fun

Capital is extremely good at turning the criticisms people make of it to its advantage. The French sociologists Luc Boltanski and Eve Chiapello have studied the way management talks to itself (i.e. through literature aimed at managers themselves), stressing its 'high moral tone': 'management literature cannot be exclusively orientated towards the pursuit of profit. It must also justify the way profit is obtained ... [it must] demonstrate how the prescribed way of making profit might be desirable, interesting, exciting, innovative or commendable.'[30] Hence there have emerged huge industries based on trying to get people to feel inspired by the process of extracting, realising and reinvesting surplus value.

Consider, for instance, the global textiles industry and the issue of sweatshops. Many British consumers are now aware that a large proportion of clothes in high street shops are manufactured in conditions that they themselves would consider intolerably bleak. This is not a happy situation and can induce severe guilt among the more switched-on, which is of course not good for business. There are various responses to this problem. One is the more direct way which is to argue explicitly that sweatshop conditions are a great boon to the world's poorest, since the alternative is starvation.[31] There is a certain degree of brutal honesty to this kind of line: don't complain about inhumane conditions in sweatshops because the manufacturers might get spooked, pulling out their investments and leaving their workers with nothing at all. This makes sense in an economic system such as capitalism where labour either has to contribute (directly or indirectly) to capital's profitability or have nothing.

The other approach is not to assuage this sense of guilt through repeated recitation of the laws of capital accumulation, but to monetise it. It is extremely common now for companies to advertise themselves on the basis of their social conscience. Coffee shop walls are plastered with feel-good posters telling customers how happy the people that grew their coffee are. Private accreditation schemes – where companies voluntarily agree to some defined labour or environmental standards throughout their supply chains in exchange for being able to advertise their conscientiousness – have taken off.

The important thing about these kinds of initiative is that, in a sense, they are a form of labour–capital conflict (in that they revolve around the tension between workers' conditions and the company's profit), but a labour–capital conflict in which labour's part is generally outsourced to the consumer. There is a risk that they marginalise the agency of labour itself, offering little role for trade unions in the monitoring and enforcement process.[32] As Nicole Aschoff argues, even a company that relentlessly parades its 'citizenship' credentials to its customers may be entirely happy to liken union membership among its own staff to herpes, or threaten them at private meetings about the dire consequences of collective organisation.[33] This is an important problem: the complexity of global supply chains (with extensive outsourcing of different production stages across different sites) means that these standards become difficult to monitor and enforce even if the company actually wants to. Consequently, local labour organising – i.e. *class consciousness* – is an important prerequisite for ensuring companies' ethical credentials are any more than a surcharge to assuage consumer guilt.[34]

Capitalists have also been trying to address the criticism that the business world is a more cynical and aloof area of human activity, with little to say to the world of genuine human interaction. This can take profoundly inane forms, such as 'wackaging', where commodities are marketed primarily as non-sentient but inexplicably jocular friends. For instance, a milkshake bottle may list its ostensibly healthy ingredients under the headline 'Get in Fella' rather than 'ingredients'. One cosmetics company likens using their hand cream to 'catching the dream bus'.* In advertising-speak this kind of infantilisation is called 'driving the conversation with the consumer'.[35] Commodities are not the product of alienated human labour, they are cute little messages between you and a friendly corporation.

This logic of the 'conversation' between company and consumer reaches a grim nadir when businesses make forays into social media. For example, in one recent instance British Gas lent its support to those mourning David Bowie over Twitter:[36] 'Morning all. A year today we lost pop icon David Bowie, time flys [sic] don't it? We're here till 10pm if you need anything. Thanks, Paul #RipDB.' On such occasions many people like to pile in by writing wittily abusive responses. The problem is that sending vitriol to British Gas's social media account still makes the mistake of acknowledging the underlying premise: that there can be such a thing as a 'conversation' between a human being and a for-profit utility company. Presumably this kind of conversation cannot be used to come to an amicable agreement over unaffordable heating bills.

In this chapter I have highlighted some ways in which capitalist processes tend to want individuals to assume a passive role: as otherwise disengaged voters, as workers who are just grateful to the job creators, as consumers who enjoys their entirely fraudulent and baseless 'conversations' with brands. Fortunately, people are usually too smart to go along with all of this. There is resistance in workplaces. People do abuse idiotic companies over social media. People can participate meaningfully in society through the electoral system under the right circumstances. So these ideological systems are not like the Matrix, consciously designed by a conniving intelligence to fool people into unquestioning obedience. Often, they are practical fixes for emerging problems, as with efforts at marketing 'responsible capitalism'. Sometimes particular attitudes are directly encouraged by politicians to create support for a particular agenda, as with the increasingly nasty language around work. And since nothing lasts forever under capitalism, these kinds of ideological fixes can always fragment, leaving angry *Times* columnists to mutter about raising the voting age.

---

* These examples taken from the blog http://wackaging.tumblr.com/.

9

Conclusion

There are three things I want to do in this conclusion. First, I will briefly summarise some of the key points I have emphasised through the book. Second, I want to examine other ideas that are currently important on the left, such as universal basic income and the notion of 'post-capitalism'. Finally, I want to consider how the arguments made here might apply to current (and rapidly changing) political events.

SUMMARY

I said in the Introduction that I wanted to make capitalism look strange. Capitalism is a system with a specific set of rules and processes, and these rules and processes lead to situations that, when looked at in wider perspective, do not make much sense. Consider the perverse and anti-human ends to which technological progress is put. Or the way 'job creation' is held up as an end in itself. Or the subordination of government policy to the 'alien powers' of confidence and competitiveness. Or the way so many people are required to spend a vast proportion of their life doing something they may find boring, alienating, exhausting, stressful or depressing, purely to furnish surplus value for someone else. To unravel these strange outcomes, there are various points from the analysis that need to be driven home.

Class and Classification

My main argument is that discussion around class should not simply focus on finding ways (however nuanced) of categorising people. Instead, I have presented a view of class that is more about understanding the relationships between groups of people who fulfil different economic roles in capitalist societies. Dividing between labour and capital would, of course, be far too binary if my goal were to provide a categorisation system into which to sort people. But this is not the objective. Instead, I have argued that 'labour' and 'capital' are not identities but processes,

which people enact, and which impose certain pressures and imperatives on them. The relationship between labour and capital, plus the
centrality of profit as the driving force of the economy, lead to demands
and pressures over which nobody really has control, and to which organisations, individuals and even government are subordinate. In Chapter 2
I used the Marxian phrase 'alien powers' to get at this idea.

Capitalists, in particular, are driven by the need to advance the
M-C-M' cycle continually. These pressures, in turn, are often the motor
of change in wider society. Look, for instance, at the extent to which
government policy, or change in the economic institutions regulating
society, are defined by the need to keep this cycle going at all costs.

There is a second response to the argument that talking about labour
and capital is simply too broad: once we recognise that the relationship between these classes imposes certain imperatives, then we can also
identify such a thing as a *labour–capital relationship*. At its bluntest, this
suggests the following maxim: in any situation where a capitalist relies
on extracting surplus value to be realised as profit, and where workers are
separated from the means of production (or from access to marketplaces,
as with supposed freelancers in the 'platform economy'), we can expect
certain outcomes. There will be a continual need to exercise control over
what the worker does with his or her working day. There will be the
recurrent conflict of interest over wages and working time resulting in
the kinds of 'small thefts' against workers as described in Chapter 4. The
worker's individual creativity and autonomy will come to be subordinated to systems defined and organised by the capitalist. There will be a
need to find some means of organising and disciplining people outside
of the labour force so that they can be called on or rejected by capital as
is required.

I am, clearly, not saying that every single workplace is a hell of control
and conflict. What I am saying is that these dynamics, though they work
out extremely differently from context to context and operate much more
oppressively in some circumstances than others, are evident *in some form*
right across any capitalist society, from the worst-paid and lowest-status
jobs through to 'elites' as in the 'knowledge' or 'creative' industries.

Government

In discussing how these alien powers operate on government, I
emphasised the idea of *adequate forms*. States have to try and mould

their policy approaches and institutions into shapes that are conducive to the continuation of the M-C-M' cycle. This is a difficult and conflictual process, and I tried to illustrate the tensions in Chapter 5, with particular reference to health and education systems. These systems, ultimately, have to be subordinated to the interests of capital. This could take the form of fiddling with their purposes to be better adapted to the 'needs of the market' (e.g. 'employability' and disappointing 'apprenticeship' schemes), or it could take the form of opening public resources up as a source of profit (e.g. with NHS privatisations or the housing market). But most of all, in recent years, it has taken the form of grinding austerity as government seeks to squeeze out more indirect surplus value on behalf of capital, lowering the costs of 'social reproduction'.

I also argued that government's role in guiding the evolution of adequate forms is made harder by the financialisation of the economy. In an effort to gain the 'confidence' of financial markets, British governments have made enormous sacrifices. In particular, they have pursued a policy of class discipline: weakening rights for labour and making people more scared of unemployment, to create a more malleable workforce better adapted to the extraction of shareholder value.

The fact that government is subject to these kinds of pressures is obviously important when it comes to discussing things like democratic participation and electoral politics. Governments under capitalism can never act disinterestedly as mediators between labour and capital, still less on labour's side, and to imagine they can do so is fantasy. This, it should be clear, is not an 'anti-voting' argument, but it is an argument against the idea that voting is, in itself, enough. The line, which has been increasingly common in recent years – that 'if you can't vote you don't have the right to complain' – is a naive and reactionary one. It rests on the false assumption that social divisions can be resolved through parliamentary means. Alien powers, and the dependence of the economy on private profit, will always tightly constrain the most radical government.

It is clear from the preceding that the first place capital has to be challenged is in the workplace. To put it bluntly, a doubling of the rate of trade union membership, and of the numbers of people willing collectively to challenge the power of their employers at work, would do far more to make Britain a better place than any conceivable general election result. The workplace is where many people spend most of their waking hours for most of their lives. Any improvement of the conditions under which people work – the amount of control they can exercise over

172 · CLASS MATTERS

their labour process, the ability to demand better terms and conditions, the level of security they have, the extent to which they can exercise creative agency – is a victory for humanity as a whole. So the most important thing people can do is to start standing up for themselves more proactively in relation to their employers, demanding considerably more from the latter, whatever the particular kind of labour they provide.

Common Non-Sense

These arguments also lead to some other points that need considering. It may be possible that, in the wake of recent political events, notably the Brexit referendum and the 2017 general election, some of the platitudinous discussion around the idea of the 'economy which works for everyone' will fade away. No political leader is going to come out and directly say 'I want an economy that only works for some', but it may be that they are more forthright and honest in designating winners and losers from the policies they are proposing. The great breakthrough of Jeremy Corbyn's 2017 election campaign was his willingness to vocalise the idea of targeting the rich to a degree which was unthinkable following New Labour. Likewise, in response the Tory press geared up for an all-out discursive assault on young people. Despite the vacuous pronunciations from self-styled moderates, the left–right divide in British politics clearly resurfaced in 2017.

This development might make the political landscape more divisive and conflictual, but probably also more honest. The interests of labour and capital do not fit well together and so people ultimately do have to pick a side. There is a growing recognition that people – particularly, but definitely not exclusively – the young, do not swallow the common sense that 'what is good for business is good for everyone'. They will come under attack for this, either being patronised or directly slandered, depending on the extent to which the media source in question wants to be considered a respectable voice. But this is a step in the right direction. I will come back to this at the end.

CAPITAL AND THE FUTURE

How does contemporary left-wing thought respond to the situation we have now? Often, its response is fairly weak. It emphasises things like higher taxation (or moving against tax avoidance/evasion), in order to build better public services. But the arguments I have made so far in this book suggest that this sort of measure is likely to remain inadequate tinkering, which does not really get to grips with the central fact of our societies: the dominance of capital over labour and government.

A more radical idea which is gaining traction (on the right as well as on the left) is universal basic income (UBI). In other words, paying everyone in the country (not just the poorest) a set amount as an absolute minimum right. On the left, UBI is presented as a response to technological change. The assumption is that technology will lead to jobs being phased out. In this sense UBI can present itself as a fairly pragmatic solution. It recognises that affluent high-skilled workers are also threatened by technology, and supposes, reasonably, that future labour markets may demand more shifts between jobs and more need to develop transferable skills. Under UBI, so its proponents argue, people could have periods outside of work in order to develop new skills without losing the ability to support themselves.

Put this way, it is a fairly intuitive prospect. Nick Srnicek and Alex Williams,[1] for instance, argue that the left should propose a two-pronged movement: the *acceleration* of the replacement of jobs through technology on one hand, and UBI on the other. We could thus move towards a system as envisioned by Marxists such as Braverman: less work is needed all round, but this is not a problem since those without work have other forms of support. In this sense, UBI could be a means of partially liberating the individual from the imperatives imposed by capitalist processes.

But there are problems with this idea. Jane Lethbridge, perhaps suspicious of the adoption of UBI by some writers on the right, raises a number of concerns.[2] For one thing, UBI can never replace proper public services, such as healthcare which is free at the point of delivery, or proper children's services, or libraries, or socialised support for the sick or disabled. Hence there is, in some quarters, a rather sinister idea that consent can be bought for the dismantling of these things through UBI – as in: 'here's a basic monthly cash handout, go and shop around for all those public services you once expected as a right'. In this sense, for all its apparent radicalism, UBI might one day turn out to be a fairly cheap way of securing continued capitalist stability while public services are retrenched further and further. The level of UBI and the conditions attached to it would, in all likelihood, be set by central government and in this sense be no more independent of capitalist imperatives than the NHS is (see Chapter 5).

Lethbridge's other critique is arguably even more important considering the argument we have made so far in this book. The idea that UBI can be a panacea completely sets aside the problem of *work*. The left version of UBI rests on the idea that it will diminish people's need to work, and in this sense will be a liberation. I have a lot of sympathy for this view, of course, given the amount of pointless drudgery within capitalist workplaces. Quite conceivably, UBI might strengthen workers' positions by making the prospect of unemployment less frightening. But this point alone cannot compensate for properly questioning the way work is conducted in capitalist societies. Why does labour have to be separated from the means of production? Why is it only able to work insofar as it provides surplus value? UBI cannot answer this.

Clearly, capitalist work relations are going to persist. Currently, it is fashionable to raise the idea of 'post-capitalism' and 'post-work', among some people on the political left.[3] The basic version of this argument goes as follows: increasingly, societies are able to produce material progress outside of the traditional capitalist work relationship, and in a way which capitalists are fundamentally unable to grasp or control. High-tech innovations are produced in flashes of inspiration or through constructive group interactions, and so cannot be controlled or legislated for by management as if on a construction line. Individuals control their expertise and inspiration, not capitalists. At the same time, new technological platforms (such as Wikipedia, or else other forms of open-source software and data-sharing technology) create scope for things to be done in a more collaborative way outside of the marketplace and outside of the control of capitalists. Therefore, we are already moving towards a society in which decentralised networks of citizens create things and govern the world around them without the input of capital. Broad societal fixes like UBI are the central prescriptions following from this argument, moving our focus away from the problem of control and exploitation within the workplace itself.

This kind of discussion is far too optimistic, mainly because it fails to recognise how important capitalist work relations still are, and will continue to be. Paul Thompson and Kendra Briken have punctured these arguments quite effectively.[4] For one thing, they point to the naivety of supposing that 'knowledge workers' cannot be controlled by capital in the same way as factory workers. Chapter 4 offers support for this argument.

High-tech firms such as Apple, Thompson and Briken argue, however much intangible 'inspiration' goes into their end product, still pursue a business model dominated by an obsession with cutting labour costs, leading to exploitative and highly controlled circumstances for workers right through their supply chains. 'Collaborative' digital platforms such as Uber are actually intensely hierarchical business models, where those that supply the labour power are under intense control, and contribute massively to the profits of company elites. As I argued in Chapter 7, new online 'means of evaluation' are pervading forms of control that are more opaque from the worker's perspective than Taylorist methods and thus, arguably, even more alienating and unfair. It is true that not all 'platforms' are like this, but such companies are not outliers of the new digital age: they constantly 'invade and seek to dominate' the marketplace, and in this effort they are leaving 'collaborative, peer-to-peer production' in the dirt.

Hence these more sunny prognoses about the potential to surpass capitalism buy into the PR of high-tech firms far too readily. When 'sharing economy' companies claim that they are non-hierarchical networks, it is obviously a mistake to believe them. Those who see a new 'post-capitalist' world emerging fetishise the ideas of 'decentralisation' and 'the network'. The emphasis is on small groups who collaborate in the production of innovative technologies which are then diffused through sharing technology, all the while in the absence of government and through breaking down corporate monopolies. The emphasis is perhaps as much to do with a desire not to be associated with failures of the past (i.e. statist Communism) as it is a genuine enthusiasm for these ideas in themselves. Besides, these kinds of highly decentralised participatory networks are good primarily for the cliques that participate in them.[5] They are never going to be strong enough to counterbalance state and capital, and so this fetishisation of decentralisation is misplaced. Better to have one strong, organised and centralised labour movement than a hundred decentralised peer-to-peer networks.

Ultimately, capital itself has to be challenged. People who act as labour need to start asking: why can't we start to organise things ourselves? Not through fetishising small-scale networks, but by demanding greater and greater control over the large organisations that dominate our society. The productive facilities that make things, the logistical networks that move things around the country, sophisticated information and communications systems. These things could be in public hands. They could be used not for private profit, but as a means of creating and distributing the things that society actually needs and wants. There would be no alien power of competition forcing people to work harder in exchange for less, or forcing governments to compromise on the quality of public services. People would not be forced to spend much of their lives in an alienating and conflictual labour–capital relationship. Technology which saves labour could be welcomed.

The election of 2017 was shortly followed by the disastrous Grenfell Tower fire. Today, the first principles of our society are private property and private profit, and anything else – such as providing safe living conditions for poor people – *is only possible insofar as it conforms to those first principles*. But we could operate differently: one of our first principles could be that everyone should have a home, and 'the economy' might have to bend itself to achieve that goal rather than vice versa. We could say the same about health or education. It is the centrality of capital accumulation as the motor of our economy that so distorts these priorities.

FINAL THOUGHTS: BRITAIN AFTER THE 2017 GENERAL ELECTION

Despite the fact that the Labour Party under Jeremy Corbyn obtained fewer seats than the Conservatives under Theresa May at the 2017 general election, it evidently came out of it very well. Corbyn's leadership had been widely ridiculed and written off, not just by the vast majority of newspaper commentators, but the most of his own MPs. May called her snap election in April 2017 because she saw a huge poll gap opening up and a divided Labour Party, and saw an opportunity to crush her opposition and usher in a potentially endless period of Tory dominance. Yet the election resulted in a hung parliament. May's authority and legitimacy to rule was massively reduced, and the Conservative Party came to look weak and scared. Corbyn's Labour Party got 40 per cent of the vote, which is almost as high as Tony Blair managed in his landslide victory of 1997. He emerged from the election vindicated against the charges that his vote would collapse, and looking far more convincing as a future prime minister than May. Why?

The first thing to note here is that May tried to use the idea of class to her advantage and it backfired. She had previously talked repeatedly about her desire to stand up for 'working-class' people, making heavy use of the 'right-wing class warrior' rhetoric I identified in Chapter 1. But there were huge and obvious contradictions in this persona, because she was clearly utterly terrified of the world of business and was never strong enough to challenge austerity and the 'free market' in any significant way. As we have seen, anti-immigrant language ultimately does nothing to hinder capital, and people who use this language in an effort to advance the cause of labour will, sooner or later, be exposed as weak charlatans. So it was in June 2017. May's claim to be representing workers, while all the while berating nurses for wanting a pay rise while on live TV, just appeared inconsistent and implausible. Pretty much the *only* thing she had to offer labour was racism, which, gratifyingly, was revealed as flimsy and unpersuasive.

The British media were utterly unequipped to deal with this eventuality. A long list of commentators, who had heaped scorn on Corbyn's supporters on the basis that were consigning the Labour Party to history, were now revealed to have been out of touch with a growing current of public opinion. Certainly, they had relied on a limited range of reference points, which they tended to see as yielding eternal and unchanging lessons. For instance, many had taken the fact that Labour lost the 1983 election on a comparatively left-wing manifesto, and won the 1997 one on a comparatively right-wing one, as evidence of some unquestionable law that Labour has to be right wing or die. This argument did not take into account the fairly obvious point that, as circumstances change, the things people are and aren't likely to support politically also changes.

In one sense, it was remarkable that Corbyn made such progress, because the platform he was running on was pushing at the boundaries of capitalist 'common sense' as it has been described here. He did not appear to accept unquestioningly that what is good for business is good for society, and that, therefore, the rich must be wrapped in cotton wool. He was unashamed about wanting to tax the wealthiest more, and had an explicitly redistributive agenda. Various nationalisations were also mooted. What changed to make this more acceptable as an electoral platform? It may be that for all its grimness, the Brexit vote had a strangely liberating effect. The 'right-wing class warrior' line unleashed Brexit as a means of making political gains out of the consequences of globalisation. Its main architects thought this would help British capital by rolling back various EU-derived regulations (see Chapter 5). But actually they (whether intentionally or not*) broke a taboo. Like a child who defies its parents for the first time and wants to do it again, the British people were apparently no longer willing to be terrified into doing what 'the markets' wanted them to do – the right wing of the Conservative Party, which sees itself as the most devoted acolyte of capital, opened the door to something else.

It is tempting to argue that Corbyn's progress was due to him reigniting the class struggle, but there are various reasons why this is very premature. First, Labour's unexpectedly good showing was at least in part due to the divisions in the capitalist class caused by Brexit. As I argued earlier, Brexit has been conducted as a conflict between different views on what is good for British capital. The Conservatives went too far in their 'right-wing class warrior' rhetoric, and scared a lot of very rich people who believe that British capitalism has to be *open*. Consequently it is in Remain areas that support swung most strongly to Labour in 2017. In strong Leave areas, if anything, things went the other way. This is not the same as a class revolt against the authority of capital. It may be that a lot of very wealthy capitalists see Labour as *less* threatening at this particular juncture than the Tories under May. Moreover, it is also true that Corbyn's own language (and more frequently that of high-profile advocates such as Paul Mason) tended to fudge occasionally towards the standard 'immigrants undermine British wages' line, which, as we saw earlier, is misleading and likely to damage rather than help the prospect of a stronger pro-labour platform. There is not yet enough self-confidence to reject these dead-ends explicitly, and this stems from the enduring power of the right-wing class warrior rhetoric identified in Chapter 1.

Second, while the Labour manifesto was praised for winning a lot of support, it was generally informed by the same 'economy that works for everyone' paradigm that I was criticising in Chapter 1. The key selling points were slightly higher taxes for the richest in exchange for better-funded public services. Once this is accomplished, the argument ran, everyone could benefit, since better health and education systems are better for business as well. This is not intended as a criticism, since to do more than this would have been beyond the pale for a British audience. It is simply to observe that it is not possible to imagine government being

---

* It probably varies depending on how much an individual wants actual power or just to be a celebrity.

run, at the moment, by people who are actively prepared to take labour's side against capital: the best we can hope for is fairly soft redistribution via the tax and welfare systems. As I argued earlier, true progress for the UK would be re-empowering labour in the workplace. It's possible that Corbyn realised this, but did not feel the population was ready for it to be at the heart of a general election campaign.

Third, there are certain weaknesses in policies that ostensibly seem radical – such as nationalisations, which moved towards the top of Labour's agenda. I made the point repeatedly in Chapter 5 that nationalisations, in and of themselves, do not necessarily mean one in the eye for capital. It is a problem for those specific capitalists who want to make profits out of public service delivery. But the main requirement of public services under capitalism is that they benefit *capital in general*: i.e. by helping with 'social reproduction' and the creation of 'indirect surplus value'. Nationalisations do not exempt public services from these functions and can just provide a more brutal means of enforcing them. As shown by the example of the NHS, government is just as likely as capital to make life miserable for those that work for it. In other words, nationalising things per se does not help us much. What matters is breaking the control capital has over our economy as a whole.

Of course, the bigger issue is as follows: let's say the Labour Party is elected on a comparatively radical manifesto, what would happen then? There would be dire warnings from capital and its interlocutors in the media that his policies would lead to a disastrous loss of confidence, investments moving abroad, labour being jettisoned to shore up profits, and so on. In fact, this started to happen after the 2017 election, with the Chancellor Phillip Hammond seeking to rally businesses into explicit support for the Conservatives over Labour, presenting the idea of a Corbyn-led government as a sufficiently existential crisis that etiquette and norms around corporate impartiality need to be discarded.[6] The closer Corbyn gets to power, the more likely this is to becoming a reality: investment strikes, dire warnings of job losses and capital flight. For now, the reason this kind of capitalist violence is relatively restrained is because business elites are terrified about what the Conservatives are doing with Brexit. In other words, Corbyn is progressing because capitalists as a class are divided: they can't decide whether a socialist Labour or a Tory Brexit is worse. This dilemma would go away if Corbyn assumed power.

Another question is whether Corbyn's own party would have the stomach for this kind of development. The right wing of the Labour

Party always used to say that they shared these left-wing principles but needed to compromise on them to get into power, otherwise those principles were pointless. Whether you accept that argument or not, there was always something disingenuous about it: even when it seemed the Labour Party does have a credible chance of power under Corbyn, the same figures were still trying to get rid of him and even, in some cases, actually pledging allegiance to his discredited opponents in the Conservative Party.[7] In other words, they do care about principles more than they care about Labour being in power: it's just that those principles are unshakeably in line with pro-capital common sense. Anyone who really wants to change the country needs to recognise that the point is not to avoid spooking business with moderate policies, but to prevent this kind of coercive power being exercised in the first place by emasculating capital. Any electoral advance by radical political parties needs to go hand in hand with increasing assertiveness by those who act as labour, and growing preparedness to assume control over the organisational and technological resources that are used to create and distribute goods and services. At the present time, with trade unionism and strike activity at historic lows, this latter part seems to be missing. This could be the Corbyn movement's fatal flaw.

But there is no point listing reasons for caution unless I suggest reasons for optimism as well. One narrative that emerged from the election was that the main cause of Corbyn's (relative) success was the high turnout among young people, which could be conveniently attributed to pledges around abolishing tuition fees and reinstating the Education Maintenance Allowance. This, in turn, gave right-wing commentators their new talking point: that young people today are entitled idiots (recall some of the quotes I offered in Chapter 8). Others make a fist of being conciliatory. The Tory MP Margot James says that 'we need to make the case for wealth creation to a new generation of young people'.[8] Ross Clark is sad about a growing disaffection among young people towards capitalism and cautions that right-wing people need to find a way of rebuilding this divide.[9] Much in Britain depends on this not happening.

In fact, it is overstating things to say that Corbynism is dependent on the young, since Labour did better than the Conservatives among various other age groups as well (according to YouGov, in 2017 one became more likely to vote Tory than Labour at age 47). 'The bulk of the Labour vote came from those more middle-aged than young.'[10] But let's accept the argument, and consider the question it raises for the purposes of this book. If it's true that young people are swinging things in important elections now, does that mean (as has already been claimed many times since the election) that age is becoming a more important societal division than class? The answer is that this might be the case *depending on what we understand by class*. If we see class as a means of categorising according to social/economic/cultural capital, then yes, maybe age is more important as a predictor of electoral preference.

But it is obvious that many people in this country, not just the young, do not like the world they are being offered: bad wages and insecure jobs, 'democratic' governments which are out of their depth when dealing with global capital, a sense of powerlessness at work and beyond. These things are widespread and they are not just limited to particular groups like the 'precariat' and other categorisations. These are issues that affect anyone who is severed from the means of production and forced to furnish surplus value to capital in exchange for a wage. It is why pensioners are likely to remain the only group who are completely immune to radical left politics in this country in the coming years. If young(ish) people are at the forefront of these changes it is because they have most to lose from a life spent in service to capital.

Notes

CHAPTER 1

1. Quoted in Phillip Mirowski (2013) *Never let a serious crisis go to waste*, Verso, p. 117.
2. Ed Miliband, 'What responsible capitalism is all about', *The Guardian*, 22 May 2013.
3. *Guardian* readers, 'Open thread: why do you keep your blinds down?', *The Guardian* blog, 8 October 2012.
4. Ross Clark, 'Corbyn has stirred the youth vote in a way that even Blair could not', *The Spectator*, 9 June 2017.
5. John Knefel, 'Bored with Occupy – and inequality: class issues fade along with protest coverage', *Fairness and Accuracy in Reporting*, 1 May 2012.
6. David Harvey (2013) *A companion to Marx's Capital volume II*, Verso, p. 196.
7. Johnathan Cribb, Robert Joyce and David Phillips (2012) *Living standards, poverty and inequality in the UK: 2012*, Institute for Fiscal Studies.
8. Nicholas Timmins, 'Public hardens attitudes to the poor', *Financial Times*, 13 December 2010.
9. Rachel Ormston and John Curtice (eds) (2015) *British social attitudes: the 32nd report*, NatCen social research.
10. John Pring, 'Anger after Reeves tells benefits claimants "Labour is not for you"', *Disability News Service*, 20 March 2015.
11. Alexandre Devecchio, 'Philippe Blond: "Trop longtemps le conservatisme a été l'otage du libéralisme"', *Le Figaro*, 21 October 2016.
12. Quoted in Alex Ross (2011) *Listen to this*, Fourth Estate, p. 231.
13. 'Rage of the working class', *The Sun*, 24 June 2016.
14. An insight offered by Ruth Milkman in her speech to the International Labour Process Conference, Sheffield, April 2017.
15. E.g. James Bloodworth, 'Labour is at risk of completely losing the working class vote', *International Business Times*, 31 August 2016; John Harris 'Britain is in the midst of a working class revolt', *The Guardian*, 17 June 2016.
16. John Harris, 'Britain is more divided than ever: now Labour has a chance to unify it', *The Guardian*, 10 June 2017.
17. Chris Curtis, 'How Britain voted at the 2017 General Election', YouGov blog, 13 June 2017.
18. Mirowski, *Never let a serious crisis go to waste*.

19. In my criticisms of Bourdieu, I am particularly influenced by Michael Burawoy; see for instance Michael Burawoy and Karl Von Holdt (2012) *Conversations with Bourdieu: the Johannesburg moment*, Wits University Press.

20. E.g. 'The biggest political divide in Britain is age', *The Economist*, 8 June 2017.

21. Guy Standing (2011) *The precariat: the new dangerous class*, Bloomsbury.

22. E.g. Robert Castell (2000) 'The roads to disaffiliation', *International Journal of Urban and Regional Research* 24(3): 519–35.

CHAPTER 2

1. Anwar Shaikh (2016) *Capitalism: competition, conflict, crises*, Oxford University Press, p. 206.

2. Karl Marx (1976) *Capital volume I*, Penguin, p. 376.

3. Ibid., p. 352.

4. Ibid., p. 381.

5. Ibid., p. 901.

6. Ibid., p. 793.

7. Ibid., pp. 896–7.

8. Ibid., pp. 873–4.

9. Ibid., p. 784.

10. Ibid., p. 484.

11. Ian Greer (2016) 'Welfare reform, precarity and the re-commodification of labour', *Work, Employment and Society* 30(1): 162–73.

12. Marx, *Capital volume I*, pp. 174–5.

13. Ibid., pp. 283–4.

14. Ibid., 481.

15. Karl Marx (1973) *Grundrisse*, Penguin, pp. 692–3.

16. Ibid., p. 158.

17. Karl Marx (1981) *Capital volume III*, Penguin, p. 507.

18. Marx, *Capital volume I*, p. 477.

19. Domenico Losurdo (2014) *Liberalism: A counter history*, Verso.

20. Ibid., p. 210.

21. Marx *Capital volume I*, p. 742.

22. Marx, *Grundrisse*, pp. 196–7.

23. Ibid., p. 649.

24. Ibid., p. 381.

25. Friedrich Hayek (2007 [1944]) *The road to serfdom*, University of Chicago Press, p. 149.

26. See Andrew Merrifield (1993) 'Place and space: a Lefebvrian reconciliation', *Transactions of the Institute of British Geographers*, 18(4): 516–31; see also Neil Brenner and Stuart Elden (2009) 'Henri Lefebvre on space, state, and territory', *International Political Sociology*, 3(4): 357–77.

27. James Meek (2017) 'Somerdale to Skarbimierz', *London Review of Books*, 39(8).
28. Ibid., p. 3.
29. Ibid., p. 6.
30. See Ernest Mandel's introduction to Marx (1978) *Capital volume II*, p. 47.
31. Karl Marx (1978) *Capital volume II*, Penguin, p. 192.
32. Ibid., p. 87.

CHAPTER 3

1. Goran Therborn (2017) 'Dynamics of inequality', *New Left Review* 103: 81–2.
2. Quoted in ibid., pp. 71–2.
3. Ibid., p. 72.
4. See Chris Bellfield, Johnathan Cribb, Andrew Hood and Robert Joyce (2015) *Living standards, poverty and inequality in the UK*, Institute for Fiscal Studies. This table drawn from data available at: www.ifs.org.uk/tools_and_ resources/incomes_in_uk.
5. Danny Dorling (2015) *Injustice*, Policy Press, data available at: www. dannydorling.org/books/injustice/figures/fig-14.pdf.
6. Anne Daguerre (2011) 'New corporate elites and the erosion the Keynesian social compact', *Work, Employment and Society* 28(2): 323–34.
7. William Brown, Alex Bryson and John Forth (2008) 'Competition and the retreat from collective bargaining', *National Institute for Economic and Social Research*, discussion paper No. 318.
8. On the correlation between union density and income equality, see David Card, Thomas Lemieux and Craig Riddell (2003) 'Unionization and wage inequality: a comparative study of the US, the UK and Canada', *National Bureau of Economic Research*, working paper 9473.
9. Keith Ewing and John Hendy (2012) *Reconstruction after the crisis*, The Institute for Employment Rights. Note that their dataset is compiled from various other sources, from which I use Simon Milner (1995) 'The coverage of collective pay-setting institutions in Britain, 1895–1990', *British Journal of Industrial Relations* 33(1): 69–91 (for years 1961–90); Keith Brook (2002) 'Trade union membership: an analysis of data from the autumn 2001 LFS', *Labour Market Trends* 110(7): 343–54; note that data after 1999 are obtained using a different methodology which necessitates caution in interpreting the data before and after this juncture – see Brook, 'Trade union membership', for more details.
10. For more data on this correlation, see Lydia Hayes and Tonia Novitz (2014) *Trade unions and economic inequality*, Institute for Employment Rights.
11. Ernest Mandel (1978) *Late Capitalism*, Verso, p. 238.
12. Chris Howell (2005) *Trade unions and the state*, Princeton University Press.

13. See Chris Wood's chapter in Peter Hall and David Soskice's (2001) *Varieties of capitalism*, Oxford University Press.
14. www.wapping-dispute.org.uk/.
15. Jane Wills (2009) 'Subcontracted employment and its challenge to labor', *Labor Studies Journal* 34(4): 441–60.
16. See Michael Terry (1999) 'Systems of employee collective representation in non-union firms in the UK', *Industrial Relations Journal* 30(1): 16–30.
17. Peter Turnbull (1991) 'Labour market deregulation and economic performance: the case of Britain's docks', *Work, Employment and Society* 5(1): 17–35.
18. Gerald Davis and Adam Cobb (2010) 'Corporations and economic inequality around the globe: the paradox of hierarchy', *Research in Organisational Behaviour* 30: 35–53.
19. Özlem Onaran (2014) *State intervention for wage-led development*, CLASS policy paper.
20. Stephen Clarke and Conor D'Arcy (2016) *Low pay in Britain*, Resolution Foundation.
21. Costas Lapavitsas (2013) *Profiting without producing: how finance exploits us all*, Verso.
22. Michael Roberts 'Thatcher: there was no alternative', blog 9 April 2013; available at https://thenextrecession.wordpress.com/2013/04/09/thatcher-there-was-no-alternative/ (accessed 8 May 2016).
23. On China, see Minqi Li (2016) *China and the 21st century crisis*, Pluto; and David Harvey (2005) *A brief history of neoliberalism*, Oxford University Press.
24. Andrew Glyn and Bob Sutcliffe (1972) *British capitalism, workers and the profits squeeze*, Penguin.
25. Tim Butcher, Richard Dickens and Alan Manning (2012) 'Minimum wage and wage inequality: some theory and an application to the UK', *Centre for Economic Performance*, discussion paper #1177.
26. Robert Joyce and Luke Sibieta (2013) *Labour's record on poverty and inequality*, Institute for Fiscal Studies.
27. For a critical summary of New Labour's trade union agenda, see Paul Smith and Gary Morton (2006) 'Nine years of New Labour: neoliberalism and workers' rights', *British Journal of Industrial Relations* 44(3) 401–20.
28. For instance John Mcilroy (2010) 'Ten years of New Labour: workplace learning, social partnership and union revitalisation in Britain', *British Journal of Industrial Relations* 46(2): 283–313; see also Helen Rainbird and Mark Stuart (2011) 'The state and the union learning agenda in Britain', *Work, Employment and Society* 25(2): 202–17.
29. Vidu Badigannavar and John Kelly (2011) 'Partnership and organizing: an empirical assessment of two contrasting approaches to union revitalization in the UK', *Economic and Industrial Democracy* 32(1): 5–27; see also John Kelly (2004) 'Social partnership agreements in Britain: Labor cooperation

and compliance', *Industrial Relations: A Journal of Economy and Society* 43(1): 267–92.

30. Andy Danford, Michael Richardson, Paul Stewart, Stephanie Tailby and Martin Upchurch (2005) 'Workplace partnership and employee voice in the UK: comparative case studies of union strategy and worker experience', *Economic and Industrial Democracy* 26(4): 593–620.

31. Greer, 'Welfare reform'.

32. Bellfield et al., *Living standards, poverty and inequality in the UK*.

33. Ibid.

34. John Hills, Jack Cunliffe, Ludovica Gambaro and Polina Obolenskaya (2013) *Winners and losers in the crisis: the changing anatomy of economic inequality in the UK 2007–2010*, Centre for Analysis of Social Exclusion.

35. Onaran, *State intervention for wage-led development*.

36. Trade Union Congress, 'Workers suffering the most severe squeeze in real earnings since Victorian times', 12 October 2014.

37. Chris Bellfield, Johnathan Cribb, Andrew Hood and Robert Joyce (2016) *Living standards, poverty and inequality in the UK: 2016*, Institute for Fiscal Studies.

38. John Bingham, 'Working families are the "new poor", says Britain's leading economic think tank', *The Telegraph*, 19 July 2016.

39. Ralph Darlington, 'Trade Union Bill: the challenge for the trade unions', University of Salford blog, 4 August 2015.

40. Patrick Butler 'DWP "punishing" low-paid full-time workers under new benefits rule', *The Guardian*, 14 April 2016.

41. Jon Stone, 'Thousands have died after being found "fit for work" by the DWP's benefits tests', *The Independent*, 27 August 2015.

42. Jay Wiggan (2015) 'Reading active labour market policy politically: an autonomist analysis of Britain's Work Programme and Mandatory Work Activity', *Critical Social Policy* 35(3): 369–92.

43. Table 2 is a simplified presentation of the chart presented in Valentina Romei, 'How wages fell in the UK while the economy grew', *Financial Times*, 2 March 2017.

44. Engelbert Stockhammer (2012) 'Financialization, income distribution and the crisis', *Investigación económica* 71(279): 39–70.

45. For key accounts see Gerald Epstein (2005) *Financialization and the world economy*, Edward Elgar; and Greta Krippner (2005) 'The financialisation of the American economy', *Socio-Economic Review* 3: 173–208.

46. Costas Lapavitsas (2011) 'Theorizing financialisation', *Work, Employment and Society* 25(4): 611–26.

47. See Engelbert Stockhammer (2006) 'Shareholder value orientation and the investment-profit puzzle', *Journal of Post-Keynesian Economics* 28(2): 193–215; and Julie Froud, Colin Haslam, Sukhdev Johal and Karel Williams (2000) 'Shareholder value and financialisation: consultancy promises, management motives', *Economy and Society* 29(1): 80–110.

48. William Lazonick and Mary O'Sullivan (2000) 'Maximising shareholder value: a new ideology for corporate governance', *Economy and Society* 29(1): 13–35.
49. Jan Fichtner (2013) 'Hedge funds: agents of change for financialisation', *Critical perspectives on international business* 9(4): 358–76.
50. Ibid., p. 366.
51. Froud et al., 'Shareholder value and financialisation', p. 104.
52. Michel Aglietta (2000) 'Shareholder value and corporate governance: some tricky questions', *Economy and Society* 29(1): 146–59.
53. Harvey, *A companion to Marx's Capital volume II*, p. 196.
54. Marx, *Capital volume III*, p. 516.
55. Ibid., p. 469.
56. Suzanne De Brunhoff (2015) *Marx on money*, Verso, p. 41; see also Harvey, *A companion to Marx's Capital volume II*.
57. See Lapavitsas (2013) *Profiting without producing*, Verso.
58. Daguerre, 'New corporate elites'.
59. Matt Vidal (2013) 'Postfordism as a dysfunctional accumulation regime', *Work, Employment and Society* 27(3): 451–71.
60. See Thibault Darcillon (2015) 'How does finance affect labor market institutions? An empirical analysis in 16 OECD countries', *Socio-Economic Review* 13(3): 477–504.
61. Lucio Baccaro and Chris Howell (2011) 'A common neoliberal trajectory: the transformation of industrial relations in advanced capitalism', *Politics and Society* 39(4): 521–63.
62. Danford et al., 'Workplace partnership'; see also Kelly, 'Social partnership agreements in Britain'.
63. See Alan Felstead, Harvey Krahn and Marcus Powell (1999) 'Young and old at risk: comparative trends in "non-standard" patterns of employment in Canada and the United Kingdom', *International Journal of Manpower* 20(5): 277–97.
64. OECD, *Employment outlook 2015*, 9 July 2015.
65. *Les status d'emploi*, Alternatives economiques poche #52, November 2011; see also Alan Booth, Juan Dolado and Jeff Frank (2002) 'Symposium on temporary work: introduction', *The Economic Journal* 113(48): F181–F188.
66. Aristea Koukiadaki (2010) *The regulation of fixed-term work in Britain*, Japanese Institute for Labor Policy and Training.
67. Nigel Morris, 'Zero-hours contracts to become main source of income for 1m British workers', *The Independent*, 9 March 2016.
68. Chartered Institute for Personnel and Development (2015) *Employment, regulation and the labour market*, Policy report, p. 6.
69. 'Involuntary temporary jobs driving rising employment', Trade Union Congress blog, 9 August 2013.
70. Standing, *The precariat*, p. 34.

71. 'Decline in employment tribunal claims continues', *Legal action group news*, 13 June 2014.
72. Matthew Lynn 'The self-employed will overtake the public sector with the "gig economy"', *The Telegraph*, 18 January 2016.
73. Ibid.
74. See Sarah Wall (2015) 'Dimensions of precariousness in an emerging sector of self-employment', *Gender, Work & Organization* 22(3): 221–36; Nickela Anderson and Karen Hughes (2010) 'The business of caring: women's self-employment and the marketization of care', *Gender, Work & Organization* 17(4): 381–405.
75. Conor D'Arcy, 'Britain's self-employed workforce is growing – but their earnings have been heading in the other direction', *Resolution Foundation* blog, 18 October 2016.
76. Jan Cavelle 'Uber drivers are missing the point of self-employment', *Real Business*, 31 October 2016.
77. Jason Moyer-Lee '"Gig workers" already have rights – all we have to do is enforce them', *The Guardian*, 5 July 2017.
78. Rob Moss, 'Dependent contractor status proposed in Taylor review', *Personnel Today*, 10 July 2017.
79. Quoted in Moshe Marvit, 'How crowdworkers became the ghosts in the digital machine', *The Nation*, 24 February 2014.
80. 'Bogus self-employment: new government measures on false self-employment', Unite the Union blog, 17 June 2014.
81. Geraint Harvey, Carl Rhodes, Sheena Vachhani and Karen Williams (2017) 'Neo-villeiny and the service sector: the case of hyperflexible and precarious work in fitness centres', *Work, Employment and Society* 31: 19–35.
82. Duncan Gallie, Alan Felstead, Francis Green and Hande Inanc (2017) 'The hidden face of job insecurity', *Work, Employment and Society* 31(1): 36–53.
83. Robert MacDonald (2009) 'Precarious work: risk, choice and poverty traps', in Andy Furlong (ed.) *Handbook of youth and young adulthood*, Routledge.
84. Felstead et al., 'Young and old at risk'.
85. Tracy Shildrick (2015) 'Young people and social class in the United Kingdom', in Johanna Wyn and Helen Cahill (eds) *Handbook of children and youth studies*, Springer Reference.
86. Kari Hadjivassiliu, Arianna Tassinari, Stefan Speckesser, Sam Swift and Christine Bertram (2015) 'Country report – United Kingdom', *Strategic transitions for youth labour in Europe*, working paper 3.
87. Lisa Russell (2014) 'Formerly NEET young people's pathways to work: a case study approach', *Power and Education* 6(2): 182–96.
88. See, for example, Charlie Brinkhurst-Cliff, 'Why don't young people want to join trade unions?', New Statesman, 22 January 2014.
89. Janet Smithson and Suzan Lewis (2000) 'Is job insecurity changing the psychological contract?', *Personnel Review* 29(6): 680–702.

90. Pauline Leonard, Susan Halford and Katie Bruce (2016) '"The new degree?" Constructing internships in the third sector', *Sociology* 50(2): 383–99.

91. On the comparison between internships and workfare which takes artistic and media work as a case study, see David Lee (2015) 'Internships, workfare and the cultural industries: a British perspective', *tripleC* 13(2): 459–70.

92. Standing, *The precariat*, p. 75–6.

93. See Annalisa Murgia and Barbara Poggio (2014) 'At risk of de-skilling and trapped by passion: a picture of precarious highly-educated young workers in Italy, Spain and the United Kingdom', in Myra Hamilton, Lorenza Antonucci and Steven Roberts (eds) *Young people and social policy in Europe*, Springer.

94. Colin Bryson and Richard Blackwell (2006) 'Managing temporary workers in higher education: still at the margins?', *Personnel Review* 35(2): 207–24.

95. See Kim Hoque and Ian Kirkpatrick (2003) 'Non-standard employment in the management and professional workforce: training, consultation and gender implications', *Work, Employment and Society* 17(4): 667–89; and Ian Kirkpatrick and Kim Hoque. 'A retreat from permanent employment? Accounting for the rise of professional agency work in UK public services', *Work, Employment and Society* 20(4): 649–66.

96. David Harvey (1990) *The condition of postmodernity*, Blackwell.

CHAPTER 4

1. Thomas Ligotti (2009) *My work is not yet done*, Virgin, p. 173.

2. Sam Greenhill, Laura Chesters and Gerri Peeve, 'The shaming of Sir Shifty', *Daily Mail*, 25 July 2016.

3. Alistair Heath, 'Philip Green's antics mustn't make us lose faith in capitalism', *The Telegraph*, 20 October 2016.

4. Simon Goodley and Jonathan Ashby, 'A day at "the gulag": what it's like to work at Sports Direct's warehouse', *The Guardian*, 9 December 2015.

5. BBC, 'Amazon workers face "increased risk of mental illness"', 25 November 2013.

6. Phil Taylor, Ian Cunningham, Kirsty Newsome and Dora Scholarios (2010) 'Too Scared to go sick', *Industrial Relations Journal* 41(4): 270–288.

7. Ibid.

8. James Barker (1993) 'Tightening the iron cage: concertive control in self-managing teams', *Administrative Science Quarterly* 38(3): 408–37.

9. Darius Mehri (2006) 'The darker side of lean: an insider's perspective on the realities of the Toyota production system', *The Academy of Management Perspectives* 20(2): 21–42.

10. Ibid., p. 26.

11. Rick Delbridge (2000) *Life on the line in contemporary manufacturing: the workplace experience of lean production and the Japanese model*, Oxford University Press.

12. See also Paul Landsbergis, Janet Cahill and Peter Schnall (1999) 'The impact of lean production and related new systems of work organization on worker health', *Journal of Occupational Health Psychology* 4(2): 108–30.

13. Wayne Lewchuk, Paul Stewart and Charlotte Yates (2001) 'Quality of working life in the automobile industry: a Canada-UK comparative study', *New Technology, Work and Employment* 16(2): 72–87.

14. Jamie Woodcock (2017) *Working the phones*, Pluto Press, p. 41.

15. David Foster Wallace (2011) *The pale king*, Penguin, pp. 379–81.

16. Sadi Mann (2007) 'Sadi Mann on why boredom at work is no longer restricted to 'boring' jobs', *The Psychologist* 20: 90–3.

17. For an important and insightful account of call centre work see Woodcock, *Working the phones*.

18. E.g. Peter Fleming and Andrew Sturdy (2011) '"Being yourself" in the electronic sweatshop: new forms of normative control', *Human Relations* 64(2): 177–200.

19. Owen Shipton, 'Fuck working in a call centre', *Vice*, 20 November 2014.

20. BBC, 'Currys interview "humiliation" as graduate "made to dance"', 5 September 2013.

21. E.g. Bob Carter, Andy Danford, Debra Howcroft, Helen Richardson, Andrew Smith and Phil Taylor (2011) 'Lean and mean in the civil service: the case of processing in HMRC', *Public Money & Management* 31(2): 115–22; Bob Carter, Andy Danford, Debra Howcroft, Helen Richardson, Andrew Smith and Phil Taylor (2011) '"All they lack is a chain": lean and the new performance management in the British civil service', *New Technology, Work and Employment* 26(2): 83–97.

22. Martha Crowley (2012) 'Control and dignity in professional, manual, and service-sector employment', *Organization Studies* 33(10): 1383–406.

23. Christopher Grey (1998) 'On being a professional in a "big six" firm', *Accounting, Organizations and Society* 23(5–6): 569–87.

24. Jodi Kantor and David Streitfeld, 'Inside Amazon: wrestling big ideas in a bruising workplace', *New York Times*, 15 August 2015.

25. Emily Douglas (2016) 'Daily Telegraph installs workplace monitors under staff desks', *HR Grapevine*, 12 January 2016.

26. Ben Farmer, 'More employees under surveillance at work', *Daily Telegraph*, 9 January 2008.

27. Olivia Rudgard, 'Why are employees using wearable tech to monitor their workers?', *Daily Telegraph*, 1 July 2015.

28. Jack Murtha, 'What it's like to get paid for clicks', *Columbia Journalism Review*, 13 July 2015; see also Anonymous, 'The secret life of a clickbait creator', *The Guardian*, 21 November 2016.

29. Shawn Long, Richie Goodman and Chase Clow (2010) 'The electronic panopticon: organization and surveillance in virtual work', in Shawn Long (ed.) *Communication, relations and practices in virtual work*, Business Science Reference.

30. Duncan Gallie (2012) 'Skills, job control and the quality of work: the evidence from Britain. Geary lecture 2012', *The Economic and Social Review* 43(3): 325–41.

31. Francis Green (2004) 'Work intensification, discretion and the decline in well-being at work', *Eastern Economic Journal* 30(4): 615–25.

32. Duncan Gallie, Alan Felstead, Francis Green and Hande Inanc (2014) 'The quality of work in Britain over the economic crisis', *International Review of Sociology* 4(2): 207–24.

33. Robert Hewison (2014) *Cultural capital*, Verso.

34. Ibid.

35. Andrew Brighton (2006) 'Consumed by the political: the ruination of the Arts Council', *Critical Quarterly* 48(1): 1–13.

36. Eleanora Belfiore (2012) '"Defensive instrumentalism" and the legacy of New Labour's cultural policies', *Cultural Trends* 21(2): 103–11.

37. Paul Thompson, Rachel Parker and Stephen Cox (2016) 'Interrogating creative theory and creative work: inside the games studio', *Sociology* 50(2): 316–32.

38. Ergin Bulut (2015) 'Playboring in the tester pit: the convergence of precarity and the degradation of fun in video game testing', *Television & New Media* 16(3): 240–58.

39. I have written on this point at great length previously: e.g. Charles Umney and Lefteris Kretsos (2014) 'Creative labour and collective interaction: the working lives of young jazz musicians in London', *Work, Employment and Society* 28(4): 571–88.

40. Umair Haque, 'The asshole factory', *Medium*, 21 April 2015.

41. Joshua Kopstein, 'Your boss can now monitor your mood on Slack, with help of AI', *Vocativ*, 18 April 2017.

42. Phil Taylor and Peter Bain (2003) ' "Subterranean worksick blues": humour as subversion in two call centres', *Organization Studies* 24(9): 1487–509.

43. Mahmoud Ezzamel, Hugh Wilmott and Frank Worthington (2001) 'Power, control and resistance in the "factory that time forgot"', *Journal of Management Studies* 38(8): 1053–79.

44. Dale Tweedie and Sasha Hollie (2016) 'The subversive craft worker: challenging "disutility" theories of management control', *Human Relations* 69(9): 1877–900.

45. Roland Gribben, 'Employment tribunals drop by 70% as staff discouraged by fees', *Daily Telegraph*, 17 March 2015.

46. Eleanor Kirk, Morag McDermott and Nicole Busby (2015) 'Employment tribunal claims: debunking the myths', *Policy Bristol Policy Report*, 1/2015.

47. Ian Greer and Marco Hauptmeier (2016) 'Management whipsawing: the staging of labor competition under capitalism', *ILR Review* 61(9): 29–52.

48. Guglielmo Meardi (2012) 'Union immobility? Trade unions and freedom of movement in the enlarged EU', *British Journal of Industrial Relations* 50(1): 99–120.

49. Kat Baker, 'British Airways' second strike injunction could damage Unite's reputation', *Personnel Today*, 18 May 2010.

50. Helen Pidd and Dan Milmo, 'BA strike cancelled after airline wins high court injunction', *The Guardian*, 17 May 2010.

51. Arjun Mahadevan, 'The Ritzy strike's back', *Rs21*, 26 September 2016.

52. Vera Weghmann, 'John Lewis Partnership: bring the cleaners into the partnership!', UVW blog, 16 September 2016.

53. Jamie Woodcock, 'Learning lessons from Deliveroo and UberEast', Pluto Press blog, undated.

54. Rob Davies, 'Ryanair pilots form unofficial union in battle with Michael O'Leary', *The Guardian*, 2 October 2017.

55. Claire Churchard, 'Trade union reforms are "outdated response", warns CIPD', *People Management*, 9 September 2015.

56. Darlington, *Trade Union Bill*.

57. BBC, 'Carr review to make no recommendations', 5 August 2014.

58. BBC, 'Southern Rail's "Tweet RMT" plea was "a mistake"', 21 November 2016.

59. Regulatory Policy Committee (2015) *Red rated impact assessment opinions (since March 2015)*, Regulatory Policy Committee, 18 August.

60. BBC, 'Construction workers win payouts for "blacklisting"', 9 May 2016.

61. Leo McKinstry, 'Unions vs workers – this is David Cameron's chance', *The Spectator*, 11 July 2015.

62. BBC, 'Conservative Party to launch own trade union movement', 30 September 2015.

CHAPTER 5

1. David Cameron, 'We've saved the economy from ruin: don't let Ed Miliband spoil it', *The Telegraph*, 25 April 2015.

2. Roberto Stefan Foa and Yascha Mounk (2017) 'The signs of deconsolidation', *Journal of Democracy* 27(3): 5–17.

3. Rys Farthing and Alex Hudson, 'What would make young people get interested in politics', *New Statesman*, 9 April 2015.

4. E.g. Ben Wright, 'There's a sinister strain of anti-intellectualism to Gove's dismissal of "experts"', *Daily Telegraph*, 21 June 2016; see also Chris York, 'Professor Brian Cox says Michael Gove's "anti-experts" stance is the "road back to the cave"', *Huffpost United Kingdom*, 2 July 2016.

5. E.g. Will Gore, 'As *Daily Mail* and *Sun* readers complain they were misinformed about Brexit, how do we respond?', *The Independent*, 27 June 2016.

6. Johnathan Freedland, 'Post-truth politicians such as Donald Trump and Boris Johnson are no joke', *The Guardian*, 13 May 2016.

7. Franco Moretti and Dominique Pestre (2015) 'Bankspeak: the language of World Bank reports', *New Left Review* 92.

8. Marx, *Capital volume I*, p. 390.

9. E.g. Ralph Miliband (1970) 'The capitalist state – a reply to N. Poulantzas', *New Left Review* I/59; Nicos Poulantzas (1976) 'The capitalist state – a reply to Miliband and Laclau', *New Left Review* I/95.

10. Theda Skocpol (1980) 'Political response to capitalist crisis: neo-Marxist theories of the state and the case of the New Deal', *Politics & Society* 10(2): 155–201.

11. Geoffrey Levy, 'The man who hated Britain', *Daily Mail*, 27 September 2013.

12. Robert Dahl, quoted in Ralph Miliband (1969) *The state in capitalist society*, Weidenfield and Nicholson, pp. 2–3.

13. Ibid., p. 56.

14. Ibid., p. 190.

15. Martin Carnoy and Manuel Castells (2001) 'Globalization, the knowledge society, and the network state: Poulantzas at the millennium', *Global Networks* 1(1): 1–18.

16. Ibid., p. 6.

17. See Skocpol (ibid.).

18. Fred Block (1977) 'The ruling class does not rule', *Socialist Revolution* 33(7): 6–28.

19. E.g. Erik Swyngedouw (2005) 'Dispossessing H2O: the contested terrain of water privatization', *Capitalism Nature Socialism* 16(1): 81–98.

20. For the most influential account of the differences between the British/American 'liberal market economy' versus the German/Japanese 'coordinated market economy', see Peter Hall and David Soskice (2001) *Varieties of capitalism*, Oxford University Press.

21. Ibid.

22. Francesca Froy (2013) 'Global policy developments towards industrial policy and skills', *Oxford Review of Economic Policy* 29(2): 344–60.

23. Ewart Keep and Susan James (2012) 'A Bermuda triangle of policy? "Bad jobs", skills policy and incentives to learn at the bottom end of the labour market', *Journal of Education Policy* 22(7): 211–30.

24. Tess Lanning, 'The real story behind the rise in apprenticeships under the coalition', *The Guardian*, 11 October 2012.

25. Phillip Toner (2008) 'Survival and decline of the apprenticeship system in the Australian and UK construction agencies', *British Journal of Industrial Relations* 41(6): 413–38.

26. Maarten Goos and Alan Manning (2007) 'Lovely and lousy jobs: the rising polarization of work in Britain', *Review of Economics and Statistics* 89(1): 118–33.

27. Keep and James, 'A Bermuda triangle of policy?'.

28. BBC, 'Most graduates "in non-graduate jobs" says CIPD', 19 August 2015.

29. Kate Page, 'Graduates in non-graduate jobs – what's the story', HEFCE blog, 12 October 2016.

30. Lee Harvey (2000) 'New realities: the relationship between higher education and employment', *Tertiary Education and Management* 6(1): 3–17.

31. Ann-Marie Bathmaker, Nicola Ingram and Richard Waller (2013) 'Higher education, social class and the mobilisation of capitals: recognising and playing the game', *British Journal of the Sociology of Education* 34(5): 723–34.

32. Denis Campbell, 'How much is the government really privatising the NHS?', *The Guardian*, 15 August 2016.

33. Nick Krachler and Ian Greer (2015) 'When does marketisation lead to privatisation? Profit-making in English health services after the 2012 Health and Social Care Act', *Social Science & Medicine* 124: 215–33.

34. Jennie Auffenberg, Genevieve Coderre-LaPalme and Ian Greer (2016) 'Success and failure in anti-privatization campaigns', unpublished working paper.

35. Nigel Morris, 'Health secretary Jeremy Hunt gains powers to shut good hospitals without consultation', *The Independent*, 11 March 2014.

36. Calum Paton (2001) 'The state in health: global capitalism, conspiracy, cock-up and competitive change in the NHS', *Public Policy and Administration* 16(4): 61–83.

37. Sharon Bolton (2004) 'A simple matter of control? NHS hospital nurses and new management', *Journal of Management Studies* 41(2): 317–33.

38. Hannah Cooke (2006) 'Seagull management and the control of nursing work', *Work, Employment and Society* 22(2): 223–43.

39. Sophie Borland, 'NHS bullying is a threat to patients', *Daily Mail*, 23 July 2015.

40. Department of Health (2015) *Culture change in the NHS: applying the lessons of the Francis enquiries*, Department of Health.

41. Press Association, 'Government faces "breaking own wage laws" unless NHS given £280m boost – unions', *Daily Mail*, 30 September 2016.

42. Jo Faragher, 'Job insecurity among public sector workers rises', *People Management*, 31 March 2014.

43. Stephen Bach and Alexandra Stroleny (2014) 'Restructuring local government employment relations: pay determination and employee participation in tough times', *Transfer* 20(3): 343–56; Kim Mather and Roger Seifert (2016) 'Police pay – contested and contestable', *Indutrial Relations Journal* 47(3): 204–19; Alistair Kleebauer (2015) 'Union concern over "undermining" of NHS Pay Review Body's remit', *Nursing Standard* 29(51): 9.

44. Anushka Asthana, Heather Stewart and Rowena Mason, 'Academisation of schools will lead to more pay disputes, union warns', *The Guardian*, 16 March 2016.

45. Douglas Martin (2017) 'Making tax and social security decisions: lean and deskilling in the UK civil service', *New Technology, Work and Employment* 32(2): 146–59.

46. John Lanchester (2017) 'Between Victoria and Vauxhall', *London Review of Books* 39(11): 3–6, p. 3.

47. Hewison, *Cultural capital*.
48. Tom Crewe (2016) 'The strange death of municipal England', *London Review of Books* 38(24): 6–10.
49. For an important theoretical statement on marketization see Ian Greer and Virginia Doellgast (2017) 'Marketization, inequality and institutional change: towards a new framework for comparative employment relations', *Journal of Industrial Relations* 59(2): 192–208.
50. Grace Lewis, 'Thousands of NHS staff made redundant and then re-hired, MP admits', *People Management*, 18 March 2014.
51. Aztec History: www.aztec-history.com/aztec-sacrifice.html.
52. Carnoy and Castells, 'Globalization'.
53. Cédric Durand (2017) *Fictitious capital*, Verso, pp. 153–4.
54. Vidal, 'Postfordism'.
55. Elmer Altvater and Birgit Mahnkopf (1997) 'The world market unbound', *Review of International Political Economy* 4(3): 448–71.
56. Jamie Peck and Adam Tickell (1994) 'Searching for a new institutional fix: the after-Fordist crisis and the global-local disorder', in Ash Amin (ed.) *Post-Fordism: a reader*, Blackwell.
57. Chris Howell (2016) 'Regulating class in the neoliberal era', *Work, Employment and Society* 30(4): 573–89.
58. Jane Lethbridge, Ian Greer, Lefteris Kretsos, Charles Umney and Geoff White (2014) *Industrial relations in central public administration: recent trends and features*, Eurofound.
59. E.g. Özlem Onaran and Giorgos Galanis (2014) 'Income distribution and growth: a global model', *Environment and Planning A* 46(10): 2489–513; see also Engelbert Stockhammer, Özlem Onaran and Stefan Ederer (2009) 'Functional income distribution and aggregate demand in the Euro area', *Cambridge Journal of Economics* 31(3): 131–59.
60. Colin Leys (2003) *Market-driven politics*, Verso.
61. Mark Evans (2010) 'Cameron's competition state', *Policy Studies* 31(1): 91–115.
62. E.g. Timothy Sinclair (1994) 'Passing judgement: credit rating processes as regulatory mechanisms of governance in the emerging world order', *Review of International Political Economy* 1(1): 133–59.
63. For more on the comparison between financial analysis and theology, see Joseph Vogl (2014) *The spectre of capital*, Stanford University Press.
64. Zsofia Barta and Alison Johnston (2017) 'Rating politics? Partisan discrimination in credit ratings in developed economies', *Comparative Political Studies*, published online before print.
65. Laura Hughes, 'Britain will cut taxes and take on EU if it tries to "punish" UK for Brexit, suggests David Davis', *Daily Telegraph*, 9 December 2016.
66. Catherine Barnard, Simon Deakin and Richard Hobbs (2003) 'Opting-out of the 48hr week: employer necessity or individual choice', *Industrial Law Journal* 32: 223–52.

67. Bruce Philp, Gary Slater and Daniel Wheatley (2015) 'New Labour and working time regulation: a Marxian analysis of the UK economy', *Cambridge Journal of Economics* 39(3): 711–32.
68. Christopher Williams, 'Theresa May backtracks on putting workers on company boards', *Daily Telegraph*, 21 November 2016.
69. Claire Churchard, 'Ban "Swedish derogation" to end pay abuses, says TUC', *People Management*, 2 September 2013.
70. Chris Forde and Gary Slater (2016) 'Labour market regulation and the "competition state": an analysis of the implementation of the Agency Worker Regulations in the UK', *Work, Employment and Society* 30(4): 590–606.
71. Frances Ryan, 'Death has become a part of Britain's benefits system', *The Guardian*, 27 August 2015.
72. Jon Stone, 'Iain Duncan Smith's Work Programme fails to find work for 70 per cent of people', *The Independent*, 21 October 2015.

CHAPTER 6

1. Rebecca Solnit, 'From lying to leering', *London Review of Books* 39(2): 3–7.
2. Dylan Riley (2017) 'American Brumaire', *New Left Review* 103: 30.
3. Catharine MacKinnon (1982) 'Feminism, Marxism, method, and the state: an agenda for theory', *Signs: Journal of Women in Culture and Society* 7(3): 515–44.
4. Quoted in MacKinnon, 'Feminism, Marxism, method, and the state'.
5. Silvia Federici (2004) *Caliban and the witch*, Autonomedia.
6. Isabella Bakker (2007) 'Social reproduction and the constitution of a gendered political economy', *New Political Economy* 12(4): 541–56.
7. Jeffry Larson, Stephan Wilson and Rochelle Beley (1994) 'The impact of job insecurity on marital and family relationships', *Family Relations* 43(2): 138–43.
8. David Bloom, David Canning, Gunther Fink and Jocelyn Finlay (2009) 'Fertility, female labor force participation, and the demographic dividend', *Journal of Economic Growth* 14(2): 79–101.
9. Julie MacLeavy (2011) 'A "new politics" of austerity, workfare and gender? The UK coalition government's welfare reform proposals', *Cambridge Journal of Regions, Economy and Society* 4(3): 355–67.
10. Linda MacDowell (2005) 'Love, money, and gender divisions of labour: some critical reflections on welfare-to-work policies in the UK', *Journal of Economic Geography* 5(3): 365–79.
11. Linda Dickens (2007) 'The road is long: thirty years of equality legislation in Britain', *British Journal of Industrial Relations* 45(3): 463–94.
12. Ibid.
13. Ibid., p. 468.

14. Bob Hepple (2011) 'Enforcing equality law: two steps forward and two steps backwards for reflexive regulation', *Industrial Law Journal* 40(4): 315–35.
15. BBC, 'Fawcett Society in legal challenge to 'unfair' budget', 1 August 2010.
16. Hazel Conley (2012) 'Using equality to challenge austerity: new actors, old problems', *Work, Employment and Society* 26(2), p. 355.
17. Ibid., p. 357.
18. Ian Roper and Ahu Tatli (2014) 'Recent developments in the equality and diversity agenda in the UK: the "big society" under austerity', in Alain Klarsfeld, Lize Booysen, Eddy Ng, Ian Roper and Ahu Tatli (eds) *International handbook on diversity management at work*, Edward Elgar.
19. Hazel Conley (2012) 'Economic crisis, austerity and gender equality: the UK case', *European Gender Equality Law Review* 2: 14–19.
20. Hazel Conley (2012) 'Using equality to challenge austerity: new actors, old problems', *Work, Employment and Society* 26(2): 349–59.
21. Ibid.
22. Claire Annesley (2014) *UK austerity policy – a feminist perspective*, Friedrich Ebert Stiftung.
23. Nick Bailey (2016) 'Exclusionary employment in Britain's broken labour market', *Critical Social Policy* 36(1): 82–103.
24. Nabil Khattab, Ron Johnston and David Manley (2015) '"All in it together?" Ethnoreligious labor-market penalties and the post-2008 recession in the UK', *Environment and Planning A* 47: 977–95.
25. Steve Jefferys (2015) 'The context to challenging discrimination against ethnic minorities and migrant workers at work', *Transfer* 21(1): 9–22.
26. Disabled People Against Cuts, 'The UN report into UK government maltreatment of disabled people has been published', DPAC blog, 7 November 2016.
27. Mike Collins and Reinhard Haudenhuyse (2015) 'Social exclusion and austerity policies in England: the role of sports in a new area of social polarisation and inequality', *Social Inclusion* 3(3): 5–18.
28. Linda Perriton (2009) '"We don't want complaining women!" A critical analysis of the business case for diversity', *Management Communication Quarterly* 23(2): 218–43.
29. Nicole Aschoff (2015) *The new prophets of capital*, Verso.
30. Orlando Richard (2000) 'Racial diversity, business strategy, and firm performance: a resource-based view', *Academy of Management Journal* 43(2): 164–77.
31. Simon Deakin, Sarah Fraser Butlin, Colm McLaughlin and Aleksandra Polanska (2015) 'Are litigation and collective bargaining complements or substitutes for achieving gender equality? A study of the British Equal Pay Act', *Cambridge Journal of Economics* 39(2): 381–403.
32. Hazel Conley (2014) 'Trade unions, equal pay and the law in the UK', *Economic and Industrial Democracy* 35(2): 309–23.

33. Linda Dickens (2000) 'Collective bargaining and the promotion of gender equality at work: opportunities and challenges for trade unions', *Transfer* 6(2): 196–7.
34. Ben Leo, 'Nigerian mum who flew to Britain to give birth to twins racked up £350,000 hospital bill – and YOU paid for it', *The Sun*, 16 January 2017.
35. Johnathan Portes (2016) 'Immigration, free movement and the EU referendum', *National Institute Economic Review* 236(1): 14–22.
36. Stephen Nickell and Jumana Saleheen (2009) 'The impact of immigration on occupational wages: evidence from Britain', *Spatial Economic Research Centre*, discussion paper 34.
37. Christian Dustmann, Tommaso Frattini and Ian Preston (2013) 'The effects of immigration along the distribution of wages', *Review of Economic Studies* 80(1): 145–73.
38. Marco Manacorda, Alan Manning and Jonathan Wadsworth (2012) 'The impact of immigration on the structure of wages: theory and evidence from Britain', *Journal of the European Economic Association* 10(1): 120–51.
39. Portes, 'Immigration, free movement and the EU referendum'.
40. Lisa O'Carroll 'Pret a Manger: just one in 50 job applicants are British, says HR boss', *The Guardian*, 9 March 2017.
41. Nickell and Saleheen, 'The impact of immigration on occupational wages'.
42. Johnathan Wadsworth, Swati Dhingra, Gianmarco Ottaviano and John Van Reenen (2016) *Brexit and the impact of immigration on the UK*, Centre for Economic Performance.
43. Gabriella Alberti (2014) 'Mobility strategies, "mobility differentials" and "transnational exit": the experience of precarious migrants in London's hospitality jobs', *Work, Employment and Society* 28(6): 865–81.
44. Barbara Samaluk (2016) 'Migrant workers' engagement with labour market intermediaries in Europe: symbolic power guiding transnational exchange', *Work, Employment and Society* 30(3): 455–71.
45. Gabriella Alberti made this point very powerfully in a talk entitled 'Why another border?' at the 'One Day Without Us' event in Leeds, 20 February 2017.
46. Richard Hyman (1975) *Industrial relations: a Marxist introduction*, Palgrave.
47. Line Eldring, Ian Fitzgerald and Jens Arnholtz (2012) 'Post-accession migration in construction and trade union responses in Denmark, Norway and the UK', *European Journal of Industrial Relations* 18(1): 21–36.
48. Ibid.
49. Maite Tapia and Lowell Turner, 'Union campaigns as countermovements: mobilizing immigrant workers in France and the United Kingdom', *British Journal of Industrial Relations* 51(3): 601–22.

CHAPTER 7

1. Derek Thompson, 'A world without work', *The Atlantic*, July/August 2015.

2. Nick Srnicek and Alex Williams (2015) *Inventing the future*, Verso.
3. International Labour Organization (2000) *Labour practices in the footwear, leather, textiles and clothing industries*, International Labour Organization.
4. Meek, 'Somerdale to Skarbimierz', p. 15.
5. BBC, 'Will a robot take your job?', 11 September 2015.
6. Arlie Hochschild (1979) *The managed heart*, University of California Press.
7. Carl Frey and Michael Osborne (2017) 'The future of employment: how susceptible are jobs to computerisation?', *Technological Forecasting and Social Change* 114: 254–80.
8. Harry Braverman (1974) *Labor and monopoly capital*, Monthly Review Press.
9. Ibid., p. 193.
10. Ibid., p. 230.
11. Ibid., p. 195.
12. Cited in ibid., p. 195.
13. Ibid., pp. 230–1.
14. Peter Bain and Phil Taylor (2000) 'Entrapped by the "electronic panopticon"? worker resistance in the call centre', *New Technology, Work and Employment* 15(1): 2–18.
15. Aurelie Leclercq-Vandelannoitte, Henri Isaac and Michel Kalika (2014) 'Mobile information systems and organisational control: beyond the panopticon metaphor?', *European Journal of Information Systems* 23(5): 543–57.
16. Ibid., p. 550.
17. Birgitta Bergvall-Kareborn and Debra Howcroft (2013) '"The future's bright, the future's mobile": a study of Apple and Google mobile application developers', *Work, Employment and Society* 27(6): 964–81.
18. Philip Schorpf, Jorg Flecker, Annika Schonauer and Hubert Eichmann (2017) 'Triangular love-hate: management and control in creative crowdworking', *New Technology, Work and Employment* 32(1): 43–58.
19. Terbor Scholz (2016) *Platform cooperativism: challenging the corporate sharing economy*, Rosa Luxemburg Stiftung.
20. Oliver Bennett, 'Rage against the machine: the trouble with self-service', *Management Today*, 29 June 2015.
21. Sue Mitchell, 'Supermarkets winning wages battle with self-service checkouts', *Sydney Morning Herald*, 26 April 2016.
22. Charles Koeber (2011) 'Consumptive labor: the increasing importance of consumers in the labor process', *Humanity & Society* 35: 205–32.
23. Lydia DePillis, 'Forget the haters: grocery self-checkout is awesome', *Washington Post*, 9 October 2013.
24. Duncan Gallie (2017) 'The quality of work in a changing labour market', *Social Policy & Administration* 51(2): 226–43.
25. Jason Moore (2015) *Capitalism in the web of life*, Verso.

26. David Levy and Daniel Egan (2003) 'A neo-Gramscian approach to corporate political strategy: conflict and accommodation in the climate change negotiations', *Journal of Management Studies* 40(4): 803–29.

27. Peter Newell and Matthew Paterson (1998) 'A climate for business: global warming, the state and capital', *Review of International Political Economy* 5(4): 679–703.

28. Eric Mack, 'How Tesla and Elon Musk's "gigafactories" could save the world', *Forbes*, 30 October 2016.

29. Steven Shaviro (2009) 'The singularity is here', in Mark Bould and China Mieville (eds) *Red planets*, Pluto Press, p. 106.

30. Fred Vogelstein, quoted in John Lanchester (2017) 'Amazon echo', *London Review of Books* 39(3): 22.

31. David Graeber (2015) *The utopia of rules*, Melville House.

CHAPTER 8

1. Srnicek and Williams, *Inventing the future*, p. 137.

2. E.g. Damian Thompson (2015) 'Shock! Horror! At LAST a BBC boss who admits it's biased', *Daily Mail*, 23 June 2015.

3. Oliver Latham (2013) *Bias at the BEEB? A qualitative study of slant in BBC online reporting*, Centre for Policy Studies.

4. Mike Berry, 'Hard evidence: how biased is the BBC?', *The Conversation*, 23 August 2013.

5. Tom Mills (2016) *The BBC: myth of a public service*, Verso.

6. Paul Hartmann (1975) 'Industrial relations in the news media', *Industrial Relations Journal* 6(4): 4–18.

7. Mike Berry (2016) 'No alternative to austerity: how BBC news reported the deficit debate', *Media, Culture & Society* 38(6): 844–63.

8. Keith Butterick (2015) *Complacency and collusion*, Pluto.

9. Simon Wren-Lewis, 'Mediamacro myths: summing up', Mainly Macro blog, 29 April 2015.

10. See Samira Shackle, 'How Newsnight humiliated single mother Shanene Thorpe', *New Statesman*, 29 May 2012; also BBC, 'BBC welfare reform show breached impartiality guidelines', 30 July 2013.

11. Theodor Adorno (2005) *Minima moralia*, Verso, p. 42.

12. Theodor Adorno (2001) *The culture industry: selected essays on mass culture*, Routledge, pp. 52–3.

13. Alain Badiou and Jean-Claude Milner (2012) *Controverse*, Seuil.

14. Ibid., p. 32, my own translation from the French.

15. Will Worley, 'Conservative changes to voter registration leaves 800,000 off electoral rolls', *The Independent*, 31 January 2016.

16. Stephen Dubner, 'Why do we vote? So we can tell people we voted', Freakonomics blog, 27 January 2014.

17. Claire Foges, 'Let's stop treating the young as political sages', *The Times* 12 June 2017.

18. Stephen Daisley, 'Labour has surrendered to Corbynism', *The Spectator*, 10 June 2017.

19. Rod Liddle, 'Shh … let your kids lie in', *The Sun*, 7 June 2017.

20. Peter Taylor-Gooby, 'Bad news for the poor: the British Social Attitudes survey shows a hardening of attitudes towards working age welfare recipients', LSE Politics and Policy blog, 27 March 2015.

21. Christian Albrekt Larsen and Thomas Engel Dejgaard (2013) 'The institutional logic of images of the poor and welfare recipients: a comparative study of British, Swedish and Danish newspapers', *Journal of European Social Policy* 23(3): 287–99.

22. Kayleigh Garthwaite (2011) '"The language of shirkers and scroungers?" Talking about illness, disability and coalition welfare reform', *Disability & Society* 26(3): 369–72.

23. Ben Baumberg Geiger (2016) *Benefit 'myths'? The accuracy and inaccuracy of public beliefs about the benefits system*, Centre for Analysis of Social Exclusion.

24. Natalie Corner, 'TV viewers blast "shameless" mother-of-four after she boasts how she spent her Christmas benefits bonus on PROSECCO and splashed out £2,800 on her children's presents (including two husky puppies', *Daily Mail*, 4 January 2017.

25. TNS Opinion and Social (2012) *Entrepreneurship in the EU and beyond: country report – United Kingdom*, European Commission.

26. Philip Johnston, 'British bureaucracy is growing out of control', *The Telegraph*, 18 January 2009.

27. Graeber, *The utopia of rules*.

28. Richard Walker and Gene Brewer (2008) 'An organizational echelon analysis of the determinants of red tape in public organizations', *Public Administration Review* 68(6): 1112–27.

29. Phil Taylor (2013) *Performance management and the new workplace tyranny*, Scottish Trades Union Congress.

30. Luc Boltanski and Eve Chiapello (2006) *The new spirit of capitalism*, Verso, p. 58.

31. Sam Bowman, 'Sweatshops make the poor better off', Adam Smith Institute blog, 29 July 2015.

32. E.g. Richard Locke, Ben Rissing and Timea Pal (2013) 'Complements or substitutes? Private codes, state regulation and the enforcement of labour standards in global supply chains', *British Journal of Industrial Relations* 51(3): 519–52; also Dana Frank (2003) 'Where are the workers in consumer-worker alliances? Class dynamics and the history of consumer-labor campaigns', *Politics & Society* 31(3): 363–79.

33. Aschoff, *The new prophets of capital*, pp. 72–3.

34. Lance Compa (2008) 'Corporate social responsibility and workers', rights', *Comparative Labor Law and Policy Journal* 30(1): 1–10.

35. Sophy Grimshaw 'Wackaging: do we want our food to talk back', *The Guardian*, 25 March 2014.
36. James Dunn, '"Go home British Gas Help, you're drunk": energy giant faces Twitter backlash after customer service tweet "hijacks" anniversary of David Bowie's death', *Daily Mail*, 10 January 2017.

CHAPTER 9

1. Srnicek and Williams, *Inventing the future*.
2. Jane Lethbridge, 'Universal basic income: further dismantling of the welfare state?', Compass blog, 6 January 2017.
3. Most influentially Paul Mason (2016) *Post-capitalism*, Penguin.
4. Paul Thompson and Kendra Briken (2017) 'Some digital delusions: actually existing capitalism', in Kendra Briken, Shiona Chillas, Martin Kryzwdzinski and Abigail Marks (eds) *The new digital workplace: how new technologies revolutionise work*, Palgrave Macmillan.
5. E.g. Srnicek and Williams, *Inventing the future*.
6. Sam Coates, 'Don't collaborate with Labour, Hammond warns businesses', *The Times*, 4 October 2017.
7. Peter Mandelson 'My party's moderates must stand by the wounded PM', *Mail on Sunday*, 11 June 2017.
8. Margot James, 'We need to make the case for wealth creation to a new generation of young people', *Conservative Home*, 11 June 2016.
9. Clark, 'Corbyn has stirred the youth vote'.
10. Jonathan White, 'Why trying to understand GE2017 as "the young vs the old" is a bad idea', *LSE Politics & Policy*, 14 June 2017.

Index